A Corinthian Endeavour

To Helen

A Corinthian Endeavour

The Story of the National
Hill Climb Championship

Paul Jones

MP

A Corinthian Endeavour

First published in 2015 by
Mousehold Press
Victoria Cottage
Constitution Opening
Norwich, NR3 4BD

www.mousehold-press.co.uk

Cover design by studioade.com

ISBN 978-1-874739-76-0

Printed by Page Bros, Norwich

Contents

	Race HQ	9
1	A Snorter (1944–49)	13
2	Robinson, Wilson and Ingman (1950–57)	25
3	Origins	44
4	The Rake's Progress (1958–62)	49
5	The Nick	61
6	The Star Wheelers (1963–74)	68
7	It Bites into the Memory (1975–79)	101
8	The Inexorable Rise of the Wheelers (1980–82)	115
9	The Enigmatic Darryl Webster (1983–86)	123
10	The Professor (1987–91)	139
11	The Hill Climb Bicycle	153
12	Dangerfield (1992–97)	169
13	Antigra (1998–2000)	179
14	The Roadman's Climb (2001–2006)	193
15	Equal Opportunities	205
16	Contemporaneity (2007–2010)	229
17	When is a Hill not a Hill?	239
18	The Stang (2011–14)	243
	Coda	263
Appendices	The Results	267
Bibliography		283

Author
Paul Jones is an occasional racing cyclist and ardent hill climber who struggles to balance the demands of writing about cycling with doing some actual cycling. He came in a long way behind Sir Bradley Wiggins in the 2014 National Time Trial Championships, once scraped a 49-minute "25" and has won a couple of hill climbs in the South West of England.

Author's acknowledgements:

I'd like to thank all of the people who have given freely of their time to talk about hill climbs. I feel privileged to have had the opportunity to have spoken with them: Vic Clark, Peter Graham, Tejvan Pettinger, Graham Sydney, Chris Boardman, Lynn Hamel, Eric Wilson, Gareth Armitage, James Dobbin, Matt Clinton and Lynn Hamel.

Thank you to Allen Janes for having a handy archive of cycling press articles and letting me spend hours holed up flicking through the binders. The support of Bristol South Cycling Club has been brilliant. Thanks to Dan Kempe, Andy Legge, George Keene, Rob and Mary-Jane Hutchinson, Dave Braidley, Steve Green and all of the other members who make it an amazing institution. This includes Ade Ridley, designer extraordinaire. Up the South!

Thank you to those people who supported me when hill climbing, even if it was just through camaraderie; people like Rob Gough, Ian Stott, Neil Blessit, all those with a supportive word, extending the slightly twisted fellowship of the hillclimber.

Thank you to Helen. There is nothing I can say that can encompass the level of support you have given and the confidence you have instilled in me. It was very nice of you to say that I could buy a vintage frame when I finished this book.

Thank you to Adrian Bell of Mousehold Press for responding to my speculative email in the first place, for being patient when I decided to get married and have a child instead of completing the manuscript, for being endlessly supportive, gently instructive in the art of a neat sentence, and for understanding what I'm trying to say, even when I don't understand it myself.

See you up the road.

'The good cyclist looks on all the world as his parish; and all his parishioners are his friends, until they prove themselves other than friends by charging eighteen pence for a shilling tea, or by similar gestures of hostility. His friends are of all lands and all people, especially if they also travel on bicycles. So his transit on earth is one long process of making friends.'

(F. Wray, *The Kudos Papers*, 1927)

'Beneath it all, desire of oblivion runs.'

(Philip Larkin)

Race HQ

On the surface, this is a book about hill climbing, a niche within a niche. The season, if not the event per se, is unique to cycle racing in this country. However, this is also a book about cycling, about the past and traditions, and how an anachronism can seem reassuring in a world of constant change. Chris Boardman frames it neatly: 'The hill climb is a wonderfully social, spectator-friendly event providing a seasonal focal point and transition into the off-season. I think they will always be enjoyed primarily by a passionate minority, but they are part of our cycling heritage and I hope they continue to be so for years to come. Not everything has to be about winning and beating the rest of the world; some things can and should simply be enjoyed for their own sake and perhaps the hill climb should be cherished in this category, something more or less unique to us.'

The key narrative components of the National Championship Hill Climb are microcosms of cycling in Britain: tradition, cycling clubs, cycle touring, the British weather, club runs, strange place names, esoteric and eccentric habits, and hills – lots of undulating, rolling, short, steep, long or shallow hills. It's an event that is not in thrall to contemporary fashion or modernity, the backwards-looking aesthetic of current cycling garb or an endless obsession with retro reproduction. Nor does it hold truck with the contemporary search for authenticity, via real ales, moustaches and beards, and things being endlessly, always 'epic' as the ultimate mark of realism. Wearing a self-consciously epic jersey will only get you so far up the Rake or Challacombe.

If there's one thing that highlights the differences between continental cycling and the insular version practised on this island, it's the juxtaposition of climbing theatres: Alpe d'Huez versus The Rake. One takes forty-five minutes, the other takes two and a half. There is no comparison beyond the obvious fact that both are stretches of uphill tarmac. And yet, they form a centrepiece to racing in their respective environments. Bike racing in any given place emerges out of the topography and climate. In France, it's mountains and fields of sunflowers. In the Netherlands, it's crosswinds and echelons across pan-flat flood plains. In the UK, it's endlessly undulating countryside with sudden, sharp and violent climbs. In the past, British cycling has suffered in comparison, in part more because we didn't quite know what to do with what we've got, aligned with a latent sense of inferiority towards the mythical narratives played out on a yearly basis on the Puy de Dôme or the Tourmalet.

In recent years there has been greater self-belief and a renewed sense of pride, both in British Cycling and in the clustered contours of the island. The inferiority has been pushed aside, success begets success, and pictures of Holme Moss, Buttertubs and the West Yorkshire heartlands, clustered with millions of spectators watching the Tour, have demonstrated the sea change. It's partly down to the efforts of people like Simon Warren, cataloguing and defining the best climbs, a modern day archivist – a Cecil Sharp of the hills. A resurgent Tour of Britain has once again embraced the rolling oscilloscope of hills and troughs, extending the length of each stage and creating unpredictable and exciting racing. But it's also in part due to the endlessly epic self-promotion of the sportif market, capturing the slobbering imagination of the modern day cycling-convert into making good use of those super wide cassettes and compact chainsets.

I've tried to explore why the National Championship Hill Climb remains such a popular event and have been lucky enough to meet and talk with the people involved, putting their views across within the history of the event. It's a story of different eras, different hills and different places, but also about the unrelenting obsessions that drive competitors, from extreme weight loss to the sourcing of obscure components and the constant quest to go faster uphill.

1

A Snorter

(1944–1949)

'You'd have thought I'd have been disappointed, but I wasn't, I was glad for Harold because there was nobody who could ride hills like him. It wouldn't have been right for his name not to have been on that trophy.'

Vic Clark is 95 years old. He has a glint in his eye and the compact, muscular build of the racing cyclist. He still spends thirty minutes a day on the turbo trainer. The thousands upon thousands of miles have shaped and determined his pose and posture. We sit in a kitchen in Kendal – Lynn Hamel's Mum's kitchen, to be precise – and talk. In fact, Vic talks, and I mostly listen. Occasionally I ask a question from my prepared list, but most of the time I sit and listen as he roams effortlessly across the years, recounting and reliving memories and experiences from seventy years ago as though they were last weekend's races. He thinks carefully about each of the events he rode. He recalls every detail of every climb, including the time splits and the opposition. He's not the only cyclist I've met who still has a recall of events from decades ago, in different lives, but he might just be the oldest. He sits upright, tea in hand, and avoids the biscuits I bought him. I bought both Vic Clark and Lynn Hamel a packet of biscuits. In retrospect this may have been a schoolboy error – they are both hill climbers and multiple National Champions; they have no need or desire for biscuits. They have the power to weight ratio of a small garden bird, able to take flight and lift upwards with grace and ease. Marks and Spencer's Belgian chocolate biscuits do not help their cause.

Vic Clark rode his first hill climb in the November of 1940. He hadn't really any idea of how to ride them, but was persuaded by the then club secretary, Charlie Viner, to line up in a club event near Daventry. Vic took the touring bag off, removed his mudguards and duly rode up the hill as fast as he could. A few hardy spectators watched, mouths agape, as he got the beating of the then unofficial British champion, Ron Gunn. In a time of austerity, the Barnet team of Ron Gunn, Glenn Thorpe and Jeff Hyams, spaced evenly apart on the card, would ride with one bike, which they would send back down the climb after each effort. Clark's time was two seconds up on Gunn. The confused Barnet riders complained that water had got into the watches and Clark believed them, but the result stood. It was 5th November, 1940. A few days later, on the 14th November, Clark's home city of Coventry was flattened by the Luftwaffe.

During the war Vic Clark worked as a toolmaker in a munitions factory. The Blitz saw the firm relocate to Nelson in the Lancashire hills. On disembarking from the train, there for the first time, he faced a long slog up a steep and cobbled climb to his digs. The effort left him wondering openly why he'd bothered bringing the bike, he certainly didn't anticipate using it. The factory was also located at the top of the hill and the sharp undulations and rolling terrain were markedly different from the East Midlands.

Luckily, Clark knew of a tricycle champion called Ossie Jackson who ran a shop in Nelson, so he sought him out as a riding partner. Early on they rode over to Clitheroe and Longridge Fell where Hebden Bridge CC were running a hill climb with entry on the line. Both riders signed on for a bit of fun, with Vic Clark again winning. It being a dry day, he began to think that maybe the timekeepers at Coventry were right. He went on to win two more on Arlington Bank in 1941: he seemed to have developed a knack for them. In fact, he went on to win nearly every hill climb he entered, without 'the proper tackle', until he got a set of sprints from Ossie Jackson. Prior to that he was riding on high pressure clinchers.

The hills and rolling countryside of Pendle changed his riding, adding a hitherto unmined strength and ability. At the end of the war, on being demobbed, he returned to Coventry to work, but his wife, Connie, stayed on in Nelson. For eighteen months he finished work at half past four on a Friday, jumped on the bike and cycled the 127 miles back to Nelson on a 72" fixed gear. Unsurprisingly, a lot of the chaps at work thought he was barmy.

'The works lorry driver had to go up to Colne and he said, "I'll give you a lift; you can put your bike on the back." I said, "No thanks Tom, I'm biking up, I'll be up there before you anyway." He passed me at Lichfield after 26 miles, and he'd say, "C'mon put your bike in the back." Then I'd see him at a transport cafe near Stone and I could see his wagon in the car park and I'd carry on, thinking, "I'll get a few miles in before he catches me again – somewhere near Congleton. If I can get to Cheadle before him I'm home and dry," because it was sixteen miles of cobbles through Manchester and Bury. I'd get there about 11.30. One weekend I took my tandem up there, on my own. Got somewhere near Stockport and there was an Army bloke thumbing lifts and nobody stopped for him, and I said, "There's room for one on the back but you'll have to work for it." He must have been a cyclist because he got on the back and I dropped him off at Burnley!'

Vic Clark is just one of the wave of cyclists of the late 1940s and early 1950s who provide a direct link back to the heroic era, prior to mass transportation when cycling huge distances was seen as far more natural and less bizarre than it was in the years that followed. There wasn't a sense that you were taking some kind of masochistic or eccentric decision; it was a means to an end in a world where car ownership was low and possession of a bike was the dominant means of personal freedom and mobility. The bicycle sustained Vic and Connie Clark's marriage in those early post-war years. It also gave him the legs and form to dominate the early episodes of the National Championship Hill Climb.

Vic Clark and Harold Worthen rode together as club mates for the Manchester Clarion, with Worthen passing on his hard-won experience to the younger rider, not least of which concerned the all-important pacing strategy*. Every era and discipline has its pre-eminent rider. In the early 1940s Harold Worthen won nearly every hill climb he entered. He was an expert over any distance and if his name was inked onto the start sheet then the course record was about as secure as a piece of porcelain at a Greek wedding. Following on in his shoeplates came Vic Clark, and with both riding latterly for the Clarion, they made a formidable outfit. 'Harold Worthern was unbeatable,' said Clark. 'For four years he won every hill climb he rode in. He not only rode, he broke records in nearly every one. And he used to finish so fresh; he was never flaked out at the top of a hill.'

Vic Clark recalled the Kentish Wheelers' Silver Jubilee event on Brasted Hill in 1943. Worthen's opening gambit was along the lines of, 'Vin Taylor and I are going down to Kent to show these Southerners how to ride hill climbs; why don't you come with us?' Clark hadn't got any digs, nor had he entered. He was talked into it, even though he was still

---

* The objectives of the founders of the Clarion Cycling Club in 1894 were 'to combine the pleasures of cycling with the propaganda of Socialism'.

riding for Nelson Wheelers at that point, by the promise of a stopover at Sandy Holdsworth's 'big mansion'. Sandy was more commonly known as W. F. Holdsworth, the prestigious Putney framebuilder. Worthen was the course record holder, but when Clark took to the climb he beat him by two seconds. The elder statesman wasn't that thrilled, in fact, 'he was really upset about it'. Clark attempted to placate him by saying it was his fault for talking him into it in the first place, before ending up with a slightly less than conciliatory 'well anyway, you're going to have to get used to this, Harold'.

Seventy years later, Clark ascribes his success to Harold Worthen: 'Harold taught me a lot; we always finished fresh... it was always described as "effortless". Mind you, it wasn't effortless, but it looked easy. Hill climbs aren't won at the start, but they are lost there. A lot of these hill climbers wear themselves out the day before, training up and down it. There's no need for that. They start as fast as they can, and this is what Bob Maitland did, but they can't hold it. At the start you can't double a man's speed – if it's ten miles an hour you're not going to do twenty – but at the finish, when he's struggling, going about two miles an hour, you can do six or eight or even ten miles an hour if you've got anything left, and that's where they're won and lost. I've watched them at the finish, and people have walked faster than what they could ride. I can tell by looking at a fella, a picture of him, how he's struggling, if he's over his bike, side to side and fighting to keep on. You can't ride through if you've got to that stage. Once you've lost your pace, you're struggling. You go slower, and slower, and slower, and the slower you go, the harder it gets.'

The following year, 1944, saw the first formal National Championship Hill Climb under RTTC* rules and regulations at Brasted in Kent. A fortnight before, Vic Clark returned to the

---

* The Road Time Trials Council, formed from the Road Racing Council, signalling the opening of membership to all cycling clubs. They sold 5,564 handbooks in the first year.

Kentish Wheelers event and won, this time in the colours of the Clarion, and again beating Harold Worthen, who was more accepting of Clark's success, at least partly because they'd been carving up the events between them for much of the season. On the biggest stage of all, fourteen days later, Harold Worthen exacted revenge by one second – he was the first National Hill Climb Champion: 'You'd have thought I'd have been disappointed, but I wasn't, I was glad for Harold because there was nobody who could ride hills like him. It wouldn't have been right for his name not to have been on that trophy.'

Twelve months later Worthen was unable to defend his trophy due to a hernia operation, leaving the door wide open for Clark. It's not specified whether the injury was caused on a typically stomach-bursting effort on a ridiculous incline somewhere up North, but it can't have helped. Worthen's win in the inaugural event was both the first and last victory for this accomplished and natural hill climber, someone who acted as a mentor to the younger Vic Clark in his formative years. Their tendency to finish fresh, without a Brylcreemed hair out of place, is in sharp contrast, even now, to the hill climber's belief that if you haven't been caught*,or haven't passed out, or haven't vomited over your lightweight climbing shoes at the top of a 1-in-4 elevation, then you haven't tried hard enough.

In the National on Dover's Hill, in 2010, I rode around the first bend and was startled to see some club members cheering me on, especially George Keene, an 82-year-old racing cyclist who had watched the 1948 event held by the Bristol South Cycling Club. I somehow managed a smile. Later George remonstrated with me: apparently having the capacity and spare energy to smile at a spectator meant I was not putting in the requisite effort. I'm not sure Vic Clark or Harold Worthen would have smiled at the ranks of spectators, crowding in on

---

* Then, as now, the effort involved in a hill climb can result in a spectacular collapse once over the line, requiring the involvement of 'catchers'.

the natural galleries, but they always 'left a bit in the tank, to ride through'. I learnt my lesson and perfected my grimace for later races, just in case one of the grandees was watching.

Four days before he was due to ride up to Chapel-en-le-Frith for the National, Clark had a vaccine jab. He had planned to ride the sixty miles from Kimbolton to his mother's, then ride up to Chapel-en-le-Frith the next day. He got up the following morning to ride the 86 miles with 'an arm as big as two', and no prospect of racing. He somehow staggered back to camp and spent a fortnight in the sickbay. In his absence the honours fell to Bob Maitland, a star of the nascent British road scene who later rode with the BSA team. Maitland is an impressively coiffed figure in photos at the time, his hair neatly parted, looking every inch the burgeoning continental rider that he so nearly became. He rode the Tour de France in 1955 for the National team alongside Brian Robinson, Fred Krebs, Ian Steel and Tony Hoar.

Vic Clark's first championship victory finally came on the steep slope of Holly Lane, out of Ambergate in Derbyshire in 1946. He was riding a custom-built Pollard with a reduced wheelbase – a 1940s equivalent of the triple triangle frame construction. He beat Maitland into second, with the Clarion winning the team prize. Clark refers to it as a 'snorter'. It's one of his favourite words to describe a tough and unpleasant hill, and it rings out throughout the conversations we had. Short, steep and unpleasant, Holly Lane is not one of the classic National courses but has reappeared in subsequent years. At the Champions' Dinner, held in the auspicious surroundings of the Royal Albert Hall, Clark took a long weekend pass from Kimbolton and then had to return with the trophy to the Camp. He had no idea where to store the expensive and large piece of silverware in a tiny RAF billet. He had to take it to the CO, who promptly enquired just where Clark had got hold of the shiny item. He told him the story and added a few extras, namely that he was very lucky to win it because he hadn't had time to train and Cambridgeshire wasn't exactly the best location for a hill climber. The trophy ended up in the coal bunker, the polished silver illuminated against the soot and blackened coal dust.

The following year Clark found himself in the uplands of Otley and had more time to train; much to the chagrin of his Air Force peers who saw him disappear off each week with the wind in his hair. They spied a ruse and were quick to jump on the bandwagon. The following week half a dozen turned out on the camp's supply of sit-up-and-begs. They'd follow him round the corner, throw the bikes in a ditch and head off into the nearest town from some recreation, avoiding Sutton Bank – 'that's a snorter, that is' – and the other climbs in the area that made up Clark's training loop. He'd do timed intervals of the Bank. On one of his first runs ('only out training') Clark beat the existing record by fifteen seconds.

In 1947 the event visited Winnats Pass for the first time. It's a climb that induces a hushed reverence from anyone who has ridden it competitively. In the early years of the National, Winnats was seen as the amphitheatre of the sport. The shape and form of the landscape presents a natural crucible of endeavour, where cyclists can test themselves time and time again on the fabled incline. If France was designed by God for stage races, then He surely had Winnats in mind as the ideal hill climb parcours. Crowds line the slopes in the galleries, cheering on their clubmen to the top, watching in surprise and vicarious excitement as the participants collapse, before being held aloft by the catchers, knees buckled and legs dragging across the tarmac like a stunned cow in an abattoir, then laid to rest on the grass verge.

A fortnight earlier there had been a dress rehearsal on the climb, marking the first time it had been used. A very much in form Maitland took the honours with a two second margin over Clark. The following week the carousel moved on to Saintbury, where Clark held the record with a very short seven minutes; Maitland won again. Clark's verdict on Saintbury is that it was 'too long and wasn't steep enough'. I've ridden it a few times, it's certainly long and has some testing ramps around the middle, but Clark is clearly cut from a different cloth. He remained unconcerned about Maitland's victory, thinking that it would lead to complacency and overconfidence, knowing that when it came down to the crunch he would pull out all the stops. Maitland was odds-on favourite, but it didn't trouble Clark. He felt the benefit of the previous encounter with the climb: 'It never worried me what other people were doing. I'd ride my own race. The fortnight before taught me just what gear to ride, where to make my effort, what pace to set, what course to take and how to ride. I'd got it all cut and dried, how I was going to do it.'

As the last man was due off the onlookers held their breath. Clark was number 90, and had opted for a 61" gear in stark contrast to Worthen's enormous 67". Vic said he was mad – 'You'll never get it up the hill, Harold.' Gear choices have changed over the years, and what seemed right in 1947 seems a bit large these days. It's hard to imagine anyone pushing such a huge gear up a savage incline.

Clark was fifteen seconds down on Maitland at 300 yards, getting a time check from a Clarion colleague placed on the verge. The gradient shifts on the bend from a 1-in-6 to a knee-popping 1-in-4. He kept the same pace all the way to the finish. The crowd shouted him up the savage incline, calling 'Hup, Hup, Hup', in time with each pedal stroke. Towards the finish Benny Foster, a club mate, shouted 'It's in the bag', and the roar of the crowd increased, and the tempo of the chant, and he kept pace with them, crossing the line some eight seconds up, the clear winner. As always, he rode through the finish, no carrying off, no stopping. He turned round in the road and saw his brother who pointed out that Vic's back wheel was dead flat. 'I'd thought that last 100 yards was a bit hard', was Clark's reply.

Vic Clark set a new course record of 3'-23.8" and beat Bob Maitland into second, with Harold Worthen in third, a fifth of a second down and ten years older. It was revenge of sorts for Maitland's win in 1945. A gift tailwind – the best and only sort – propelled the riders up the narrow valley with the sound of silk tubulars on the uneven road surface ringing in the ears, a serene silence that comes from having the wind behind. Clark remembers the course fondly: 'It's a true test. The National Hill Climb should always be held on Winnats, and as an alternative, the Nick O'Pendle.' Some 65 years later he cites it as his best ride – 'it was never beaten'. Very few riders ever got inside four minutes on the 983-yard ribbon of penury that is Winnats.

The following year Vic Clark sealed his hat trick and dominance at the discipline with a champion's display on a technical and difficult, if not that steep, course. In a rare foray down south the event was organised by Bristol South Cycling Club. Even now it's unusual for the event to be held south of the Midlands, or perhaps south of Dover's Hill. A local rider, Les Cattell, riding for the host club, rattled the form book with a blast up the gritty surface of the climb, using his local knowledge to gauge both the undulations of the course and the two most difficult technicalities: tyre pressure and gear choice. Every year races are won and lost by these two decisions. In 2012 BSCC pocket rocket Glyndwr Griffiths took second behind short-course monster Rob Gough at Catford. In the spirit of Les Cattell's race some sixty years previously he let an onrush of air out of his tyres at the last minute, in order to cope with potential wheelspin, elevating himself to the podium for the first time. His tendency to push himself so hard that he retches green bile and his eyes seem to explode also helps, although I'm not sure Vic Clark would have approved.

On Weston Lane Clark geared above his competitors with a tall 66", coping effortlessly with the gradient, the greasy surface and the mist blowing up from the valley to win with ease. In pictures from the event he is the embodiment of fluency and balance, arms bent at the elbow, head level, muscles taut rather than straining and eyes firmly on the prize. The bell on the handlebars is a quaint affectation and it's certainly strange to see an unnecessary weight on a hill climb bike, but it was the law. Beneath Clark's superlative performance lurked a nagging sense of diminished powers. It wasn't apparent to those around him, but he knew it. He was still winning hill climbs but the margins were being steadily eroded. Instead of five or six seconds, it was a second or two. Clark attributes the reason for this to moving back to Coventry from Nelson, from the peaks to the flatlands of the Midlands. He no longer had the hills to train on, although it didn't stop him setting a course record of 4'-04" on Dover's Hill.

It was the following year that the difference became apparent. Back at Winnats for the second time, two years to the day after the first running, and the weather conditions couldn't have been more different. Gone was the beneficial tailwind, replaced instead with a snarling and savage headwind, blowing the hapless riders back down the hill. Maitland started halfway down the field and managed 3'-50.8", at which point the wind got up and it began to pour with rain. Clark was struggling, by his own admission, and his choice of 62" was a bit big. He came third with 3'-55", with W.E. Penvose splitting the two. Don Spink crashed in the first few yards to finish just outside the top ten.

In 2012, at the age of 94, Vic Clark attended the Championship Hill Climb in the pouring rain on the Rake. By a rough calculation he has managed 300,000 miles on his Brooks B17 saddle, bought new in 1942 and reblocked in 1947. In 1948 alone he managed 23,000 miles. His is a life in cycling.

2

Robinson, Wilson and Ingman

(1950–1957)

'The standard of climbing when we were riding was very open. There was an awful lot of talent all at once, vying for the big one: Bill Holmes, Bill Bradley, Norman Shiel, Brian Robinson, Peter Graham, Bob Maitland...'

The early part of the decade saw the country move shakily out of the period of post-war austerity. The bike industry and cycle sport as a collective experience changed. The battle between the BLRC and the NCU was gradually nearing a rapprochement which would be sealed at the equivalent of a cold war summit by the end of the decade with the founding of the British Cycling Federation. The insular complexion of British cycling had begun to shift on its axis. In 1955 a GB outfit containing two hill climb champions rode *la Grande Boucle*. It was a slightly ill-fated excursion, with many of the roadmen struggling to cope with the pace and unrelenting nature of the contest. Most had gone by stage 8; Maitland lasted another day, and the mountains did for Krebs and Mitchell. Robinson finished a creditable 29th and Hoar was the *lanterne rouge*. I doubt at that point he could ever have imagined a day when the Tour would come within spitting distance of his hometown of Ravensthorpe, and that he would be a key part of the team responsible for bringing the biggest race on the planet to West Yorkshire.

The genie was out of the bottle and the appeal of continental racing continued to exert a pull on the best of the UK's roadmen, and the best of them began to achieve a palmarès measured in stage wins and podium places in monuments. Brian Robinson's third place in Milan–St Remo in 1957 came on the back of a victory over Louison Bobet in the GP de la Ville Nice. Graeme Fife's book, Pioneer, is aptly named. Following hot in his tyre tracks was Tommy Simpson, who headed to Saint-Brieuc in Brittany in the 1959 season to try and gain a professional contract.

Rewind to the beginning of the decade and a young Robinson was taking up the mantle thrown down by Bob Maitland and striving to win the 1950 Championship Hill Climb on Barber's Hill, leading out of Llangollen. In keeping with the severity of effort and the near death experiences of many of the riders, the hill is named after the town barber and schoolmaster, Thomas Edwards, who was by all accounts a bit quick to anger. He settled a full and frank exchange of views with his wife over whether to boil or roast a neck of mutton by cutting her throat with the tools of his trade, before running out of the door towards Cross Lane. The schoolchildren saw Maria Edwards running around with blood spurting all over the place so raised the alarm.

The barber ran across the open fields to the top of one of the many climbs overlooking the town. He was caught and hung on a gibbet at the top of Moel-y-Geraint, which has since been known as Moel-y-Barbwr. Two hundred and eleven years later it became the location for an equally cut-throat event, with the participants lined up on bicycles to make good their escape from the insidious clutches of gravity, the barber of physics. With its history of savage violence and murderous brutality, it seemed an apt setting for a hill climb. The press and clubmen concurred, in part because of the particularly steep finish. Ron Stringwell took the title with a startling performance. He was a surprise at Llangollen, unfancied before the event and number six on the start sheet. His was a particularly lonely ride up, two DNS and two DNF either side. He ended up being the second rider to reach the summit. Vic Clark came eighth in his last event, finishing with a record of 35 wins from 71 hill climbs, with second place in 19 others. Bob Maitland's merry men took the team prize for the Concorde RCC.

Ronnie Stringwell had some previous, although not that much, with a tidy fifth place the year before, when a fresh-faced Brian Robinson, a few days shy of his twentieth birthday, took third place for the Huddersfield RC with a performance on the hill which gave notice of his potential. He entered his two years of National Service the following year. Stringwell had also won on Holme Moss, which became a favourite stamping ground for Brian Robinson over the years. It's very much an Alpine climb in gradient, if not in terms of duration, and is best climbed on a 60" to 63" gear.

The following year the action shifted further south, to Saintbury on the Cotswold escarpment. It leans against the same brow as Dover's and the two formed a seasonal double-header run by the Warwickshire RC until 2012. They are barely a mile or so apart. Saintbury favours an unrelenting tempo and perfectly judged pace, whilst Dover's tends to reward a shorter, explosive effort. Whilst the event has visited Saintbury since, Dover's has been the more popular of the two.

In 1951 Robinson had been riding well, improving over the season and giving glimpses of his strength and determination. He rode to seventh place in the Isle of Man International and tenth in the NCU mass-start championships, preferring to sit outside of Percy Stallard's BLRC. A week earlier he had scalped Stringwell in a snowstorm on Holme Moss, with both men climbing up in awful conditions through a Kirklees white-out.

Things were more clement down south and the championship and the autumn sun shone kindly on Broadway, where 'foregathered the cream of the country's ascenders to do battle for the season's biggest honour, and between them... they shattered the hill record and left each other gasping in the magnificence of their efforts'.* As the morning progressed and the starters worked their way through the card, the wind picked up and gathered in strength. Three particularly hardy souls opted to try the fairly new-fangled idea of 'variable gears', but without success, not even grazing the top twenty. The early running was set by mass-start champion Peter Procter, riding for the Army Cycling Union. Two weeks previously Procter had beaten Robinson on Saintbury and taken the hill record. Maitland rode a 67" for eighth place, a touch overgeared and about 5" taller than most.

Robinson gave it everything, 'a fantastic bundle of energy was simply hurtling up the hill'.** He came in thirteen and a half seconds up on Procter, utterly spent and had to be lifted from his machine, legs shaking and lungs heaving. With only Stringwell to come he was looking good for the title.

Stringwell had not seen the hill before riding it, he'd walked it the previous day, but that was it. Stringwell's ride showed his form and strength over the longer ascents and was good enough for a new course record of 6'-26". This was despite the vicious headwind blasting down the climb, wickedly punishing the field over the open 300 yards at the top. He proved to be too strong for his peers, with Robinson taking the silver medal.

After two near misses, the inevitable happened in 1952 on Mow Cop in Staffordshire. Now a climb familiar to legions of

---

* George Pearson, 'The Champion Rose to the Occasion, *Cycling*, 1/11/51
** *Ibid.*

sportif riders huffing up the hill in wayward, demented zigzags, it's also known as 'the killer mile', a 1-in-4 ascent through the village. Brian Robinson was 22 and midway through his National Service with the King's Own Light Infantry. In a year of staggering achievements, it was clear that he would shortly be forsaking the short and savage climbs of the Cotswolds for the epic mountain passes of the continent. Robinson had tied for eighth with Jacques Anquetil at the World Championships, come fourth in the Tour of Britain and had ridden the road race at the Helsinki Olympics. In the summer he had also raced the Route de France, an amateur version of the Tour, climbing up over many of the same mountain passes. In subsequent years the Route was won by Lucien Aimar and Robert Millar. It was superseded by the Tour de l'Avenir.

It's clear that in those early years the Championship was an ambition for Robinson. He had inched his way up the podium, one step at a time, and was determined to achieve the top step before embarking on a professional career. Once the race was done he intended to focus entirely on road racing.

It was a warm and breezy late autumn day, perfect hill climb weather. The surface of the Mow Cop was loosely gravelled, making progress slightly more tricky and wheelspin a distinct possibility. Gear choice varied widely, with Robinson on a light 57", Jim Pentecost on a 58", but some riding as tall as a 62". Roy Keighley made his first appearance in the National Championship riding for Shipley CC. He had all the attributes of the successful mountaineer, coming in at a compressed five feet and four inches, and weighing just nine stone. He turned over a 54" gear with a high cadence, legs blurring with rapidity and grace, his style 'effortless'. After three wins in his first six open hill climbs he took third place on the day in 3'-44.2" and was heralded as a champion of the future. It fell to Jim Pentecost to disrupt the West Yorkshire hegemony. Pentecost was the man of Catford, with three wins to his name and he liked the short stuff. He stole less than a second on Keighley to clamber onto the second step. Brian Robinson tightened his straps and found a couple of seconds grace on the chasing pack to take the title he craved. Stringwell ended up on the wrong side of a tenth of a second, coming fifth to miss out on a hat trick of wins. Robinson's outfit, the Huddersfield RC, won the battle of the West Yorkshire clubs and took the team prize back to the Colne Valley for the second year in succession.

In 1953 Brian Robinson turned professional and tilted his gaze to bigger and brighter things. He joined the Ellis Briggs road team, home of the 1952 Tour of Britain winner, Ken Russell*. The team was linked to the shop in Shipley, started in 1936 by Leonard Ellis and Thomas Briggs. They are still going strong and still sponsor a road team. My mum recently bought a bicycle from them. I'm not sure she was aware of their illustrious history and significant role in the emergence of British Cycling from the civil war of the 1950s, or the beginnings of mass-start racing, removed from the alpaca and coded courses at 5a.m. But she likes her new bike very much.

Robinson rode the Tour of Britain as an independent or semi-professional, the same status shared by Bob Maitland riding for BSA. He came fourth in 1953, then second behind Eugene Tamburlini in 1954.

In Robinson's absence, the National Hill Climb became a straight bunfight between Roy Keighley and Stringwell. P.S. Boyd came third, but a good eight seconds behind Stringwell, who had been nursing an ankle injury since the previous November and was close to packing it in. Roy Keighley jumped to the top step of the podium with a convincing five second win. It was a transitional year. The complexion of the Championship and British cycling was changing: Brian

---

* Ken Russell won the GC of the 1952 Tour of Britain, riding alone, with no team support and an Ellis Briggs support car that couldn't keep up. He won several stages and fended off the best efforts of Ian Steel's 4-man Viking outfit, not to mention some of the best riders in Europe. On the run in to the final stage his crank worked loose. The Belgian Michel Michaux gave him his bike, with cracked forks, and Russell completed the stage to win the title. He acquired the nickname 'The Lone Wolf'. It remains a staggering achievement and Russell is one of the unsung heroes of British cycling.

Robinson was pursuing his ultimately illustrious career amongst the professionals; Keighley and Stringwell's powers were waning. Maitland, Stringwell and Robinson had carved up the first seven championships and many of the headline open events over the years, but the door now opened to a new generation, and two climbers came exploding out of the gate: Les Ingman and Eric Wilson.

Sixty one years later, Eric Wilson still lives in the lee of the Rake. It's an appropriate location for a whippet-thin hill climber. He speaks clearly, with a rich and sonorous voice – it's in the way he says 'colour', with a longer, richer double L in the middle, and the lilting northern Z of Rossendale. It reminds me again that I'm from the South, for better or for worse. Yet again I chose Marks and Spencer Belgian biscuits as my icebreaker. I think he appreciated them.

Wilson's early cycling experiences were forged in the Boy Scout movement under the watchful eye of Jimmy Gaines, his local Scoutmaster. For Wilson, growing up deaf, the bike offered an escape from harsh and judgemental surroundings: 'You don't know you're deaf like you do nowadays. I was on my own, people ignored me, kids thought I was thick, slow, there was something wrong with me. It didn't matter if I was riding the bike or walking on the hills because I didn't need to worry. I was content with my own company. I used to ride an awful lot on the bike.'

Jimmy Gaines was a devotee of all things continental and several times had been over to watch the Tour. Wilson was one of many to benefit from his love of cycling, which he passed on through the Scout movement. 'After one ride he gave me some magazines from the Tour; it showed Coppi and Bartali going up the cols. Cycling then for me involved a lot of "playing Tour".'

It's also apparent that as well as a passive involvement in cyclo-sport, Gaines had a more modern eye for detail: 'As far as I know he never raced, but he was very knowledgeable: he'd alter our positions, make sure the bikes were mechanically sound. He said to me, "Eric, you'll be all right on the bike but don't think about racing yet, join a touring club." He told us to get plenty of riding in. "Don't ride at the edge of the road, that's where you pick up your flints and what have you. When you're drinking, don't slap a lot down, drink frequently." He was passing knowledge on.'

Wilson is quick to undermine the contemporary notion of the singular hill climber: 'A lot of us who were climbing in those days, we were not specialists. We were cyclists of many colours. I rode TTs up to a 100, mountain time trials and grass track. Pete Graham rode track as well. We'd go to Fallowfield and watch Reg Harris win by half a millimetre if he could get away with it.'

All the while Wilson was riding the local club circuit up and through Rawtenstall and around the hills, tackling the 10-mile course in football shorts and a tartan wool shirt from Blacks of Greenock, usually with mudguards and a Carradice adorning his Raleigh Sports all steel bicycle. 'There wasn't a sodding thing on that bicycle that wasn't steel'. He'd glance covetously at a club mate's Flying Gate. They have a tight wheelbase and hold a place in history as one of the ugliest bike frames ever built. In the end, he opted for a Pierce point lugged, chromed Rotrax, a bike more befitting the challenges of the Holcombe circuit, 37-and-a-bit miles with not much flat. The idea of tackling it on a three speed close-ratio block, 16-17-18, goes some way to demonstrating the changes in equipment over the last seventy years. Long rides and away days were their bread and butter: 'We'd be off all day, dropping into a café or pub late at night, sometimes 9 or 10 o clock. There were no point in rushing home; there were only the wireless.'

At his first competitive '10' Wilson put in a startling time. He was riding for the Wheelers, the touring faction, far removed from the racing club down the valley. At the finish suspicious rumours circulated, that the young tyro had 'turned short', and it was only after further results and strong rides that the air of scepticism abated.

It's reminiscent of Vic Clark's first hill climb; the sound of a cat being casually placed amongst the pigeons. Young Eric had accidentally thrown down the gauntlet to the local roadmen: 'The following Sunday the two clubs met up together, accidentally, in Skipton. We were going over towards Harrogate, and it was, "Come on we'll ride together". Word went out, "That touring lad's with us". And the pace increased and kept increasing. Over Blubberhouses – it's not severe but it's long – there were about three others left. They just upped the pace, then they attacked, and I responded to the attack and unfortunately when I put the pressure on they couldn't keep up. It was then that I realised I could climb because I finished about a minute and a half clear at the top of Blubberhouses. I just kept it going, not off the saddle. It would demoralise the person attacking, I found I could respond still sat on the saddle while they were thrutching and blasting away. If I wanted to get rid of anyone I would do that. Sit on the saddle, then increase the pace, and they didn't like it. They are thrutching off, their eyeballs on the stem, and I'm sat there as though I'm not suffering.'* With an awareness of his ability to float uphill, Wilson began putting in entries for hill climbs, heading to Otley for his first event in September 1954. Double national winner Ron Stringwell was the scratch rider. Wilson's performance caused ripples of interest outside of his native Lancashire; he scalped Stringwell by 17 seconds – an enormous margin – which immediately put him in amongst the favourites for the National on Holme Moss. As if to emphasise the point that he was amongst the big boys, Norman Shiel, a world class pursuiter and master of the '25' – the first British rider to go under 55 minutes for the distance – was his minute man. The biggest challenge was to come from the smallest rider, the 5ft 4in Les Ingman, and their

---

* "thrutching" derives from "thrutch" – a narrow gorge or ravine. It's a term used in Lancashire and northern England meaning to push or press, especially among cavers or climbers.

nascent rivalry looked set to animate the race for the next few years. Robinson had gone, Keighley and Stringwell were seen as the old guard. In contrast, Wilson was on a blistering streak of form and Ingman had a glittering palmarès. He had ridden the 1952 Olympic Road Race, won the Isle of Man mountain time trial and won at Catford the year before.

The fickle weather of Kirklees threatened to undo the efforts of the riders. The rain steadily increased and the temperature fell as the race unfolded. Ingman put in a hernia-inducing time of 6'-46.2" on the long drag up the side of Holme Moss. Wilson arguably had the worst of the weather, and with Brian Haskell six seconds down it became a battle between the two. Neither rider had ridden the hill before and they could perhaps have chosen a more benign day to break their duck. A crowd lined the slopes even in the thickest of the weather; although the notion of what a crowd looks like on Holme Moss has been recalibrated by the Tour's most recent visit. Nevertheless, the serried ranks of caped spectators watched on in reverence as the thinly-clad riders shook off the worst of the elements. Wilson dug deep at the top, the sinews in his arms drawn tight, gripping the drops with an eye on the time, but the seconds slipped away with the raindrops across the face of his wristwatch. After a season in which his form dipped and rolled, Ingman had done enough to take the title back to the Paragon in their jubilee year; they became the first London club to win the title.

It's easy to imagine that Wilson would be happy to have achieved so much in a debut season, but remembering it, sixty years later, he sees it differently: 'I had something to live up to on Holmes Moss (he adds the 's' on the end of Holme) and I got beat by 1 and 5.* I was absolutely gutted. I felt terrible that I'd let meself down, let other people down. I did one thing wrong, I stood up nearly all the way, but I wasn't trained up to a seven minute climb – the climbs that I prefer are undulating, like the Rake if it were twice the bloody distance. So I decided,

---

* One and one-fifth of a second.

the next championship I'm going to make sure my training is based on the time the climb will take, not the distance. Every hill climb I rode after that I trained for the event. I was very much disappointed. I was the favourite. I didn't even know who Les was.'

The following year looked set for a rematch and to add spice to the encounter a host of other contenders had crept out of the woodwork. Stringwell and Keighley returned, along with Stan Brittain, who had ridden the World Championships the year before. Owen Blower was on the start sheet and Arthur Pursey made the journey up from the Medway delta, fresh from a brace of Catford wins, along with Jim Pentecost, the master of Catford's Brasted Hill. Paddy Hoban, World Cyclo-Cross Champion, also took up the challenge. It had all the hallmarks of a vintage year – but with one notable absence. Ingman was unwell and unable to compete. It robbed the event of the rivalry of the previous year, but the strength of the field held the promise of fireworks. Ambergate is an awkward climb and it requires careful judgement. National grass track champion Brian Sandy diligently showed how not to tackle the climb; igniting out of the blocks like a burst of flame, only to burn out near the top and dribble across the line. In the absence of Ingman the pendulum swung decisively back towards Eric Wilson. He sat upright on the bike at the start, relaxed, his mouth hanging open, thin arms bent slightly and gloved hands clutching the tops, one lever on the right, half-taped bars, a bandage round his right knee, with foppish hair and glasses.

Wilson lacked the confidence of a year ago: 'I was not very happy at all. Bill Bradley came up to me and said, "You don't look right happy," and I didn't feel confident. Bill said, "You'll win." Things like that make all the difference.'

In pictures taken at the event Wilson's knee is bandaged. Earlier on in the season he was touring with a group in Wales when they had to scramble over some rocks on a gravelly bit of road. It was a nasty scrape: 'I caught it on a rock, got an infection and I had a septic leg, poisoning me system like nobody's business. I were having to bathe it about three times a bloody day. Ointments, penicillin wouldn't shift it and I had this thick horrible bandage and shouldn't really have been riding I don't suppose.' He managed to shrug off the injury; the only saving grace being that it was a wound rather than something muscular.

Wilson sauntered up the 4-minute hill as the last man, a slight eight stone and seven pounds. Under ideal conditions a huge crowd of over 4,000 stood in rapt admiration, before unleashing a primitive roar of encouragement, swelling in noise and tone as he climbed onwards. At the last gasp it became clear that the North versus South battle would be settled by a true champion's ride. Wilson had won and exorcised the ghosts of hill climbs past, taking three seconds from Roy Keighley. He had also earned his place at the Champions' Dinner, where his thoughts turned to Jimmy Gaines: 'I was able to say thanks when they had the presentation down in London. I took Jimmy; he met all these stars, the champions, and we had breakfast with Norman Shiel and he was so pleased, and I was too, that I could say, "Thanks Skip" for the bits of advice and holding me back.'

The Champions' Night was a big occasion in those days. Nowadays it takes place at a hotel somewhere in the Midlands. In the heyday of time trialling it was the Royal Albert Hall: 'It was really so frightening, you'd leave the box and they'd give you instructions, there are two gangways and they tell you which one to go to, there's all this activity behind you and you're in a concrete corridor, stood at top of steps and there's this mass of people and they sound this bloody trumpet while you walk down the thing. But it's an experience; you feel privileged. I was gobsmacked, I felt humbled – this just for riding a bloody bike race. This is what you feel, I'm not that good to deserve this treatment, you can't imagine that all that trouble had been gone to for the group of us, the national champions. I still have, to this day, and use the second prize. It had to be of an engraveable nature and was of no sporting connection whatsoever. It's a Parker 51 propelling lead pencil that I use in my sketch book and I've been using it since 1953. It was worth two guineas, I've got the pen that goes with it that I got the year after. That was three guineas.'

With one win apiece, Ingman and Wilson were back on the start sheet at Saintbury in 1956, both vying for a brace of championship wins. Saintbury is seen as a roadman's hill, but the changes in gradient serve up a level of challenge beyond the more consistent longer climbs. It requires careful judgement to cope with the length and subtle variations in pitch. The longer the climb, the more important pace becomes, and the more difficult to judge. The sun shone kindly, allowing respite and showing a different side to the Cotswolds from that seen in 1951. Accepted wisdom leant towards a 65″ gear. For a technical and difficult climb it seems like a big gear – like most things, cadences have increased and gear inches decreased over the decades.

Bill Bradley was the first to squeak inside Ronnie Stringwell's course record with 6′-25.8″, pushing a mammoth 69″ gear up and over the steepest sections. Ingman worked his way up the climb, alternating between being up and on top of the gear, dancing on the pedals, then sitting down and measuring out the rhythm and cadence when the gradient allowed. The tunnel of onlookers at the top were astounded as news of the time filtered out: 6′-13.8″. Ingman paid for his effort, just as Robinson had suffered five years previously. He rode through the tunnel of vicarious spectators before collapsing into the crowds and then onto the bank. The gathered clubmen looked on in stunned admiration at the transparent effort and the physical cost; the world caved in around the climber, utterly spent from the explosive effort of the last section of the climb. Ingman lay prone at the side of the hill, in amongst the leaves and grass in the lea of the bank, tended to by friends from the Paragon. The protective cordon allowed him to breathe, refill his oxygen starved lungs and gather himself.

All the while they waited for the figure of Eric Wilson to emerge from the depths, rocketing up onto the Cotswold escarpment. Trepidation was mixed with excitement. It would require a monumental effort to surpass Ingman's time, but Wilson was the only rider capable of doing so. Waiting for the scratch rider is the definitive moment in every championship, the last man capable of winning and reordering the podium; it's a moment of nervous tension. Every neck craned to catch the first glimpse of the rider appearing through the trees, the roar and swoop of sound preceding his journey upwards and giving notice that the challenger and champion was coming. The effort and pressure built, the veins and aorta fluttering into a frenzy to transport oxygen through the blood, but slower than the body needed, as is the case with every battle against gravity when everything is given and nothing more remains, only the steady decline into oxygen debt. He rode inside the old course record, but ceded 3.8 seconds to Ingman; the title returned to Norwood. As Wilson puts it, 'the rotten beggar came back and won again'.

The pendulum duly swung back the other way in 1957. It was a horrible day on Winnats Pass, leading the onlooking Vic Clark to comment, 'When I set that record the wind was blowing up the hill just as strongly as it was blowing down against the riders today'.* It was by some distance the slowest of the four Nationals to have been held on the climb. It wasn't a particularly blustery day, more an unceasing session of constant wind rolling down the gorge. The spectacular and steep-sided walls served only to send lacerating currents of cold air into the isolated competitors, battling gravity and the elemental fury of nature. The first five hundred metres were translated from the purity of the hill climb into a purgatory of despair. Each rider was forced to reckon with the sudden physical reality of the headwind and the invisible and unyielding hand of nature, making the competitors double and then redouble their effort,

---

* George Pearson, 'Winnats Pass at its Toughest', *Cycling*, 31/10/57

simply to counteract the additional and darkening forces. It was only with the ascent into the galleries, typically three or four deep, that there was any respite from the bullying wind. The slight change in the angle of the climb helped and the last few hundred yards offered a vague hope of getting on top of the gear and starting to put some power out, rather than churning and forcing and struggling and grinding to the top. The only problem was the gradient beneath the bike, which more than made up for any subsidence in wind by rising to a 1-in-4. Gear choices were correspondingly low, with 51″ being the favourite option.

'It wasn't a welcoming climb, Winnats,' said Wilson. 'I used to like walking on the climbs or riding gently before the event, sometimes three times. I liked to feel the hill, to become part of it. Winnats always seemed a stranger, it never seemed a friendly hill to me. If I was using a Cyclo sprocket it would have to be a bloody tough climb, because I'd always use Villiers because of the perfect fit on the chain.'*

Many confessed they would have happily gone into the 40s if they had the necessary cogs; Bill Holmes captured the mood for many in his first national championship, with 'big opponents, a big crowd', but definitely no "big gear".' Discretion is the better part of valour. In unfriendly conditions the 'true test' became one for only the strongest of riders. Photos show spectators with gaberdines blown out, hair ruffled, standing at an angle to counteract the gales.

Also on the startsheet was Tommy Simpson, looking to secure the double after taking the BLRC title on Mam Tour Gap a few weeks previously. During the great schism between Percy Stallard's BLRC and the NCU, the BLRC ran a parallel hill climb championship. On occasions riders attempted the double, but by and large the RTTC event remained the 'blue riband' championship with the BLRC event attracting a smaller

---

* Cyclo made a larger sprocket than the largest Villiers, thereby offering a lower gear.

field. The event had been held on Holme Moss and Winnats, before settling on Mam Tor.*

Simpson lined up for his tilt at the title, only to be turned away by the observer for having no lockring; a 'compulsory fitment' then and now. By all accounts, particularly his own, Simpson was incandescant:

> '...half a minute... ten seconds... then Shaw said, "Mr Simpson, you have no locking ring and will be disqualified if you start like that!" I heard the timekeeper saying, "Five, four, three, two, one!" and jumped off the bike in a complete fury. How I did not throw it at Mr Shaw I shall never know. "You stupid little nit!" I shouted. "Just because I won the BLRC hill climb you want to disqualify me. That's how you go is it? You're too small to beat anybody and you take it out on them that way!" I called him all the names I could think of and he just stood there and took it. As I paused for breath he said, "Mr Simpson, if you calm yourself and find a locking ring you can start." He was marvellous and I wished that I had the same self-control... I rushed off madly to find someone who might lend me the missing piece of equipment... I threw myself up the hill and caught my minuteman in about 500 yards and then blew up.'**

He lost over five minutes in the kerfuffle of the late start, which was added on to his effort, a pedestrian 4'-15.2", the sting taken out of any competitive edge.

Eric Wilson wonders what might have been: 'I can remember freezing at the bottom. You know you're going to turn that corner and it's going to hit you. There was a bloke stood there

---

* Winners included Geoff Clark (a founder member of the BLRC, with Stallard) in 1946 on Holme Moss, Len West (another founder member of the League) in 1948 on the same climb, Tony Murray in 1950 on a wind-swept Winnats where only 18 of the 28 starters managed to finish, and Brian Haskell on Mam Tor in 1956. Tommy Simpson won in 1957, before Peter Graham did the double in 1958.

** *Cycling is my Life*, Tom Simpson

with a tie sticking straight out. I was pleased, but rather at the back of my mind I wonder if Tommy would have won it.'

Simpson or no Simpson, Eric Wilson was undoubtedly the man for the day. He had proved his worth as a devastating hill climber and the course suited him more than at Saintbury. In the absence of Ingman there could only be one winner. His 3'-56.6" shook off the challenge of Arthur Pursey, the great white hope from the South, and the only other rider to get under four minutes. This contrasts with Clark's course record of 3'-23.8". The thirty second swing on the day shows the difficulty of the climb when the conditions turn. Peter Graham, a near neighbour in Rossendale, recorded a shade over four minutes, serving notice that there was a new kid on the block.

Wilson finished second the following year at Bathford, then some way down at Winnats in 1959, where the omnipotent Bramley Wheelers outfit took their seventh team title in succession. He stormed back on Saintbury in 1960 to take his third title and move level with Vic Clark. Moreover, his Rossendale took the team prize: 'I was pleased and we won the team; they probably pulled their socks off more than what I did. Roy Ashworth was a tryer, but he must have given absolutely a hundred and five percent. Barry Clegg was always a tryer. I was pleased for them. Bramley Wheelers had ruled the roost for yonks and it was really close.' The hegemony of the West Yorkshire team had finally been broken.

The third counter for the Rossendale, Roy Ashworth, was interviewed by a local journalist following the success of the team. The writer innocently asked if he might be selected for the Olympics, to which Ashworth replied, 'There's a good chance.' His light-hearted comment made waves across the valley where Wilson worked, selling spring mattresses: 'The boss called me in. "Well done Eric, on the… what is it… the hill climb? Don't think you're bloody getting any bloody time off for going to Australia. You can forget it!"' It was a different era: Stan Brittain, who won a silver medal in the team road race at Melbourne in 1956, is alleged to have lost his job on account of the time off. It's unthinkable that it might happen now.

The years following his success on Saintbury seem to represent a dying of the light. It's hard to explain why people ride hills in the first place, and perhaps easier to articulate why they stop – it's hard and unforgiving. It's easier not to do hill climbs. The 1962 excursion to Catford, a short sharp climb, meant nothing to Wilson and in the National on Winnats in 1963 he felt that enough was enough. In 1964 he rode a truncated calendar, only entering the Nick on account of it being the club climb and an opportunity for a drink in the pub afterwards. The National didn't figure in his reckoning and there were three weeks to go until the end of October. As is often, or at least sometimes the case, when we are at our most relaxed, we do well, and Wilson surprised himself with his time in the club event. He sent off an entry, first class carrier pigeon, and set about getting race fit in short order.

'I'd been developing a form of running whereby you'd run hard for five yards, then relax, then another five yards, and I tried to develop it for the bike. I knew how long the hill would take, three to four minutes. Pulse pedalling, I called it, in four minute sessions. I started off, accelerated gradually for eight revs, held it, then on top of that for another eight revs. Then do that for four minutes. Then do it again. I'd do it on a gradual gradient over Rochdale way. I was doing 18 miles per hour when I finished; your speed goes up and you're trying like bloody hell, and I thought it would be a bit of a winner. After three weeks of four minute sessions with a good recovery break between I felt fitter and faster than I'd ever been.

'They'd increased Peaslows, yippee, it levelled out then went on at the top. I really felt that I was going to win and I wanted to win because I wanted to pack it in. I think it was about three seconds, but it should have been more because the guy that I was catching, I should have passed him but I thought, "I can't do that, pass him on the line", so I eased off. I knew I were up because I'd had the check.'

On a diet of three weeks of proto-intervals, a lot of self-belief and some pedigree, Wilson took the title for a record fourth time. The headline in the Comic hinted at another secret weapon in his armoury: 'Puff Puff Wilson Wins Again.'

'I smoked, but not as much as everyone used to think I did. I used to always light a fag when I finished the Championship. It became a bit of a ritual.' After setting a new standard with four wins, Wilson slipped quietly into cycling retirement and a life in the cycling industry.

3

Origins

'The man who will systematically walk all the hills in his way, is a dead thing, devoid of all self-esteem, courage and enterprise.'*

Early hill climbs were viewed as a test to see who could get to the top; riding a fast time is less important when you're riding a penny farthing. There is something utterly terrifying about the prospect of a fall from an 'ordinary', comparable to throwing yourself out of a second storey window. Road surfaces were unmetalled, a caustic mix of gravel and debris, some compacted, some not, and it wasn't until 1888 that J.B. Dunlop patented the pneumatic bicycle tyre. As early as September 4, 1880, the Surrey Bicycle Club promoted a hill climb on Reigate Hill: 'The gradient averages 4 ½ in every 100, and the steepest part is 12 in 100. Total length from "The Grapes" Hotel, Reigate, to the Suspension bridge, 2.640 yds. Total rise, 420 ft. Forty-one riders in all got up, G.H. Coleman, of Leytonstone, being credited with the fastest time, 4 mins. 40 secs., but the clocking was questioned.' As if riding an

---

* J. Handel Barr, 'Hills', *Cycling* 1897

Ordinary uphill wasn't challenging enough, 'H.L.Cortis rode the hill with one arm in a sling.' *

In London the Hornsey and Canonbury Cycling Clubs combined in 1881 to organise an event on Muswell Hill, heading from the Victoria Hotel to finish at the Drinking Fountain. Throughout the 1880s more and more open events took place and hill climbing emerged as a distinct and challenging discipline. Prior to 1886 times were less important, particularly if the gradient was a challenge. Reports stated simple achievements, such as, 'Nineteen numbers got up. No times were taken'.

Things began to change with the advent of the safety bicycle; getting to the top was no longer a fortuitous fluke or the preserve of one or two riders, and a better method was required to ascertain the winner. In 1886 Finsbury Park CC ran an Open on Muswell Hill in London, with P.L. Breysig winning in 2'-45" from H.B. Saunders. No mention of machines was made. 1887 saw the *Sport and Play* magazine promotion at Weatheroak: 'Gradients 1-in-12, 1-in-10, 1-in-8, 1-in-6 ½, 1-in-7, 1-in-8, 1-in-10. Length, 1,060 feet. Surface Bad.' Frank Moore won from A.J. Wilson, both on safeties. Arthur James Wilson was a founder of the North Road Club, a key instigator in the Road Records Association and a tandem trike record holder to boot. He was also the editor of *Bicycling Times* and the *Touring Gazette*. The *Athletic News* promotion took place on Wizard Hill near Alderley Edge, with A.M. Dutton winning from T.W. Grace in 5'-1½". Other events took place at Mowacre and even across the water on Lucan Hill in Ireland and at Carisbrooke on the Isle of Wight.

The Catford Hill Climb didn't start until comparatively late, in 1887, but the event is lauded because it is the oldest continuously held bike race in the world. Where other opens and even clubs have fallen by the wayside, the Catford

---

* *The Badminton Library of Sports and Pastimes: Cycling*, (Ed.) Duke of Beaufort, 1892

continues: longevity is its unique selling point. In later years it has been part of a double header with the Bec CC hill climb taking place nearby. Riders compete at Catford first thing, then finish with the Bec CC promotion on White Lane. The Catford climb doesn't take place in Catford, but on Yorks Hill, and while it isn't long, it is horribly steep. The average gradient is 12%, with two nasty 25% ramps. The gradient is made more challenging by the greasy, leaf-strewn surface which leads to excessive wheelspin. It's 707 yards in old money, and it has been 31 years since Phil Mason put the course record on the shelf with a 1'-47.6". In short, it's a mulchy corridor of dreams and nightmares, and the event is a magnet for all of the clubs in and around south London.

The Sunday of the race sees club runs deviate and head for the hill. De Ver Cycles, the Addiscombe, the Paragons of Norwood and Dulwich all make the pilgrimage. It lures the capital's resident professionals and some returning roadmen, all keen to have a tilt at the coveted trophy from Catford and then take home the cash on offer at the Bec. Rapha Condor and Sigma Sport usually field a smattering of riders and David Millar made it his last ever race in 2014, somehow drawn to the romanticism of the event. He came 21st. It's a get-together and an end-of-season blow out, the last hurrah for the summer bikes before the nuclear winter.

In the first year only twelve riders made it to the top with eight on safety bicycles, three on trikes and one brave soul on an ordinary. In 1888 the Catford climb took place on Westerham, with W. Chater Lea wining convincingly from T. Simmonds. Chater Lea won again on Titsey Hill in 1889.* Bertram Blunt was first tricycle and A.V. Puckle first ordinary. The names speak of moustachioed men in alpaca and plus fours, pipe-smokers and Victorian gentlemen, enacting a form of muscular Christianity on their way to the top (or near it). It's a shame there aren't more people called Puckle or Bertram these days .

---

* Several hills were visited in the early years in the quest for the perfect challenge.

In 1890 Chater-Lea had to settle for second behind Felix Greville. No doubt he was kept busy by the formation of his bicycle component company in the same year – a Chater-Lea cottered crankset is a thing of beauty.

By 1891 the Catford C.C. gave notice of their event with a plaintive request in the cycling press: 'A stiff hill wanted':

'Hill climbers will be glad to hear that the annual mountaineering contest of the Catford CC takes place this year on July 18th. The club has not yet fixed on a hill and will be glad to hear of one which is as stiff as Westerham, Titsey or Toys. The contest this year will be full of interest, as pneumatic tyres have never yet been tried in an open hill contest.'

The club opted for Waller Hill, near Caterham, but continued the search for the definitive parcours.

In 1922 the event visited Brasted Hill, which became an early favourite and was used 21 times. C.F. Perridge won for the first time, usurping the reigning champion: 'It would appear that F.M. Dowell is nearing the end of his unchallenged supremacy in the climbing of steep hills, for the old crack could on this occasion only finish fifth.' Physical decline, a large crowd and a tough challenge were the key ingredients: 'An orderly crowd of visiting clubmen formed an appreciative gallery which, however, did not make any noticeable difference to the pitiless influence of gravitation.' So wrote *Cycling* in its report of the event.

Alongside the Catford climb, it is clear that the sport was growing in popularity. The November 3rd, 1933 edition of *Cycling* provides a glimpse of a healthy hill climb calendar taking up a full page: Merlin CC promoted on Chalk Hill; Aylesbury Wheelers went for Cop Hill; Wolverhampton Wheelers chose Orton Hill, where Percy Stallard came second; Notts Castle BC chose Blackberry Hill; Audenshaw YMCA displayed their muscular Christianity at Alderley

Edge; Bournemouth Arrow CC cast off at Fisherman's Hill and the East Anglian CC tackled Ringland Hill.

In 1936, after 15 years on Brasted, Catford CC visited Yorks Hill for the first time, apparently on the suggestion made by *Cycling* the previous year, and E.W. Hussey, the 'Finsbury Park crack', won a seventh successive title. *Cycling* reported that he 'smilingly sped to the top with graceful ease,' using a futuristic oval-shaped chainwheel, while on a greasy and dark day, 'several riders wrapped cord around their tyres to counteract the effect of the autumnal mulch.'

How to cope with wheelspin remained the biggest problem. In 1937 only 16 of the 92 riders made it to the top, but 1940 was even better – or worse – with only four making the complete ascent. In the only Championship event on the course, Peter Graham combatted the problem with a grass track tyre. Others simply ran very low pressures, as low as 50psi. Crowds loom down on the riders, lined up on the steep sided banks three or four deep. It's a spectacle unlike any other. As a rider, it's hard to see beyond the faces encroaching inwards and impossible to think about anything in the din of cowbells and baying of a good-natured crowd.

Steve Marchant compensated for his lack of a National win by being the fastest man at Catford on six occasions, but it's Max Pendleton* who has the long-term bragging rights with eight wins. The current king of the hill is Rob Gough, winning four times in a row, until Matt Pilkington got the better of him in 2012. The climb has a mythic quality in the south-east, particularly amongst those who favour the shorter stuff, but in raw terms, it lacks a certain something – probably 200 yards – which would make it genuinely popular as a challenging climb outside of the south-east. As a spectacle though, only the Rake on a National Championship weekend comes close.

---

* Max Pendleton, father of Victoria, National Grass Track Champion and King of Catford.

4

The Rake's Progress

(1958–1962)

'On a hill you just stop, you've had it. You start to weave about, you're gone, and it's like death. The last 50 yards you can't hear, see or think, everything's burning and killing. It's just a question of whether you can put up with it.'

In 2012 the National returned to the Rake for the third time. It is a short and extremely savage climb with an assured place in hill climbing folklore. This is mostly down to the 1-in-4 section which runs up towards the finish. The mythic status of the Rake is enhanced by the presence of a handrail for pedestrians attempting to walk up. One of the reasons it has become so popular is because of the unstinting efforts of the organiser, Peter Graham. My feelings towards Peter Graham are slightly ambivalent; this has absolutely nothing to do with him personally – he's a fine chap – and everything to do with his piercing honesty when commentating. He sits in a panoptic gazebo on Rakefold from whence he gazes down, a latter-day Zeus on Mount Olympus, skewering the performances of the competitors in dulcet northern tones. His withering comments are boosted by the kind of PA last seen in a working men's club in Rossendale accompanying a buxom karaoke singer. Each rider is succinctly defined in incisive northern vernacular for the enthusiastic mob on the hardest section of the climb.

I felt things were going well in the 2012 National – only because I hadn't hit the hardest section of the hill. The verb 'hit' is apposite in this case; up until that point the gradient is manageable at pace. It doesn't hurt too much on the initial 10%, the slope levels off nicely and the gear turns over efficiently. The road then turns sharply to the right and any pretence of dignity and *souplesse* is shattered in an instant as everything closes in, including the crowd, in a kaleidoscopic collapse of vision. Beforehand I'd agonised over which cog to go with on the back. The only issue I had was that switching out to a 19 would mean a bit more of a faff. I left the 18 on there. I was anxious when it transpired that two of the fastest men, Matt Clinton and Pete Tadros, had gone a bit lighter, but, nothing ventured, nothing gained, I felt. My optimism was misplaced and I struggled to turn the pedals. Any hope that I had lurking in the back of my mind that I at least looked like I was going well was deflated in the time it took Peter Graham to finish his sentence: 'And here's Paul Jones of the Bristol South, riding fixed, and… and… well, it definitely looks a bit overgeared does that…' It cut through the wall of sound and it's one of my defining memories of the day; but in a curious way it's a positive one. By no means does Peter Graham reserve his acerbic comments for those making up the middle and lower reaches of the card. Jim Henderson received the same treatment, both when coming third and when winning it; a disembodied and unmistakeable northern voice drifting down across the top of the course, the damning and chastening words hanging in the air and reaching the ears of the struggling rider: 'he seems to have gone a cog too big there'.

When it comes round to the District, they tend to plump for the Rake, and it's Peter Graham who organises.* Each club is affiliated to a geographical 'District' which offers regional oversight of all aspects of time trials and hill climbs. When I spoke with him in mid-August before the championship he was wading through a huge number of entry forms. This is the organiser's lot; pages and pages of forms, selecting the entrants, setting out the field in keeping with regulations, but also allowing for the idiosyncratic slant that some tend to put on things.** Graham has been an undoubted force for good within the sport, doing what every racing cyclist should do: giving a bit back, with interest. He has involved the wider community in the promotion, harnessing a disparate group of sponsors and offering huge cash prizes, or even a Rolex watch, to anyone who took the course record. For a while he publicised the event as the 'richest cycling race in the world', with a potential prize fund of a thousand pounds for two minutes and eight seconds of work. In the end Jeff Wright somehow managed to take the record and the shiny timepiece. His course record still stands.

As well as bringing the razzmatazz and some of the excitement with his promotions in Ramsbottom, Peter Graham has also been responsible for the jerseys. He is scathing in his opinion of the 'silly cap' awarded to the winner. It's certainly gold and shiny. He is also adamant that the champion deserves to be recognised by the public for what he is. Peter Graham pulled on the BLRC jersey in 1958 and he was thrilled to bits; his face lights up even now to think of it. In 1999 he commissioned the jerseys for the event, with Jim Henderson being first to wear one. All went swimmingly until 2011 when British Cycling objected to the jersey being given away in a CTT event. As it stands, British Cycling hold the prerogative

---

* Each club is affiliated to a geographical 'District' which offers regional oversight of all aspects of time trials and hill climbs.

** Things have changed slightly now that the CTT has recognised that there is this thing called the internet, whch can be quite useful and will not lead to the downfall of bike racing forever.

for the national champions' jerseys. They seem to feel that it might demean the jersey in some way, shape or form, perhaps become part of a wider trend to litter the country with the red, white and blue bands. This ignores the growing tendency of new riders to happily don the polka dot jersey or rainbow bands whilst labouring up the Horseshoe Pass in the 34:32 at around 3mph. It also ignores the fact that the hill climb championship is inconceivably tough and deserves wider recognition. Peter Graham is right, British Cycling are wrong. It doesn't seem to have been a problem; hill climb winners only wear the bands in hill climbs. No-one gets confused.

The Rake is Peter Graham's back yard. He has won there, trained there, organised there. He knows everything there is to know about the course and those who have ridden it. The Rake was first used, apocryphally, by Bury Cycling Club in 1929. They held a competition to see who could make it the furthest up the incline. Eventually, a cyclist made it to the top and it subsequently became a race to the line. Back in the mid 1950s, the Rake was more of a training climb than anything spectacular. It has grown in affection over time. With low traffic counts and a plethora of suitable courses across the area, it was simply one of a number of testing events littered throughout the season. And back in 1957 Peter Graham was animating the race from within, not without.

In and amongst my journey around the country to meet with hill climbers various, I made my way to Rochdale, on the edge of Manchester, to catch up with Peter Graham. It was the middle of a February deep freeze with Arctic weather buffeting the North of England. I presume the North is always like this. I nearly slipped and broke my back on a treacherous ice moraine after taking a wrong turn in the driveway by his house. I took Peter Graham some biscuits. He gave me a wry Northern look. I think he thought I was daft or peculiar or both. It's not really the done thing in Oldham for grown men to be giving each other biscuits. He put them to one side and I suspect they are still there: the strange gift from the chap from the South where they do things differently. Despite my *faux pas*, he spoke freely on and off the record, was generous to a fault with his praise of others, but is not afraid of punctuating his speech with the odd titbit or nugget of salacious gossip regarding an erstwhile rival, suffixed with a casual 'off-the-record of course', to which I nod, conspiratorially. He is short in stature, not tiny, but compact, with the muscular arms and a sculpted jawline still evident. There is no wattle neck of age, only a sprightliness and age-defying physique that reflects the countless miles ridden – and still ridden. Once a hill climber, always a hill climber; the hill climb was always the discipline he excelled at and he's also mentored a number of younger riders, including Vince Smith and Lynn Hamel.

Graham first became aware of his potential to defy gravity in a Withington Wheelers event in 1952. Eric Wilson lived just up the valley and the area was full of elite roadmen. He was then called up for national service where the bike racing helped smooth things over, just as it had eased Vic Clark's passage through the military. Graham won the RAF championship at an obscure camp in the Midlands and this helped him train more; the officers were happy to support any handy athletes and allow them the pass they needed to train – as long as they were winning and therefore holding up the good name of the Air Force, especially in an inter-service capacity. By writing to other associations and asking them to set up 'afternoon 10s' with an invitation to ride, a day out from camp could be secured with some juicy travel vouchers. The travel vouchers were then sold on at a profit, as the team would ride to the event and ride home again.

For a while Graham was sharing a billet with the evergreen John Woodburn and Dave Marsh. Later he got to commuting from Rochdale to Kirkham and back every day, about 35 miles each way. He daren't be late for his supper so he used to pedal 'like the clappers' to get home and avoid an angry Dad. Turning in seventy miles a day, five or six days a week on a fixed wheel, he rapidly became very fit and started to overtake his companions, including the prodigiously gifted Woodburn, who had been staying on camp. In the Preston Wheelers '25' at Brock he managed a super-fast 58'-36", in contrast to Woodburn's 1hr-02'.

Towards the end of August the hill climb training would start, typically riding 'gently gently' round a circuit involving a three mile climb which they rode up like men possessed, before finishing off by dropping down into Ramsbottom and heading up the Rake three or four times. The next morning he could hardly stand. I doubt there's anyone who knows the Rake like Peter Graham; he trained on it with Eric Wilson and others and tells rich anecdotes of half-wheeling savagery amongst the club fraternity, none prepared to give any quarter.

In 1962 Graham was riding up in the dark with Ken Nuttall on his wheel. Nuttall was a multiple Milk Race stage winner and later came second in the National Road Race in 1964, before heading off to the continent. Nuttall had intended to ride the National so he doorstepped Peter Graham to find the climb and do some training. They were both pushing each other hard, as friends tend to do when riding together; there is a silent pleasure in the unspoken battles between training partners. They ended up side by side, both leaning over the front of their bikes, each rider swaying unsteadily from side to side, teeth clenched and hands tight on the hoods. The two milky braze-on lights on the front were not even enough to illuminate the surface ahead, merely two equidistant and shallow, pulsing pin pricks of light. Up ahead in the dusky twilight they could see a figure silhouetted against the gas lamp at the top, making his way down the climb. The only thing the figure could have seen were the two lights moving in and out towards each other, swirling in the near dark, accompanied by ragged, rasping breaths, in tandem, and out of rhythm: 'He pressed himself right back against the wall in total fear, and it was only when we got level with him that he realised what it were. He said, "You daft buggers, you'll bloody kill yourselves doing that," and he tottered off holding onto the handrail, down to the pub.

He must have thought it was a monster or something coming up out of the black pit. Even in the dark I could see he was afraid.'

In his first outing in the National Championship event in 1957 Graham came fourth on Winnats. To cope with the vicious headwind he switched his 46 tooth chainring for a 44, lending the larger ring to Bill Holmes whom he proceeded to beat by one second. He apologised profusely for years afterwards. The same year Graham also rode the BLRC event, riding out from Bury to Castelton with a headwind all the way. He was late and very nearly missed the start. With no time to consider the intricacies of gear selection, he simply based his gear choice on Brian Haskell, who always went for a gear that was too tall, and took off about two or three inches. Haskell was a sheet metal worker and a strong rider with an international pedigree. Without any real reconnaissance, Graham took the hill at about 90% effort and was undergeared on the last section. Tom Simpson took the win by three seconds. The year afterwards, having been demobbed, Graham went back up to Mam Nick for a second crack. He spent the weekend at Castleton, heading up and down every inch of the tarmac, and managed to reverse the result by the same time difference. Tommy Simpson was not pleased. There was no shaking of hands; he headed off immediately.

On the back of his BLRC win, Graham headed south for the 1958 Championship in high spirits and in search of a rare double. The West DC organised the event and found a new hill, choosing to ignore Lansdowne Lane. The edges of Bath are dominated by steep climbs out of the Avonvale Valley and Monk's Lane edges upwards from the bottom. The initial steepness gave way to a shallow finish; as a result most of the crowd clustered lower down to see the agonies of the nastier section of the course. Graham succeeded in doing the double where Simpson had failed just a year before. He professed himself dissatisfied with his choice of gear, 56", in contrast to Bill Holmes' 54", but in fact it suited him to a tee. Both Holmes and Bradley showed their form from riding the World Championship by taking third and fourth place. With the exception of Don Tanner in fifth and then Pete Baldwin in tenth, the southern riders were outclassed by the northern invaders.

In 1959 the event returned to Winnats for the fifth time. The wind was again roaring down from the top to the Speedwell Cavern at the bottom, slowing times and making it miserable for the competitors. Russell Foster opted for a 47" gear over erstwhile postman Gordon Rhodes' 52", covering significantly less distance with each turn of the pedals and having to spin his way from the bottom to the top. Rhodes was eight seconds down on Foster at halfway and received a time check from a spectator on the climb. Rhodes responded with an almighty dig and somehow made up nine seconds over the top to beat Foster by a second. Peter Graham had been odds-on favourite to retain the title. He'd bagged Vic Clark's course record a fortnight previously and beaten Rhodes three times. A week before Russell Foster had also put five seconds into Rhodes over a shorter climb. Rhodes' victory was a shock. He had finished a creditable eleventh the year before, but on Winnats his club mates and supporters, including Brian Robinson, felt that he had judged his form perfectly for the biggest race of them all.

The 1960 season was a big step up for Graham and he rode much more, taking part in the Manx international, local BAR and 12-hour, and then the Tour of Yugoslavia for the National team with Norman Baty, a successful Milk Race rider.* By the time he got home he looked, by his own admission, like 'an underfed rat'. He was worn out by October and hadn't had his customary August 'lull'. A resurgent Eric Wilson made it a hat trick on Saintbury. Even the press accounts commented on how Graham looked 'extremely tired'.

---

* Norman Baty won six stages of the Milk Race between 1962 and 1968. His brother, Bill Baty, was also an accomplished roadman, twice national champion and winner of a stage of the Milk Race in 1960.

Graham's experiences of the continental peloton were telling. During the Tour of Yugoslavia he had aimed for the mountain prime, riding at his own pace and ignoring the others. It wasn't steep but it went on and on. After half an hour there were only two left, 'a little Bulgarian who kept jumping away', only for Graham to pull him back: 'We got to a bend, and he put his hand in his back pocket and he pulled out what I can only describe as a golf ball and he put it in his mouth. So I jumped and thought he can't hold on with that in his mouth; he can't breathe. And I dropped him. Within three minutes he came past me as though there were no climb. And whatever he took I do not know. He just disappeared.'

Wilson's win in 1960 was marginal, a fifth of a second over Graham in second place, and whilst it represented a strong ride from Graham over the longer parcours of Saintbury, it was the next year that Graham returned to winning ways. The contrast between the high Yugoslavian mountains of 1960 and the National Hill Climb of 1961 could not be more acute. The event headed south to Yorks Hill, home of the Catford Hill Climb. He rode round looking for it the day before, not realising the brevity of the climb, and it was only when someone said they'd been up it twice that he realised. Graham was riding a Pennine made by Johnny Mapplebeck and had stuck a Dunlop Number 6 grass track tyre on the back. Like Max Pendleton and many other riders of the era, Graham liked the grass track, partly because the pure sprinters struggled after a few laps.

Once he'd worked out where he was, Graham went up and down at least seven times on a tiny gear, picking his racing line, looking carefully at every inch of the surface, identifying the slippery sections. During the season Graham had recruited an old friend whom he stationed at the side of the climbs at the point of no return; whereupon he had to absolutely turn himself inside out in pursuit of glory. The friend, Jack Spencer, wore a horribly bright and fluorescent cape. The plan was carefully considered and measured out. However, early in the season Jack believed that his companion was underestimating his abilities, so he would amble a few yards down the hill, extending the 'death zone'. Graham would pass him and then unleash hell, only to suffer and start to heave as he neared the finish, worrying that he'd mistimed the effort. Eventually he got him to stand still.

Russell Foster was back in the running and Graham closed him out by two tenths of a second, with Dave Patten in third. It was generally seen as too short for the Northern specialists, but Graham proved them wrong and got himself back to the top of the podium. It didn't go smoothly for the other illustrious Northerner, and the reigning champion, Eric Wilson: 'I was terrible at Catford. Way way down. It just wasn't my climb. It was greasy, you couldn't perform, or I couldn't.'

In 1962 the race visited the Nick O'Pendle for the first time. It's a surprise they ever went back again. At times the windswept edge of Pendle Moor can be an unforgiving and cruel place with no shelter on the barren scrub. The Rossendale Road Club had been holding their event on the climb for 13 years without experiencing anything like the conditions they had in the last weekend of October 1962. The invisible enemy roars across the Lancashire moorland with an untethered fury, strong enough to sweep riders from one side of the road to the other. The witches had sent down a furious hex.* It was extremely unpleasant and cold; too cold for Alan Ramsbottom who flatly refused to ride.** Barry Hoban stood at the side of the road, his continental tan gained from a summer spent in the peloton taking 16 wins, standing out amidst the pale and ashen northern crowd. He also opted not to ride into the teeth of a betwitched gale somewhere on a hill in Lancashire.

Spiteful gusts of wind blew down the valley with such force that riders were all but stopped in their tracks. The fickle and changeable nature of the wind meant that not all riders

* The 1612 Pendle Witch Trials cast a long shadow over the area, as well as providing some excellent opportunities for tourist revenue.

** Ramsbottom went on to ride for Pelforth and Peugeot in an illustrious career on the continent.

experienced the full horror. Eric Wilson, riding for host club Rossendale, requested an early time from Phil Livesy: 'I said, "Look, Phil, put me off number 60. I'll put such a bloody time up that they'll give up hope, that's my plan, I'm gonna do a stormer up there." But it was a terrible start. It was bucketing down, it was cold, there was a river pouring down the sodding hill. It was a horrible, horrible, horrible day. And I finished and I recorded the fastest time of the first 60. It then stopped raining, the wind dropped and the sun came out for virtually the last 60 riders. I was the only one that got it. And I thought, "It serves you bloody well right." That's honestly what I thought. That eleventh was a cracking ride under the conditions.'

The pushers drew the short straw, lurking in the depression at Sabden, at the foot of the climb, struggling to hold riders upright in the north westerly wind. Given the parlous weather, it was more than a surprise when an 18-year-old in only his second hill climb, Dixon Miller of Southport Road Club, climbed the 1,324 yard hill to take an astonishing third place. Russell Foster shaded the teenager out by a minimal fifth of a second, before Peter Graham edged him out by the same margin in one of the closest races for many years.

As well as the weather and the closeness of the podium, Bill Baty added his own contribution to the ongoing narrative of the National. He sought to answer a question that is asked from time to time: 'Why do I need a saddle in hill climbs?' Baty, along with his brother Norman and Peter Graham, had ridden a big event in Harrogate a few weeks previously. Nearing the finish the selection had been made and there were about a dozen still in contention, including Tommy Simpson and Stan Brittain. Two-bolt Campagnolo Record seatpillars were making their first appearance, and anyone who has ever tried to adjust one of these seat pillars with its strange spanner will confirm that they are a devil to get right. As the road went up, the group climbed, then freewheeled round the bend before all getting out of the saddle to accelerate out of the corner. As they rode, *en masse*, stamping on the pedals, a shiny leather saddle went sliding slowly across the road. Anxiety struck the honking peloton, with each rider simultaneously and collectively wondering if they still had a saddle to sit down on.

Peter Graham takes up the story: 'Everybody was thinking, "Bloody hell, is it mine?" and we all sat down gingerly – and it was Bill Baty's. He just stuck it in a big gear and stood on it all the way to the finish and he just held us off. So when he rode the hill climb championship he thought, "Well, I'm not going to need a saddle." How he got over the cattle grid I do not know.'

Bill's judgement on the experiment given to the scribe at *Cycling Weekly* tells you all you need to know: 'I've done a daft thing, I've done better than this in an overcoat.'

Wilson confirmed the anecdote with reference to Baty's 'previous': 'He would do anything for a laugh that lad. He probably sat on the post. He rode a criterion round Heaton Park and on the track going round he punctured, and the next time you see him coming round he's on a lady's touring bike.'

Peter Graham attributes his success to reconnaissance on the hill and a hefty dose of research, making notes on gear choices in previous events. It goes to show the huge number of variables facing any hill climber. Ultimately, he knew how to raise his pain threshold and go over into the realm of oxygen debt. With the next year's event due to return to Winnats Pass, there were few prepared to bet against Graham taking his fourth title. But little did anyone know that the discipline of hill climbing was about to be redefined by the greatest specialist the sport has ever seen.

5

The Nick

'As we travelled, we came near a very great hill, called Pendle Hill, and I was moved of the Lord to go up to the top of it; which I did with difficulty, it was so very steep and high. When I was come to the top, I saw the sea bordering upon Lancashire.'*

The austere landscape of Pendleton Moor towers intimidatingly above the Lancashire village of Sabden, with the squat and square houses sitting silently at the bottom of the valley. An approach from Clitheroe or Padiham involves a steady climb up to the exposed heath, before a precipitous drop into the heart of the settlement; ahead the road stretches onwards and upwards, a scar pointing to the blind summit of Pendle and the 'Nick' sliced into the sandstone plateau. It has beguiled and alienated visitors for many years, 'the celebrated mountain of that name extends and stretches in a long but interrupted descent of five miles, to the water of Pendle, a barren and dreary tract'.**

---

* Pendle Hill is closely linked to the Quaker movement after George Fox experienced 'visions' on the moorland.

** *The Wonderful Discoverie of Witches in the Countie of Lancaster*, Thomas Potts (pamphlet), 1613.

The moorland harbours dark secrets, none darker than the Pendle Witch Trials of 1612. As it has on Barber's Hill, in Llangollen, the landscape has become intertwined with myth. The coldly liminal nature of Pendle, a place forgotten somehow by time, is reinforced by Thomas Potts' contemporary record of the trials: *The Wonderfull Discoverie of Witches in the Countie of Lancashire*:

> 'He who visits Pendle will yet find that charms are generally resorted to amongst the lower classes; that there are hares which, in their persuasion, never can be caught, and which survive only to baffle and confound the huntsman; that each small hamlet has its peculiar and gifted personage, whom it is dangerous to offend; that the wise man and wise woman still continue their investigations of truth, undisturbed by the rural police or the progress of the schoolmaster; that each locality has its haunted house; that apparitions still walk their ghostly rounds.'

It was, and still is, an isolated parish, with the complex spiritual history of the community serving to reinforce their isolation; Whalley Abbey was dissolved in 1537, leading to an absence of guidance in superstitious and troubled times. The saga of the Witch Trials began when John Law, a pedlar, met Alison Devize on the road to Colne. She asked for pins, he refused, she cursed him. Metal pins were rare, expensive, and used for magical purposes and things like the charming of warts, divination and amorous cures, all of which may have explained the anger surrounding the failed purchase.

Moments later Law had a debilitating stroke and lost the power of speech. He later complained of having been injured by a witch and the terrifying wheels of 17th Century justice lumbered into operation. Feuding between families, including the evocatively named Demdike and Chattox clans, led to accusation and counter-accusation and a broadening of the literal witch hunt. Many of those implicated in the case identified themselves as witches, insofar as they were folk healers, a common feature of parochial life.

Alison Devize told all to the interrogating JP, Roger Nowell, in a sensational tale of fancies and familiars. A hysterical outbreak of rampant commercial rivalry between the two eighty-year-old matriarchs, Old Chattox and Old Demdike, saw accusations of witchcraft shatter the veneer of calm within the sleepy village.

> 'If the former had skill in waxen images, the latter could dig up the scalps of the dead, and make their teeth serviceable to her unhallowed purposes. In the anxiety which each felt to outvie the other, and to secure the greater share of the general custom of a not very extended or very lucrative market, each would wish to be represented as more death-dealing, destructive, and powerful than her neighbour.'

A hex, the use of clay figures, extortion money paid in oatmeal, maleficent sickness and marks on the skin left by the Devil himself, formed the internecine catalogue of complaint between the feuding families. After four hundred years the sinister events have been sanitised. You can drink the local ale, 'Witches' Brew', or take the X43 bus along The Witch Way. You can buy any number of witcherly trinkets in the shops of Clitheroe or Padiham. Or you can enter purgatory, not on a broomstick, but on a bicycle, and enter the North Lancashire Road Club hill climb up the Nick O' Pendle. The 2012 event coincided with the 400th anniversary of the Witch Trials, and whilst the actions of Demdike and Chattox have become immortalised over time, events on the Nick have acquired a latter-day superstitious status amongst the hill climb fraternity.

The ascent starts at the bottom of the valley in Sabden Village. It then climbs 460ft up to Pendle Moor. The initial section up to the cattle grid is a blank wall, eyeballing the competitor on the line. It levels off briefly before a final charge up and around the corner, out of the line of sight. Like all stern hill climbs it has a cattle grid; seemingly put there to disrupt any sense of rhythm or pace and to test the structural integrity of the lightest wheels and silk tubulars. It's 1324 yards of torture and more than once the conditions have been extremely unkind to the riders.

In 1970 a violent maelstrom of hail, wind and rain assaulted the second half of the field. But it was in 1962 that the Pendle hex bit deeply with the worst weather for any National, before or since. Only the 1980 running on the Horseshoe comes close. The wind blew through the cutting and swiped riders across the road. The angry and betrayed hand of the martyred witches could be sensed pulsing through the valley in the form of a gale force north westerly. Spectators huddled for warmth against cars, narrowing the gap for the riders in an unclosed road, with heavy traffic causing problems.

Despite the past, the fear of the curse, the inclement weather and the shivering cold of the Lancashire Moors, it remains a favourite hill climb for many. Usually I head up north once or twice during the season. My mum lives in Bradford so I pretend that I'm coming up to visit and just happen to have the bike in the car, and just coincidentally happen to also enter a series of races at least two weeks in advance. She's quite taken to watching the desperate privations of the thin people though, and as a runner seems to relish watching other people suffer for a change. I was lured across to the Nick by Carl Helliwell and Ian Stott after riding the Nelson Wheeler's event on Annal's Cross in 2010. They said, 'You'll have to come and do the Nick, it's a proper climb is that.'

The Blackburn CTC are a sizeable contingent with an irrational love of hill climbs and a long track record of success in the event, taking both team prizes and medals with Ian Stott. Look out for their blue jerseys on the hills, and listen out for the vocal encouragement they give each other. Annal's Cross is a gentle gradient and doesn't take long. I once held the course record for about 16 minutes, after which Mike Cuming tore up the hill in his Rapha Condor kit and put it on the shelf.

It sits on the other side of Pendle Moor to the Nick and contrasts sharply with its longer and steeper cousin. I drove over with my wife, who likes nothing better than standing on a freezing cold or damp hillside for half an hour on a Sunday morning when most of the populace remains six inches under a duvet. It's one thing dragging yourself to a hill climb on a freezing cold October morning, it's another thing altogether if you drag the family along as well. The descent down to Sabden filled me with a sense of dread. I knew I had either to come back up the steep and horrible road we were descending, or take the savage arrow up ahead that climbed out the other side. Neither looked appealing. I hoped it was the latter on account of the wind direction.

Chris Boardman enjoyed himself on the Nick. He set the course record that remains untouched. Jim Henderson also has strangely fond memories of the climb: 'I really love that one. It's got quite a good bit in it where it's straight for quite a while. It doesn't hide away from you, it invites you to come and have a go.' In the second of his hat trick of student championship wins the witches' hex struck once again. It was beyond rainy; torrents of water flooded down the road from Pendle Moor and there were barely any spectators. Even the parents of the foolhardy students knew better than to stand in the rain for an hour or more, watching their sons and daughters do something inexplicable; it was left to a few foolhardy souls to offer encouragement: 'Mike Mallon from Tyne Velo was there at the side of the road in absolutely soaking rain, shouting, "Goo on Lad... Goo on Jim, Cooorse reckud Jim", really yelling out in this thick Geordie accent. It was the first year I'd ridden Tour of the Peak, and he was riding and we were way out of our depth. Like me he was best in his club, did road racing, liked the hills, and we both got dropped early on and ended up doing 40 miles of this Premier, round and round.'

A month later and he could be heard suddenly shouting from the side of the road, cheering on his fellow cyclist. Jim Henderson identified the oddly solipsistic nature of the hill climb season; but also the paradox. He charged remorselessly up the climb in total isolation, kept company by the horrible weather and the hill and nothing else. When suddenly a figure emerged for a few brief moments, apropos of nothing, an apparition from a completely different time and place, removed – almost plucked from a different existence, and placed down at that spot next to a cattle grid by an invisible hand. These are the people you don't see afterwards, only later, at the next race, in a slightly different place. You don't see them all year, and suddenly faces loom out from the verge.

With the Nick O' Pendle, Henderson freely admits that part of what attracts him to it is 'the difficulty... it's not easy, it's the exact opposite of track racing, where it's all just there'. And I think he means that the track, especially Newport or Manchester, is a controlled environment, with changing rooms and showers, then the warmth of the pine boards and the overhead lights, the precise timing and the starting gates, the lines demarcating the divisions with clinical precision.

Something about the Nick seems to enable riders to push themselves beyond their typical limits, beyond even the fragile parameters of effort so frequently exceeded in a hill climb. Tjevan Pettinger, the 2013 National Champion, has come close to Boardman's record, benefitting from a generous tailwind push: 'I remembered doing Nick O' Pendle and I got within four seconds of Boardman's record in the National. I pushed myself further than in any other race. After about a minute I was light headed, going into the zone, I was dizzy, on the limit, it was a fantastic experience.'

The Nick O'Pendle has a road curving upwards and a latent elemental fury contained within the geography and the environment, which on the right day or the wrong day, can elevate a challenge beyond the realms of possibility. It encapsulates the sport within a hilly, violent, and mythic narrative. The climb is firmly anchored in the past and in the landscape. And the temporary and ephemeral hill climbers come to do battle, and go again, and it's reliably the same, insofar as it's utterly unreliable from year to year, and consistent in the shape of the challenge it provides.

2012 saw the 400th anniversary of the witch trials. I feared a catastrophe. The most it managed was a punctured tub for John Findley and a moderate headwind. It will be back, with a supernatural desire to challenge and inflict pain and suffering, just when we least expect it. The hex is dormant.

6

The Star Wheelers

(1963–1974)

'He could be very funny and could be very intense as well. I suppose that was why he was so successful. If he did anything he did it properly.'

It's easy to forget the relative obscurity of cycling as a sport prior to the current spectacular bike boom. The occasional blip saw a rider flirt with recognition: Reg Harris achieved fame in the 1950s, Robert Millar may have been familiar to one or possibly two people outside of the sport and Tommy Simpson came closest to transcending cycling and achieving a wider fame, winning BBC Sports Personality of the Year. But as a general rule, the most successful racing cyclists could pass unrecognised in the high street. Cycling has been a dark art practised by strange men in odd, figure-hugging outfits: black alpaca at dawn somewhere on the A38. The sub-genres of the event gave new meaning to the word 'niche', and hill climbing was of little renown outside of the pages of the *Cycling Weekly*. Head to a hill climb this October and ask the sallow stick-men if they have heard of Tommy Simpson or Sir Bradley Wiggins and they'll nod, sagely. Ask them the same question, but regarding Granville Sydney, and the chances are they won't have a clue who you're on about.

Granville Sydney stands above everybody (metaphorically, if not literally, being another relatively small and compact rider) in the history of the championship thanks to his matchless capacity to race up hill at incredible speeds with an unfettered violence of effort. He seemed able to go beyond the depths of physical exhaustion in order to repeatedly find something extra and exceed the limits of physical or mental comprehension. Granville Sydney appeared suddenly at Winnats Pass in 1963, taking the title from Peter Graham and equalling the course record. He won more championship titles than any other rider – six in ten years – and along the way accumulated ten championship medals. He rode for the Huddersfield Star Wheelers, who in the process became the most successful team in the history of the event. At his side throughout was his brother Graham, an accomplished roadman and master of the shorter climbs, especially the Rake. In 1967 Granville and Graham somehow tied for third place on Winnats. A diptych in the Comic was accompanied by the caption, 'Terrible pair, brothers alike even to beards and climbing styles, Granville (left) and Graham Sydney (right) – we think!'

Despite their similarities on the bike, they did many things differently. Graham worked as a travel agent; Granville was a systems analyst. Granville's season revolved around the hill climbs. Over the winter he did a lot of touring, running, circuits, but didn't really start till February, then he rode through. Graham was training on January 1st with everybody else. Graham favoured the shorter lumps, The Rake, or Winnats. Granville would ride anything, and usually win.

It's difficult when researching a book not to feel an affinity with some of the people and characters that you meet. It's even harder when your impression of that person is forged through photos and contemporary news reports, along with reminiscences from close friends, fellow competitors and family members. You read into everything you find and begin to form a representation of a character, but it's a shadow of a character, a representation in newsprint and faded photos. Over the course of writing and researching, Granville Sydney began to acquire an elevated status in my mind; he crept gently into my psyche and I found myself becoming increasingly captivated by his character. Odd things happened. I grew a beard in readiness for the hill climb season, just as Graham and Granville had done. I resolved to do as many on fixed wheel as I could in one season. I made the pilgrimage to Jackson Bridge for the first time to ride the Huddersfield Star Wheelers Open Hill Climb – also known as the Granville Sydney Memorial Event.

Hindsight in cycling allows us to look back at the past and make judgements on things. We can look for evidence of a rider's later success or subsequent decline and nod sagely as though we knew all along, even though we didn't see it at the time. We can also look for signs of incipient tragedy, tell-tale marks of pathos. Hindsight and myth tell us that Tommy Simpson was a rider doomed by a Sisyphean ambition that drove him to exceed his limits. Contemporary news reports speak of a chipper and dandy character with a sense of humour and an idiosyncratic nature that somehow counterbalanced the thirst for success. Whilst Team Sky might point to the blue line on their jerseys being the thin line between success and failure, in reality, for those outside of the scientific and controlled modern side of the sport, the dividing line between success and failure has been less clearly controlled, more of an ephemeral scratch drawn across the surface of a lake than a razor sharp stripe on a black background. In hill climbs the variables cannot be controlled. The capricious October weather, the dark mechanical forces that respond to the stresses and strains of extreme torque with petulance and anger and the fragile nature of the solipsistic climber all conspire against the rider in pursuit of victory. The margin for error is too narrow. The hill climb requires extraordinary sacrifices. Anyone wishing to compete at the sharp end needs a degree of mental and physical fortitude beyond the demands of other forms of racing.

A friend said recently that as much as he tries to push himself to the extreme when riding uphill, his head doesn't let him go beyond a certain point. I suspect it might be the same for me. I'm certainly no Vic Clark: I can't cross the line fresh and still put time into my co-competitors, neither can I defy the base needs of my body – for oxygen and respite – by pushing through into a place where collapse becomes the inevitable ending. I've come close, once being nearly sick at the top of Haytor. But I wasn't sick; I felt mildly nauseous. I rode through; I didn't collapse onto the verge as though struck by lightning. It's easy to see a metaphor within the sport, within each race, of a death or near-death experience. In fact, it's often cited in literal terms; 'I completely died out there today.' 'I died on the hill.' 'My legs died.' 'I was dying a thousand deaths.' 'I felt like death.' 'My legs were dead.' 'I obliterated myself.' David Harmon speaks the lingua franca of suffering: remarking on a rider's attack in the Vuelta in 2012, he excitedly said, 'He's killing them, he's actually killing them.'

The cover of the *Cycling* on 1st November, 1969 is taken up entirely by a picture of Granville. It was an era when *Cycling* valued and valorised all competitive branches of the sport, identifying the rich, end-of-season narrative of the hill climb as being distinctive and newsworthy, rather than other stories, like the endless self-promotion of their 'classic sportif', with the narcissistic 'suffering' of their staff writers or editor being the narrative of choice. It's telling that in October 2014 the comic opted for a large masthead on 'how to lose weight', but gave no mention of the hill climb photos buried within.

On the cover of that issue in 1969 Granville is small in stature but with a latent explosive power coursing through two tensile and taut legs, steeled like hawsers. The blocky initials of the Huddersfield Star Wheelers are woven in flock upon the shoulder, Airlite Continental hubs and lightweight tubulars offer the latest advantage in weight and rolling resistance. But there are some eccentricities. The beard and the unshaved legs are exhibits one and two. His eyes are fixed firmly up the road, his face etched with the strain of the gradient, as a bystander (looking suspiciously like Ralph Wilson) gazes intently at the drivetrain – checking the gear maybe? His *souplesse*? Or perhaps just vicariously enjoying the pain and degradation of the hill climb, like most spectators.

In team photos, alongside either Adrian Hinchcliffe or Dave Petroykus, but always with his brother Graham, he's smiling and in the centre, arms around the other two. It's a classic pose, often re-enacted by any amateur cyclist who is part of a winning trio in the local chipper. In this case there's a warmth and sparkle in the eyes. Another evocative image is taken from Sowerby Bridge, the local climb and a stone's throw from Halifax. It's also a tough one, rising up steeply like any classic northern wall, before easing towards the finish. Granville Sydney is in full flight, leaning forwards over the bike and out of the saddle with hands on the drops. He is at one with the machine and the gradient and charging relentlessly upwards. The bike is impelled uphill with a tense and unrelenting force. He's wearing his HSW shorts, and the hairy legs are there again, and he is wearing a striped breton-style shirt. He liked to do things his way. And then there are the last pictures of him from Dover's Hill, crossing the line at an angle, face contorted by the pain of having achieved something no-one else has managed to do, before or since.

The photos are laid out across Graham Sydney's coffee table. He hasn't strayed far from Huddersfield, where the brothers grew up. If you've ever ridden anywhere in West Yorkshire, you'll know it's hilly. The words on the map are a roll call of lumpen parcours: Ripponden Bank, Jackson Bridge, Mytholm Steeps, Shibden Wall, Luddenden Lane (and Raw End Road), Thwaites Brow, Cragg Vale – each climb a litany of suffering written in the lines of the ordnance survey. Graham still rides regularly, preferring longer tours and leisure rides to the controlled savagery of the hill climb, exploring the roads and rolling beauty of the limestone and shale inclines around High Peak.

Like many other cyclists of the time, the bulk of the Sydney brothers' riding was touring all year round. It's a common thread. With the current emphasis on sportif riding, supported tours and riding a piece of carbon fibre lightweight road smut, often outside of club colours, it's easy to forget just how much touring and youth hostelling used to be a central part of British cycling. A regular feature in *Cycling Weekly* highlighted a particularly pastoral route or an unusual stopover. The 1968 preview of the National on Winnats is as much an exhortation to pause whilst touring and visit the Speedwell Cavern as it is to watch the race or compete: 'Going to the National Hill Climb Championship? Then how about making it a subterranean stopover?' It somehow juxtaposes the languid charms of W.H. Davies, 'A poor life this if, full of care, we have no time to stop and stare', with the desperate fight against the clock of the hill climb.

The boundaries between leisure riding and competitive races were blurred. People rode to races much more frequently, armed with a set of wheel carriers and a Carradice. Graham Sydney's bike, for at least some of his championship rides, was a converted tourer. Frequent cycle-touring was seen as a fundamental way of building up the miles and acquiring endurance fitness. Both Graham and Granville rode a fixed wheel tourer with track ends, making light work of the hills along the way. Amongst the club fraternity they were known as 'Big Jim' and 'Little Jim', nicknames acquired through 'The Goon Show'. Granville had a similar sense of humour to one of the main characters and used to imitate 'Singing Spriggs', who would warble 'Jim' repeatedly. People christened him 'Jim'. When Graham subsequently joined the club he became 'Little Jim'.

The fulcrum to change the club from one that wasn't serious and was mostly concerned with 'just pottering about really', into something more assertive and competitive, came from Gordon Rhodes, the National Champion in 1959. Rhodes was a member of the Huddersfield Road Club. On Sunday runs Granville Sydney found he could keep pace with him on the climbs and gradually learnt how to gauge the effort from the older rider before being drawn into road racing. Rhodes' unheralded and unexpected success encouraged Granville to give it a go. Most new road racers dream of winning their first event, or suddenly and strangely finding out they are really good at it, and whilst there is a sense that hill climbs can turn up the odd unfancied rider due to the high degree of specificity in the event, it's not a common occurrence. Nevertheless, the skills needed to compete successfully on a hill are uniquely different from other disciplines. After an unspectacular ride in 1963, Granville Sydney won the title at only his second attempt.

1963 was the first time the event had visited Sabden to take in the Nick O' Pendle. It has since become a firm favourite amongst the cognoscenti and is a daunting and difficult climb, even when conditions are benign. Throw in a brutal combination of angry, fractious weather and a crowd keen to witness the privations of the competitors, and you have an extremely tough first championship. Granville Sydney rode well to come 22nd, two places behind his mentor. It was a creditable ride, but nothing that gave notice of things to come. His brother Graham, a couple of years younger, opted not to ride. He was not yet convinced by the discipline and had only ridden one event that year. Granville rode over to the Nick from Huddersfield with mudguards on. The route climbed up and over the moors before dropping down the steep valley with the view of the Nick up ahead, a thin silver sliver of torture. At the sign-on in Sabden he tried to stay warm whilst preparing the bike, removing any excess bits, but not the bell, before heading out into the grasping fingers of the fickle wind to get absolutely soaked and assaulted by the weather. The West Pennine, led by Peter Graham, took the team prize. Granville's effort was played out in isolation with no fellow club members other than Gordon Rhodes. He then rode back home to complete a seventy mile round trip with a savage hill climb in the middle. He must have thought it was a good idea, or had managed to block out the traumatic memories of the event and decided a second attempt was in order the following year.

Over time there are transitional points for cycling clubs. It can happen all at once, with the involvement of Jack Fletcher bankrolling the ailing Manchester Wheelers, for example, and turning them into the foremost racing cyclist club in the country, or it can happen more organically, as first one club member begins to road race, then another, then a few more. The camaraderie and feeling of competition can coalesce and create something that is bigger than the sum of its parts. There is an argument that those halcyon days of club life are disappearing, and it's an argument that rumbles on. Graham Sydney observed: 'If you look at a start sheet these days there aren't any names of towns on the lists; it's sponsors and shops.' There is clearly an increasing disconnection between place and identity, although it's not only cycling that suffers from this. People move around and drive further, they cope with geography in different ways, home becomes where you live rather than where you are from, and community becomes a noble ideal, rather than an earthy reality. It's ironic, in the context of a sport where local knowledge can be paramount, that the friendly localism of the club scene is less significant than it used to be for many people. The Huddersfield Star Wheelers of the early 1960s grew together and a spirit of adventure and excitement coursed through the veins of the racing men and women.

In 1963, Granville and Graham Sydney began road racing more often. They took their training seriously and looked at getting a hill climb outfit together. Within the club a few more came on board, including a young Adrian Hinchliffe, followed by Dave Petroykus. Whilst training is easier for some when riding on their own, and I possibly count myself in that bracket, it's probably easier to motivate yourself and enjoy it if there are others to share the experience. Being a team counter in a race increases the desire to succeed. The fellowship of the road and the wheelmen is an understated and important aspect of the sport. Road races, including the occasional Star Trophy event, and time trials quickly became a part of their diet. Towards the end of the season the brothers' attention, Granville's especially, shifted towards the hills. Where Graham had only ridden one the year previously, this year he took part in a few more and the club won the team prize on Peaslows for the Withington Wheelers' event. With the National looming a few short weeks away they stuck their entries in via first class post.

Peter Graham was bidding for a fourth title when the event returned to Winnats in 1963. The Huddersfield riders were unseeded, with Granville at 25 and Graham 119, separated on the card to give them enough time to send their shared bike back down the hill.

It was a Hilton Rigley and was very responsive and stiff with pencil stays. Graham was slightly shorter, but didn't bother adjusting the saddle height – 'You wouldn't be sat down on Winnats at any rate.' The form book didn't suggest an upset was in the offing; Granville had been beaten fairly soundly by Peter Graham in three earlier hill climbs, including the Upperthorpe event on the same hill, where he lost by half a minute – a huge margin in a four-minute climb. He gave no suggestion that he might trouble the timekeepers later on in the season. The conditions were relatively calm and mild with a breeze gently helping the riders up the incline. It's hard to escape the arduous nature of the Pass, even in helpful weather, and K. Nipress of Hull Thursday succinctly summed up the struggle: 'It was easier than I thought, it's just half-killed me instead of murdering me.'*

---

* Dick Snowdon, 'The Hill Climb', *Cycling*, 30/10/1960

It was clear to those near the bottom watching and doing time checks that Granville was motoring. His speed was visibly quicker than previous competitors and a murmur of acknowledgement rolled up through the galleries as he passed. Hunched low with hands on the drops and legs turning over the gear with muscular force and simplicity, he reeled in his minuteman and took a further 24 seconds out of the hapless J.G. Turner of Midland C and AC. He crossed the line to equal Peter Graham's course record.

Whilst the ride was impressive, the spectators and pondering clubmen saw it more as a sign of a particularly fast day and were eagerly expecting both Russell Foster and Peter Graham to do something spectacular. Granville was rightly pleased, having come 20th the previous year. Peter Graham opted for a 51", in contrast to Granville's 55", preferring to spin and pedal rather than push the big gear over. Despite his belief that he 'could beat it easily', it slipped away in the last fifty yards and he came in four seconds down in 3'-22.2". 'Sydney's Record Shock' had taken the title back to Huddersfield and left his fellow competitors, the spectators and the press reeling in surprise.

The following year on Peaslows in County Durham the starting positions were reversed, with Granville in the scratch rider's position and Graham off at the crack of dawn. For a couple of years they continued to put a note in with their entries until eventually the bike was stolen. To replace it Granville got a new track frame and Graham adapted his touring bike, but even then they found themselves apart on the card because organisers assumed they were still sharing. They might occasionally stick a knobbly grass track tyre on the back to cope with the mulchy surface of steep Northern Lanes.

But it was the unseeded Eric Wilson, now a sprightly 31 and in his retirement year, who took an unexpected but not unmerited win, with Granville third. The strength in depth of the Star Wheelers, abetted by Adrian Hinchliffe, saw them take the team prize. Granville's podium finish proved the previous year was no fluke, but also stoked the fires of competition: he was determined to come back and win it again.

A significant year in the history of the event was 1965 when the race visited Dover's Hill for the first time. The brothers came to like Dover's, which featured regularly over the years and has been used as recently as 2010. Back in 1965 they'd never ridden it before, so the four Star Wheelers went down during the summer and spent a full day on the hill, checking out the gradients and the different gears needed, leaving nothing to chance. It reinforces the idea of preparation being the key to success. They mapped the course in their minds and when October came round were ready to put their planning and preparation into action. Graham Sydney recalled the excursion: 'We used to think about the last point after which you had to go all out for the finish. Quite often our intermediate times were slower, but we'd gain a lot by the end. We'd find a point where, from here, it's flat out for the finish, and have it a little bit longer for the National, following advice from Gordon Rhodes, who said that the crowd will carry you over the last hundred yards. I thought, "I hope he's right". On the day we found a small driveway with some mushroom shaped stones. We didn't think we'd be able to see it with the crowds, so we put one of our supporters there and then any Star Wheelers that came past he'd shout "Mushrooms!" People thought he was mad but we knew the significance.'

The course record of 4'-06.4" had been set by Vic Clark in the very first open event ever held on the hill, 17 years before. In 1965 Clark returned to Weston-sub-Edge as the organiser for the National. The field contained a number of promising riders, including Les West and Max Pendleton. Rain and a strong crosswind greeted the early starters, which complicated gear choices and led to wide variations. Stuart Holdsworth in the new Condor RC colours opted for a 59", and coming in just outside the course record created ripples of anticipation and anxiety and a sudden rush to change cogs. Les West, star of the road, stuck with a 69″ and paid a heavy price. He struggled to turn the gear and hold it to the line for tenth place. Graham was the first of the brothers to go, putting in a strong ride for fifteenth place, but complaining that his 62″ gear was 'too high'. Peter Graham fared better, to tie with Ron Martin, 0.2 of a second outside the record. It left only Granville. He opted for the same gear as Les West. He must have had an inkling that he could turn it over; gear choice was usually a collective decision for the Star Wheelers. A poor start with wheelspin on the bottom corner gave no indication of what was to come. Granville accelerated remorselessly up the incline, on top of the gear and the gradient, crossing the line in four minutes dead to take his second title in three years.

The see-saw nature of the Championship was underlined over the next three years. On Winnats in 1966 Granville was clear favourite to gain a third title, but Pete Greenhaulgh, who Graham Sydney affectionately described as 'a one-year wonder' on account of him 'winning everything that year', stormed up the pass, shattering the course record in the process with 3′-11″ and also took the team prize back to East Bradford. It wasn't the whole story though. At the start of September whilst out training, Graham Sydney and six other club mates were hit by a car. Graham was off the bike for six weeks and had no chance, finishing a lowly 27th.

The race returned to Winnats the following year, but again Granville failed to make the top step of the podium. In a quirk of fate, the Sydney brothers somehow tied for third in what *Cycling Weekly* dubbed the 'Battle of the Beards'. It was a sterling ride from the younger brother and his highest placing, a marked contrast with the previous year's disappointment. The club had three counters in the top eight, with Steve Whitely rounding out the team. It was a show of strength, but a nagging disappointment for Granville to have missed out. It was one of the toughest championships in living memory, with the winning time over thirty seconds slower than the previous year. Paul Wildsmith rode himself into the ground and was laid out on a bright yellow cape to continue the struggle for air. It took him twenty minutes before he could summon up the mental and physical strength to speak.

Former champion Peter Graham surrendered to the inexorable march of time and bowed out gracefully, some way down the field. He knew it was time to retire, and is not shy in discussing the effect of age on hill climbers, even now: 'To me, veterans shouldn't ride hill climbs. You can get by in a flat time trial and look like everybody else. But on a hill climb, when it's steep, they look distressed and uncomfortable. They don't look good, veterans climbing hills, they look distressed, and "pitiable" is the word that comes to my mind.' Despite that, Peter Graham ignored his own sage advice and returned to ride a few more events in later years. He maintains he did them for a friend in a bike shop in Bury and he had to ride the frames. He was forty odd at the time, and finished in the top half of the field, but admits that 'your lungs turn to shredded wheat when you get older'.

The third fallow year for Granville was again at Dover's in 1968, where Pete Gannon won. Like Max Pendleton who came tenth on Winnats in 1966, Pete Gannon was an accomplished grass track rider. He was also a handy roadman and a close friend to the Sydney brothers. Granville went further into debt than he had previously, his familiarity with the climb and determination to succeed allowing him to ignore the horrible pain and lack of oxygen in pursuit of a third title, but it was not forthcoming. With Graham inside the top ten, the Star Wheelers again took the team prize.

After 1968 though, things changed; Granville won four of the next five championships. It was a purple patch that saw him elevated from contender and worthy champion, to becoming the greatest hill climber in the history of the event. In the process he established a record that has still not been beaten. The run started in a relatively subdued fashion on a strange dual carriageway and military road at Llywel. Occasionally the District responsible for the Championship makes an odd choice. It's happened as recently as 2011, when the Buxton CC opted for Long Hill over any one of a baker's dozen of more suitable climbs in the area. The 1969 event is chiefly memorable for its lack of any memorable features. The Star Wheelers took their fifth team title and Granville won by three seconds from Claude Kierley – unusually a southern rider. An image from the time depicts an exhausted Granville lying prone on the roadside with Wendy Hinchcliffe looking over him, a guiding hand holding the blanket around his shoulders. Max Pendleton had his best placing of fourth and Graham came eleventh. It was not a full field and it wasn't a vintage year. Unsurprisingly, Llywel has not seen a race since.

What Llywel lacked in substance and atmosphere, the Nick more than compensated for in 1970. In fact, it possibly added a bit too much. It was the kind of day that was probably worse for the spectators than it was for the riders. A torrent of run-off water poured down the road, forcing the riders out into the middle as onlookers huddled together in rain capes or under umbrellas, trying to escape the worst of the wretched weather. It seems foolhardy to organise a race up a hill on the site of a mass hanging of 'witches' a day or so before Hallowe'en, and the devil himself could easily have ordered the fury that rained from the sky. Granville was in imperious form, the only man inside four minutes, and was lifted from the bike at the end in a state of catalepsy. Graham also rode himself into the ground and had to be propped up against the timekeeper's van to recover.

But in a race that turned hardened athletes into shaking, ashen shadows, even Granville admitted being almost overwhelmed by the conditions: 'Three quarters of the way up I almost decided I had had enough. I was ready to pack it in and say no more climbing.'* His girlfriend, Jean Lockhead, cheering him on at the side of the road, tipped the balance and he carried on, turning over the 59" gear to destroy the

---

* Sid Saltmarsh, 'Anti-Gravity Granville', *Cycling*, 31/10/1970

opposition. She ran to the top to welcome him with a victory hug. Jean had no problem with the incline, she was an international runner.

In 1971 the event moved to a 'roadman's hill', a comparatively new phenomenon. The Horseshoe Pass is a steady three-mile climb out of picturesque Llangollen and around the 'shoe' before finishing at the Ponderosa Cafe. It's close to Barber's Hill but lacks the savagery of its neighbour. Since 1971 it's been a popular event and is run by Fibrax Wrexham RC, attracting a large field each year. It is perhaps closer to a mountain time trial, taking nearly ten minutes to ascend, with rhythm and pace being the significant elements rather than explosive force and power. As a result it piqued the interest of the roadmen. Dave Lloyd and John Clewarth of Kirkby CC took to the startline and the Star Wheelers' hegemony was clearly under threat. The long wait for a Southern victor – not since 1955 had the trophy left the North – looked set to continue. The Kirkby team were seen as the pre-eminent road outfit of the era, a forerunner of the Manchester Wheelers and a hothouse for new talent. The complexion of the event had changed.

The relatively shallow gradient also opened up an entirely new conundrum that has come to bedevil contenders over the years: equipment anxiety, and more specifically, the burning question of whether to ride gears or fixed. In the warm-up event, earlier in the season, Clewarth took the course record with a 91" biggest gear and a range across the block. For those used to riding fixed, especially those who knew next to nothing else, it had the potential to become a stumbling block. International roadman Phil Bayton, John Clewarth, and Granville Sydney stood as the three main contenders. In the end, the strength in depth of the Merseysiders saw them take the team prize and Granville finished in fourth, outside the podium placings for the first time in seven years. With hindsight Graham admitted they perhaps should have ridden gears; his choice of a 69" was fine apart from the last quarter of a mile, where the road flattens out and a tailwind lifted the riders over the line.

Debate as to whether the Horseshoe Pass was a suitable climb for a National Championship rumbled on in the pages of *Cycling*, until Graham Sydney had the last word: 'We are generally referred to as hill-climb specialists and the majority of us, Granville included, consider the Horseshoe to be a completely fair and good hill…A climber should be able to adapt to any hill…I have nothing but admiration for the rider who gives up all chances of a career to be a good bike rider. Next year we're back on Winnats…We will win the team prize and "our kid" will regain the title he deserves.'*

Graham Sydney's letter also alluded to the disquiet felt amongst the traditionalists that somehow the Kirkby riders were 'cheating' by focusing exclusively on cycling and blurring the distinctions between the amateur and the nascent professional.

The late autumnal chill and a return to Winnats offered an opportunity for revenge in 1972 as the Kirkby CC returned to do battle with the specialists again. Winnats Pass was established as the 'blue riband' course, the true test, and Granville's fifth title both realigned people's perceptions of the event and his phenomenal ability to defy gravity. Beards were much in evidence, with the hirsute Paul Wildsmith giving Granville and Graham a run for their money in the hairiest hillclimber competition. Granville won on account of his permanently unshaved legs. He took his fifth title with a 3'-23", giving him almost a four second beating of Clewarth, who felt his 57" was generally the right choice, although 'when the wind hit me I stood still'. The capricious and swirling wind made life difficult for the starters and made it tricky to select a gear. Dave Lloyd was back in fifth and Graham Sydney charged up to tenth place. The Huddersfield Star Wheelers also took the team title back again, their seventh. Winnats was lined from top to bottom with crowds; Granville climbed through the narrow causeway of spectators. His forceful style parted the tunnel

---

* 'Commentary', *Cycling*, 11/12/1971

of people and he flew through the finish. His ability to bury himself in the pursuit of victory and ride against the fear of failure seemed to become more marked each year. He was out for the count for nearly 15 minutes, unable to stand, see or talk after his effort. All colour drained from his face and the effects of the race were clearly evident in his pallid and blank expression. Both Clewarth and Lloyd were up relatively quickly, drained, but functioning. Granville's semi-conscious state was a ghostly and worrying sight for spectators. He somehow managed to exert the last ounces of energy in the very last seconds of the last race of the season, year after year.

In 1973 Granville was looking for his sixth title, with the team in the hunt for an eighth to establish a new team record (the Bramley Wheelers were also on seven wins). A full field, replete with strong roadmen, gathered in the Cotswold village of Broadway to renew their acquaintance with Dover's Hill.

Organiser Vic Clark spaced the seeded riders throughout the field like a time trial card, with the intention of maintaining a level of interest right through the event. When number 10, Dave Pitman, broke the hill record it certainly woke up the crowd. Forty minutes later Paul Carbutt, a classy roadman and very much a dark horse for the title, also went under the old time. The race was on. Little Jim edged under the 4-minute barrier, putting in his counter for the Star Wheelers and equalling the '68 record, before the champion on the Horseshoe, John Clewarth, tore up the variable gradient to record the fastest time. Charlie Porter added his ride to the team effort, leaving only Granville and Paul Wildsmith to come. The reigning champion started slowly before accelerating up through the 1-in-7, past the shout of 'Mushrooms', before scorching up and over the steadily easing gradient to win by nearly three seconds. He was always in control of the ride, knowing where to make the effort and how to tame the climb. Every inch of the surface had been mapped in the minds of the Star Wheelers with nothing left to chance. He crossed the line, almost fighting with the bike, extracting every last molecule of energy from lactic-filled legs; with hands and arms in a vice-like grip on the bars, head at an angle and mouth agape, sucking in oxygen. The crowd looked on in awe and admiration, aware that they were seeing something special on the leafy surface of a Cotswold lane.

Moments later he collapsed into the grass verge, without the energy to stand or speak or breathe, the privations of the effort written in the furrowed brow and contorted features, the sallow, empty eyes and painful grimace. Having pushed himself beyond the parameters of endeavour, it took even longer than the year before at Winnats for him to come round, to acknowledge the achievement, recognise his surroundings and hold a conversation with the concerned faces looking over his prone body on the grass. There was a tangible sense of concern, bemusement, and admiration amongst the spectators at the damage done, the extremes of effort and the utter physical collapse. At 32 years old he had taken his sixth title. The press had run out of superlatives to describe his form and dominance in the event, settling only for 'Master to the Last Gasp', and 'What can you say about Granville Sydney that has not already been said?'*

Granville had become a part of the event's folklore. His unshaven legs, running socks, occasionally eccentric jerseys and full beard, combined with a savage and yet elegant display of hill climbing prowess each and every weekend throughout the season had made him the most successful rider in the history of the event. He had fought off all challenges, including international roadmen, over a ten year period. His racing was orientated almost exclusively around the hill climb season, with a later start than others, followed by a lull and then a relentless build up to the Championship. In the aftermath of his sixth title win, most expected a repeat performance in the following year's event on Holme Moss. In the most shattering and finite terms, it was not to be. In February 1974, Granville Sydney killed himself.

---

* Sid Saltmarsh, 'Master to the Last Gasp', *Cycling*, 3/11/1973

In 2012 his brother spoke about Granville's death: 'It was a complete shock for me. I was married at the time. I had absolutely no idea at all. Anyone who's dealt with suicide knows you get this horrible guilty feeling, especially when you had no idea. And I still don't understand it to this day. I didn't feel sorry for him, I felt sorry for my parents, and everybody else that was around to survive the aftermath. The initial bit after was really quite difficult, especially when I had to go into a road racing changing room; people treat you differently. The ones you want are the ones who treat you normally, maybe ask about him, something like this. Some people don't know what to say so they blank you out, and some people can be hostile in a way, strangely. But most were fine. I'd been around a long time and got a lot of friends on the road and track.'

It's clear that Granville was set to ride on and he still had a lot to offer. He was 32 when he last won and the margin of victory on Dover's suggested he had every chance of repeating it the following year. Instead, it was Graham who had to decide whether he wanted to carry on and take part in an event where the absence of his brother would dominate his thoughts and experiences, over and above the presence of other riders: 'If anybody was going to stop riding hill climbs it was me. I said every year, "I'm not going to ride these anymore." Initially, when it first happened, it was a hard time. I did wonder whether to carry on racing, or riding, but it was probably the release really, most of my friends were into cycling, so I just kept going. I probably trained harder than ever that season, and I had quite a good year. As it got nearer, I almost thought as though I was defending his title for him. Primarily I wanted to win it for myself, but I wanted to do it for him as well. By October there was no chance I wasn't going to ride.'

The Huddersfield Star Wheelers decided that a memorial event would be a fitting tribute and the organisers hoped an intense competition would honour Granville's contribution to cycling. A ceremonial ride through Holmfirth preceded the race, before a wave of the flag signalled the beginning of a mass-start, two mile hill climb up Greenfield Road. Graham Sydney took seventh, and then won the second race, a conventional time trial up the same hill. He received the trophy from Beryl Burton and it provided a fitting and emotional tribute to his brother.

The National on Holme Moss offered a further opportunity for catharsis and somehow to provide a degree of context to complex and harrowing emotions, barely eight months after Granville's death. The weather had other ideas though. It was blowing a gale with rain and hail attacking in diagonals across the hillside. In the cycle of horrible hill climbs, it was up there with the Nick in 1970 and Winnats in 1957. Graham opted for a 66″, but he was over-geared and couldn't get it turning over. He wasn't the only one, with riders struggling to get moving on the lower bends of the climb. Brian Pownall was all but brought to a standstill. At the finish Graham turned round and got straight back into his car in an attempt to get warm.

Joe Waugh won, riding a three speed block to give a 54″, 59″ and 66″. He was a relative newcomer, a fresh-faced 22-year-old who had spent the latter part of the season riding the Tour de l'Avenir, where he had been the first rider over the Tourmalet. When I mentioned this to Graham, some 43 years later, he laughed. 'That's cheating that is… it's no wonder he got up Holme Moss.'

Both Granville and Graham Sydney and the Huddersfield Star Wheelers enriched the Championship. Granville was enigmatic, funny and intense, both knowing and unknowable. He was and still is the most successful rider ever, transcending the limitations of the individual's physique to conquer a range of climbs. The success of the Huddersfield Star Wheelers can be seen as a key moment in British cycling prior to the steady changes and inexorable march of sponsorship in the decade to follow. They were the last great club team from a parochial and rigidly amateur era. Graham Sydney, Dave Petroykus, Adrian Hinchcliffe and Granville Sydney all lived within six miles of

Huddersfield. They rode together, socialised together and were the embodiment of the fellowship of the road. Granville Sydney epitomises the discipline of hill climbing, but in many ways he was a representation of cycling in Britain – an esoteric and slightly awkward relation to a glamorous continental cousin. His six titles remain the benchmark, and though people have come close, his achievements have not been surpassed.

Hill climber on Rockingham, Northamptonshire

Vic Clark riding his Pollard frame at a Coventry CC 25-mile Promotion in the early 1940s

Vic Clark on his way to victory in 1948 on Lansdowne Lane

The crowded galleries on Winnats

Granville Sydney on Winnats in 1963

The startline of the Catford Hill Climb in the early 1950s

Graham Sydney on
Winnats in 1963

Granville on Winnats

A triptych of pain

The Horseshoe Pass in a friendly mood for the 1971 Championship

A miserable day on the Nick O' Pendle, but with a full crowd

Granville Sydney winning on the Nick O' Pendle in 1970

Ralph Wilson, second on
the Nick O' Pendle in 1970

Graham Sydney fights against gravity at
Deep Lane, Huddersfield

The last of Granville Sydney's six titles,
at Dover's Hill in 1973

Joe Waugh in full flight

7

It Bites into the Memory

(1975–1979)

'Until that season, I'd been a tourist, pure and simple. I'd been talked into competition.'

Whilst Joe Waugh's win on Holme Moss in 1974 might be seen as a victory for the roadmen and the returning continental professional, legs honed into mahogany by a succession of Alpine passes, then Gareth Armitage's emergence in 1975 has something more distinctively British about it. Whilst many cyclists are talked into competition by friends and fellow roadmen, or perhaps a wife or husband trying to get them out of the house, very few people stumble unknowingly and innocently into competition only to find themselves at the very highest level. Apart from Gareth Armitage.

Gareth Armitage comes from Oldham. The Greater Manchester area is populated with racing cyclists, especially to the east of the city where it sprawls out greedily towards the Peaks. Knock on any door in Rochdale or Oldham or Clayton and the chances are there's a steel lightweight out the back (of the back-to-back, of course) and the man or woman of the house is a member of the Oldham Century or West Pennine or another northern racing club. This is where Gareth Armitage has lived and ridden all his life. Armitage's first bike came, oddly enough, from a second-hand car dealership over the road from his house. He'd been eyeing it up on his way to and from school before finally managing to scrape together the pocket money to buy it. Apparently someone had traded it in against a new Robin Reliant; moving from two wheels to three in one easy sweep, but possibly without going any quicker. It was almost certainly easier to reverse the bicycle than it was the Reliant.

Armitage used his new steed to ride from Oldham to Hathershaw and back for school. The routes into cycling in those days were perhaps clearer and the role the club played more significant. If you wanted to ride more, you joined a club. There were no sponsored outfits for anyone who fancied riding in a fancy bit of kit. He joined Oldham Century CTC and had absolutely no intention of racing. In fact, that's probably too strong, Gareth Armitage probably didn't even imagine that racing was something that you might do on a bike. It's not so much that it was thought about and discounted, it just doesn't seem to have entered his imagination. His intention was to ride his bike as often as he could and get as far away from the city as time and energy would allow.

Membership of a cycling club transformed his teenage years and added an endless potential for escape, providing a limitless freedom and the joyous feeling that comes from being out on the bike, far from home. It's an innocence familiar to anyone who has loaded up a Carradice and ridden out of the front door with a destination in mind and about ten hours to get there. It's also a testament to the transformative capacity of the bicycle and the seemingly limitless freedom it confers on the owner. The contrast of the Peak District and the Yorkshire Moors to industrial and post-industrial Manchester cannot be overstated.

After school Armitage began working full-time for British Aerospace and the bike created breathing space, allowing time and space from work. The weekends were spent in the welcoming arms of the club, doing anything from fifty to seventy miles. He describes it simply: 'I was 15 or 16 years old, going out for hours and hours into the countryside with a kind of freedom. Kids these days don't experience anything like that. When I think of the places I went to, it was phenomenal. There wasn't the same amount of cars or transport; it was much more pleasant to be on the roads. I remember touring North Wales, over Sarn Helen, right over the hills and mountains, along a track, out into the middle of nowhere.'

And he's right, something has been lost over time, and it's not just the sensation of quiet roads, but the 'love of travel, speed, fresh air, natural beauty; a quick escape from ugliness'.*

The rites of passage associated with cyclo-touring have dissipated; it's seen now as one for the older rider, the one with the extensive beard and SPD sandals, disposable income and a lust for high-end bicycle frames. A generation has missed out on the incredible sense of freedom that can be had from waving goodbye to your parents on the doorstep and then riding out, across and up onto Exmoor, or over the Trough of Bowland, away and beyond all the vestiges and pressures of life, up a track and across mountains until a day later you find yourself in the middle of nowhere, in an isolated bunkhouse accompanied only by a set of tired legs and an expanded mind.

One thing is apparent; throughout the late sixties and into the early seventies Gareth Armitage was riding his bike a huge

---

* W. Fitzwater Wray, A *Vagabond's Notebook*, 1908

amount and not thinking anything of it. He was riding to work, touring, doing the Oldham Century Easter breaks, September breaks, Christmas tours, Youth Hostel weekends, much like Granville and Graham Sydney – much like members of any cycling club anywhere in the country: 'We were just mad keen on touring; we just loved to be outside and we enjoyed the country. It was a love of being outside.' You can't underestimate the huge mileage being done, providing a basic and enduring level of fitness, especially in the light of what was to come.

When he married young the bike continued to serve as a means of escape from the long working week, but this time his wife came too: 'We just toured every year. If we weren't with the club on tour then we'd book our own; two fortnight holidays, youth hostelling. I've got all the YHA stamps and badges I used to collect. We just had a fantastic time. We'd do Devon and Cornwall, the Cotswolds, The Lakes, Dales, North Devon, it was absolutely fantastic. I'd always book the youth hostels ahead, there was no way of not making it, sometimes they were eighty or ninety miles apart.' In between the tours Armitage began to ride out with the local roadmen, hitting the training circuit: up Ripponden Road, straight down to Denshaw, left and up, then back round a couple of times, proving his legs on the pacier rides.

In 1975, at the age of 23, he decided to test the waters and start racing. One of the lads on the weekly rides happened to mention that he appeared to be a bit handy on the hills and suggested he might like to try his luck in a road race. He gave it a whirl. Several club members were heading over to the Isle of Man Festival of Cycling and Armitage went along for the experience. The Manx International and the Festival of Cycling on the Isle of Man attracted the very best riders from the continent. Previous winners included Jacques Anquetil, Shay Elliott, Andre Darrigade and Tom Simpson. Armitage admits to being 'green to everything. I didn't have a clue who I was riding against, I had no idea of the history of it or anything.' He was third in the prestigious Manx Arms and sixth in the Mannin Veg. He was a third category roadman with the Cyclists' Touring Club logo still emblazoned on his arms.

From that point on things became a little bit different. He worked closely with Phil Buckley, who had the experience and wherewithal to help guide the inexperienced Armitage, handing on tips and tricks, as well as the all-important advice regarding cogs and gearing in the run up to Armitage's first attempt at a hill climb season. He came third in his first open event at Frodsham, then hit a winning streak that saw him win most of the ones he entered from that point on. All hill climbers have a preferred gradient or type of hill. For Gareth Armitage, it was the really unpleasant and extremely steep ones, and it didn't really matter how long or how short or how unpleasant and steep they were. At 5ft-4ins and eight and a half stone, he could explode out of the blocks and be up the hill before most people had even got up to speed, but crucially he could also turn in a great ride on the longer, shallower climbs because of his road background and levels of endurance honed through thousands of miles of touring. I'd venture to suggest that he'd probably ridden most of the hill climb courses in the country on a fully laden tourer at some point in the previous eight years, and probably ridiculously quickly, and probably without realising.

It's clear that Phil Buckley is a key figure in Armitage's life. The role of the coach is an important one, whether as mentor or technical guru. Buckley performed a vital role; waiting and lifting him off the bike at the end of each race, when he was unable even to get his feet out of the straps. It's an evocative memory: the coach holding up his young protégé, physically supporting him, out of necessity, at the very point when he has given everything he can. There's something physical and emotive about the bond between the two at that precise moment. And in a living room in Oldham, when we met to talk about his career, 40 years on, Armitage's voice cracks as he remembers. The emotional connection has lasted over time, and I feel guilty about awakening such powerful memories.

Time marches on, it subtracts from us each day and the past becomes an ephemeral and fading imprint, a dissolving and sun-bleached photograph on a window sill to be found years later, the edges blurred and features somehow diminished as we search for the meaning that we knew was once there. There's a sense that all of us dream of riding alone across the top of mountain passes, achieving a lengthy and mythical palmarès that will live on beyond our years, that we will somehow defeat the ravages of time and provide a narrative of force, etched in granite. And yet very few of us win anything, ever, let alone anything sufficient to leave a mark. But both meaning and longevity can be written and found in the simplest of memories; subtle experiences have lasting depth. Phil Buckley waiting at the top of a climb, a few feet beyond the tenuously drawn chalk line, arms outstretched and ready to catch, provides a moment in time that lasts. There is a profundity in the smallest of gestures that outlasts us fully, in the reality of doing a small, good thing and the positive effect it has on someone else. In every club there is someone to catch us when we fall, to help us back on the bike and see that we are there to carry on and learn from the experience, or to say nothing and only listen. And the club lasts forever, long after the team has folded and we are gone. And within the brief moment that Gareth Armitage's voice wavers, and reluctant, but then necessary tears form, I sense the value of friendship and paternal guidance and how much this means.

With Phil Buckley at his side, Armitage began preparing for the 1975 National Championship on the Nick O' Pendle. Prior to the event, despite his considerable success in the short hill climb season, he didn't suffer from nerves. There was no expectation or pressure, he just went out and did what he had been doing for the previous six weeks. He gave it everything he possibly could right from the count and made sure when he got to the finish there was absolutely nothing left in the tank at all: 'I don't know what it was, I just had the knack of knowing where the finish was and I knew I could get it all out.'

The weather helped matters. It was an unusually friendly day on the Nick, and the esoteric and slightly odd hill climbers were out in force: it was a day for beards and moustaches. In contemporary pictures Armitage can be seen peeking out from behind a sturdy pair of Raybans with a huge moustache clinging to his upper lip. It was the 1970s after all. A time of 3'-49.5" was enough for the win, suggesting a headwind conspired to slow the pace and ensure Eric Wilson's record was safe for another year. However, Armitage managed to see off one of the strongest fields for many years. Elite roadmen Paul Carbutt and Joe Waugh were beaten into second and third respectively by the comparative newcomer. Graham Sydney finished fifteenth in this, his last event.

His win wasn't entirely unexpected, with the Manx results and several hill climb victories suggesting he was the favourite for the title. Furthermore, the Nick isn't the type of climb that rewards a 'lucky' rider, something Paul Wildsmith attested to at the time. Armitage himself confesses that he was 'just amazed, in a state of shock, it was just a blur really'. He rode a 59" gear in murky but benign conditions, made it up the cattle grid and then tried to wind it up as he tore past the galleries of people and up into the blind corner that heralds the finish.

The Oldham Century were delighted with his win and sent him a card which he still has today. In amongst the signatures one message stands out: 'Watch out! We're out to get you!' It's affectionately meant, but there is a grain of truth therein. Overnight he had become a marked man, especially if the road looked like it might start angling upwards. In short, the experience changed his racing and cycling forever. In 1974 Gareth Armitage was a cyclo-tourist. In 1975 he was the National Champion. The innocence had gone in a moment, and things would never be quite the same again: 'I'd be out with Jack Kershaw*, Bob Barlow and John Kenworthy, they'd make me sprint past, gun it on the climb. We'd drop in and

---

* Kershaw was second in 1973 on Dover's Hill.

out of Hebden Bridge, racing up climbs and sprinting for signs.' There are cyclists, and there are racing cyclists. Gareth Armitage was suddenly in the latter camp, racing for lamp-posts, albeit with a saddlebag.

The significance of just how far things had changed hit home at the Championship the following year. When I initially made contact with Gareth Armitage over the phone to request an interview he was effusive and friendly. One of the first things he mentioned was the Horseshoe Pass in 1976. He said, with an almost audible sigh, 'There isn't a day goes by when I don't think about it and regret the race.' Listening back to the audio record of our subsequent interviews I can hear the register subtly shift, as though he had opened a door to a previously locked room that hid all the unopened bills and other scary things. It's tangible in his voice. The next time we broached the topic, in person, he voiced two monosyllabic words surrounded by a brooding silence on either side – '*It hurts*'. The pause speaks volumes. He gathers himself to revisit the memory of an event he'd rather forget, but cannot: 'Because you've done so well, you want to prove yourself again, and show to everybody that it's not a fluke.' He has a knack of saying things simply and with a stark reality: 'It bites into the memory.' And it unquestionably does, as he fights against the unwelcome tears of regret. It's more than that though: revisiting the past in acute relief with a stranger armed with a list of his victories and a series of quotes and pictures, is an unsettling and emotional experience.

They'd had all the equipment checked beforehand. Ron Kitching, the legendary distributor of almost everything relating to the bicycle, had provided some juicy bits and pieces. Derek Clarke had trued the lightweight wheels, with 28 spokes on the front and 32 on the back; the tubulars were aged and ready. They had also stayed down for a few days in Llangollen, heading up and down the Pass more than a few times, working out the gentle subtleties of the gradient, building on the knowledge gained from a visit two weeks before. He felt good and strong.

The Horseshoe Pass is one for gears. Even Granville and Graham Sydney would admit this. Most riders went for a narrow block on the back with a variation on a close ratio, 14-18 and a 48:52 double ring. To be honest, it's not that different from the kind of gears people rode back then anyway, when men were men and 'compact' wasn't even an idea, let alone an industry standard. A charitable tailwind helped the riders up the hill. Emboldened by a lift from the breeze as he came up and around the 'Horseshoe', along with the general feeling of being on top of the gearing and riding well, Armitage moved the shifter to put it in the big ring. Disaster struck: 'It immediately unshipped. I was messing about with it and trying to get it back on and losing momentum, so I had to turn round in the middle of the road without putting my foot down, to avoid disqualification, and go down fifty to a hundred yards before I eventually managed to get it back on, and then I had to watch for other riders coming back up so I didn't impede them, then turn round again, try and get some momentum back, pile on the pressure and go back up. I kept it in the big ring because I was that frightened of unshipping it again and the adrenalin, was going but I felt so annoyed with myself and frustrated. I felt so good before that.'

He came fifth, in spite of the catastrophe. Looking at the time lost, it's entirely feasible that the twenty-five or thirty seconds might have put him in second, a few seconds down on an effervescent and very strong Joe Waugh, fresh from the Milk Race where he'd ridden in support of Bill Nickson's successful bid for victory, who took the title with panache.

At the finish he was inconsolable, wanting to be left alone in disbelief and frustration, blaming himself for the gear change. His hunched and isolated figure lay bent double at the roadside, wrapped in a blanket and shrouded in despair. The heightened sense of pressure was in complete contrast to the previous year's event, with much of it carried by Armitage himself: 'I was expected to do well; all the lads were down there; I'd been winning hill climbs. I was doing four in a weekend, riding to one in the morning, then the afternoon, the same Sunday.' Eighteen months ago the only pressure he felt when cycling was the slow race to reach a youth hostel before nightfall. It had been replaced with a nail-biting concoction of anxiety and an omnipresent fear of failure.

The following year the race returned to Winnats for what would be the last time. A series of landslips two years later led to the closure of the A625, which in turn led to an increase in traffic density over Winnats Pass. With a shake of the unstable shale topography the crucible of the sport was lost.

Gareth Armitage, along with everyone else, is unequivocal in his reckoning that Winnats is the one, and true to form, the precipitous valley played host to another epic battle. This time the cycling gods frowned on the unsuspecting Joe Waugh. In a cruel echo of Armitage's fate 12 months previously he managed to unship his chain *twice*, before borrowing a bike from someone in the crowd to complete the climb in 79th place. The steepness of the ascent exacted its usual high price on the competitors: Kevin Reilly rode through the line and collapsed onto the ground, chest heaving in asthmatic paroxysms. He lay down as though dead, eyelids fluttering, with no sign of a response for nearly ten minutes. An ambulance was summoned and he was driven away, breathing in oxygen in an attempt to restore the depletion. Wheelspin afflicted all the competitors, even the forceful Paul Carbutt nearly vaulted over the bars whilst trying to force the pedal stroke.* He too collapsed over the line into the sodden grass: 'Look at me, here I am covered in mud and sitting on top of a mountain. It used to be a gentleman's sport!' he opined afterwards.**

Armitage opted for a big gear, nearly 57", and struggled against it, shouting and screaming in pain as his legs

---

* Carbutt seemed capable of riding almost any distance: a silver in the hill climb; the 100-mile time trial record; and in 1979 the Land's End /John o' Groats record -47hrs, 23mins and 1sec, despite being accused of speeding by the Cornish constabulary.

** Dennis Donovan, 'Youth Goes Top in Hill Climb', *Cycling*, 5/11/1977 confronted the unforgiving cadence needed to maintain pace and rhythm, and he fell, prone, onto the ground at the death. He was gracious in his praise for the 19-year-old John Parker – a 'tremendous talent'. But the win he craved the most, along with the recognition and the reality, had eluded him again. He was pleased to get a medal for third place and would have liked to have won, but had a sense of relief after the previous year's debacle and felt like he was back in contention. His sister and mother had come to watch. Neither had been to an event before to see him race, and it felt very special.

The mid to late 70s saw a gradual but marked change in nearly all disciplines of cycling. Armitage had become increasingly aware that the boundaries between professional and amateur status were becoming blurred. Many of the Liverpool riders were semi-professional, going out all day training and putting in big miles, particularly those from the Kirkby CC, with Dave Lloyd being an example. At the time Armitage was doing twelve-hour shifts, including nights, then coming home and struggling to find the time to get out on the bike. The quality and strength of the field was improving year on year; the roadmen were attracted by the prestige of a national title and it had become a part of their calendar. The championship was no longer the preserve of the bandy-legged, unshaven, sallow, specialist hill climber. John Parker had ridden the Etoile des Espoirs in France and a young Steve Joughin rode in the colours of the national junior road champion. Paul Carbutt was third in the Milk Race, and Winnats was his last race before turning pro for Viking. Steve Joughin signed on the dole in order to pursue his dream of a professional contract – in his autobiography he jokingly refers to it as the 'DHSS performance plan'.

The upsurge in interest made the 1978 event a tough one to call and a full field turned up to do battle in the Cotswolds. After getting half a day off work, Armitage drove down on the Friday night in a Mini Clubman Traveller. My parents used to have one; the back doors open outwards like a barn and the bodywork is timbered. It's like driving a very small mock-tudor house. Somehow, in a 'how do you get four elephants in a mini' type of way, he managed to squeeze all the equipment and a wife into the car and they headed down the M6. Armitage didn't find it hard or steep in comparison to the northern climbs. In fact, he honked up it, going virtually flat out for the entire distance. Dave Lloyd rode a pursuit bike, which seems strange in retrospect, and probably seemed strange at the time. John Parker looked strong; he'd come no lower than fifth in his last four races on the continent and was there to win. Armitage looked fresher than he had on Winnats – the climb didn't exact such a horrific toll on the body and mind. It's arguable that the nature of the finish, where it eases off into a sprint, allows some dignity into proceedings.

He made good his desire to regain the title and to prove himself again on the biggest stage, taking a substantial six seconds out of Chris Miller in second. Perhaps the questions Armitage sought to answer with a second title win were more imagined than asked; certainly there was no indication of doubt in the press. A crestfallen and slightly ungracious John Parker left immediately afterwards and did not stay for the presentation, wanting to be left alone. It was Gareth Armitage's last ride in the colours of the Oldham Century. In 1979, immediately ahead of the hill climb season, he became the first of many elite riders to join the Manchester Wheelers. Something strange was happening in the North of England, and the genteel world of the Wheelers was about to be singularly transformed by an individual called Jack Fletcher.

Up until 1979 the Manchester Wheelers was a club in decline, losing members and money. They decided to take action to reinvigorate the youth policy and transform the Wheelers into a 'sponsored' club. Long-standing club supporter and Trumann Steel magnate, Jack Fletcher, offered financial support. After some initial ructions, the deal was inked in July 1979. It was too late for the road season, but just in time for the climbs. Dave Aston recruited Gareth Armitage to ride with Brian Lowe and Steve Wilkinson in support. Armitage won 12 out of 12 hill climbs in the run up to the 1979 Championship race on Haytor Vale, but most were considerably shorter and less steep.

On the day they won the team prize and Armitage took third place. Haytor is a long, and challenging climb, with several changes in gradient before it crests out on the top of Dartmoor. It looked like a battle between the roadman and the specialist, with Longbottom and Williams vying for the title. Jeff Williams, riding for GS Strada Lutz and boosted by his Olympic selection, stormed up the climb, tackling the changes in gradient with ease and staying on top of the gear, rattling up the final steep pitches to the highest point of the moor. He won with a still unbeaten course record of 12'-44".

Within a year Armitage had been joined by Mike and Jeff Williams, Steve Joughin and Peter Longbottom. Rarely, if ever, had such a pool of talent been recruited for what was ostensibly a 'club' team, and an 'amateur' one at that. It's no surprise that there were financial inducements offered to the riders. A hill climber chasing four events over a weekend could stand to recoup much more than their race entry and petrol fees. For Armitage, joining the Wheelers was a difficult decision. Leaving the club that had nurtured him, supported him and, above all, a club that he felt a key part of, was not an easy step. But with the cost of travelling to events and the need for equipment, pragmatics won out; the head ruled the heart.

After Haytor Vale in 1979, Armitage returned to the Nick in 1980, taking a bronze medal. He then left cycling in 1981, almost as abruptly as he had arrived. He stopped competing on the bike and started running instead, completing marathons in a mind-boggling 2 hours 45 minutes, just for fun, before slipping quietly back into his life, a world away from savage inclines and lung-bursting efforts. As the National Hill Climb Championship lurched into the new decade, its complexion was about to change forever. Jack Fletcher had transformed not only the Manchester Wheelers, but also the direction and shape of British cycling for the next ten years.

8

The Inexorable Rise of the Wheelers

(1980–1982)

'Handsome prizes to be danced for.'

The stage was set, via the largesse of Jack Fletcher and supporting force of Trumann steel, for the Manchester Wheelers to dominate the British club scene for the next ten years – with the exception of a blip caused by a young, rakish rider in the colours of Rutland Cycling Club – Malcolm Elliott. Ironically, he lived and rode in Sheffield, a town synonymous with the stainless stuff.

It's difficult to reconcile the two images of Malcolm Elliott: the winner of the Durham round of the Tour Series in 2010, at the age of 49 years young, with the winner of the National Championship Hill Climb in 1980 at 19 years old. In terms of longevity, he outstrips even Jens Voigt, who has been telling his legs to shut up for a paltry 25 years or so. Elliott still looks sprightly, still retains the luxuriant blonde highlights and pop star looks, having never fully shaken off the 1980s in terms of his image. Whilst he was known as a sprinter, there's little doubt that Elliot can climb, especially the shorter stuff. The 1989 Tour of Britain prologue took place on the Law in Dundee, a spiralling roadman's climb of 174 vertical metres, looping up and around the extinct volcano. The field included a young Laurent Jalabert, Paul Curran in his first year as a professional riding for Percy Bilton, Martin Earley, Sean Kelly fresh from his third place at the World Championships, Robert Millar – who had successfully seen off Pedro Delgado on the climb to Super Bagnères at the Tour that year, and Phil Anderson. The grainy VHS images show quill stems, Rolls saddles, pedal straps and hairnet helmets very much in vogue, and the occasional slightly aero-looking item as an indication of the sudden lurch into a post-Lemond world.

Paul Curran was 'on a ride', according to Phil Ligget, edging out Jalabert and Early, but Elliott rode them all into the ground. He had form, having won the red points jersey at the Vuelta earlier in the year, then stages at both the Tours of Burgos and of Galicia the month before, but the margin of victory was impressive, taking twelve seconds from Curran, who finished runner-up.

Elliot waited impassively on the start ramp, with wisps of blonde hair sticking through his black and white hairnet helmet, his Teka jersey a riot of blue, red and yellow. He stayed seated for most of the climb, with elbows bent in the perfect position, back slightly curved, turning over a big gear right up until the last 50 metres, when the final effort began to take its toll. He climbed out of the saddle and was fighting against the bike just to force each pedal stoke through faster and ride through the line. Once across he fell off the bike and rolled onto the floor, eyes closed, chest heaving, arms outstretched. A helper cushioned his head with a towel, the fight for oxygen continued. Later, still slightly breathless, he admitted, 'I really psyched myself up for this.'

It's possible that the six minutes of the 1989 prologue might even be on the long side for Elliott. One of the longest standing records in hill climbing is his time on Monsal Dale of 1'-14.2"; no-one has got within four seconds in the years since; a significant margin over such a short climb. The record was previously held by Tom Simpson. Elliot's time is comparable with Phil Mason's untouchable mark on Catford; not even Rob Gough can erase that one from the books.

He initially joined the Sheffield CTC, but found it a bit pedestrian, and having seen a road race in the centre of Sheffield in 1976, sought out the Rutland CC for a greater challenge. In 1977 he began racing much more seriously, including the junior road race championships at Blenheim, coming second. He was making waves, none more so than when he beat Paul Swinnerton and Urs Freüler, a super fast track rider and later winner of 15 stages and the points classification in the Giro d'Italia. In February 1980 he headed out to Troyes to ride for UV Aube. Elliott was working at Tony Butterworth's in Sheffield when Harry Hall rang to see if he might be interested in riding on the continent. Joining one of the French feeder clubs was seen as one of the few routes into continental cycling, most famously the Athletic Club de Boulogne-Billancourt, where Stephen Roche was riding at the same time as Elliot signed on for UV Aube. As Elliot puts it, 'The professional scene back home was dormant and to make any sort of impact you had to live and ride abroad.'*

In between spells abroad and a close season in Sheffield, Elliot returned to tackle the National Hill Climb in 1980 and 1981. After the lengthy and challenging excursion to deepest Dartmoor, the championship returned to more traditional ground for the start of the new decade, with a visit to Sabden and the Nick O' Pendle. The rain, typically for Pendle, was slicing down in punitive, freezing spittle. With a low, dank mist glowering through the valley and shrouding the top of

---

* Malcolm Elliott with Jeff Connor, *Sprinter*, 1990

Pendle Moor, the cheers of spectators drifted down the climb like disembodied voices, spectral echoes of the witcherly past. Dave Gabbott of Clayton Velo, the promoting club, went off first, deciding that three wheels were better than two and turning in a highly creditable 4'-42.6".

Armitage, Williams and Steve Joughin seemed a shoo-in for the team prize, with the likelihood being that the title would end up in the blue and white of the Manchester Wheelers as well. With such a strong field, Eric Wilson's 20-year record of 3'-37" was under threat. Manx rider Joughin was first to equal Wilson's time, eyeballs popping out at the severity of the effort, catchers grabbing the flailing limbs. He was on the lightest gear of the heavyweights, a 59.7", and made a hushed confession to Keith Bingham of a training regime of 'Guinness and wine and discos'.*

In the time between Joughin's ride and the later seeds, word got out of the lighter gear and the car parks echoed with the sound of lockrings being loosened and cogs swapped. Joe Waugh was the first to try – and fail – to dent Joughin's time, missing out by three seconds. Elliot then took up the challenge, charging up the hill on a 61" gear to claim the course record outright with a 3'-34.4". A new mark would need to be set for the title to be wrested from the youthful Elliot's grasp. Armitage tried and failed; the demands of family life had curtailed his training, but there was a common theme in the narrative of Armitage's season: 'That's the story for most of my races; Elliot has reduced my wins.' Elliott had won six hill climbs in the run-up to the big one. Armitage did manage to dislodge Joughin to go inside the old record, but still two seconds adrift of Elliott. It left only Williams to go.

In terms of preparation for the event, Williams relied on his season's base. It's a common approach: after six months of racing it's a question of maintaining some top end and then

---

* Keith Bingham, 'Elliott Snatches Title as Williams Breaks His Nose', *Cycling*, 1/11/1980

clinging on until the last weekend of October before the off-season can begin. Calamity struck when warming up on the road: he was hit by a rider coming down the hill after they both turned in the same direction: 'We hit head on and he nutted me.' In the list of things to include in preparing for the National Championship, I'm not sure 'Break nose in collision with other competitor' is high up on the list. He abandoned his warm-up and sat immobile in his car to staunch the bleeding. After an hour Williams took his place on the line and blasted out of the gate. He was four seconds up at the cattle grid, then barrelled across the flatter section before things came unseamed on the steep ramp to the finish. A huge crowd gathered across the banked galleries at the top, ten deep, standing higher and higher along the natural amphitheatre, roaring and willing Williams on. He struggled to breathe and the gains evaporated, crossing the line an agonising tenth of a second down on Elliott.

Interviewed by Keith Bingham in *Cycling*, Elliot gave an indication of the level of effort required on the steep and tough climb: 'That is the fiercest climb I've ridden. It was the hardest I've ever tried and at the top I went through the catchers and rolled on over the top. I was nearly at the bottom before I realised I might not be able to ride back up again. So I just leaned against a car until I recovered.'*

Further down the field Peter Graham came in 56th, ignoring his own advice about riding hill climbs when a bit past your prime.

The following year those optimistic for a re-run of the 1976 event on the Horseshoe, bathed in glorious sunshine with a friendly tailwind, were in for disappointment. If anyone was hoping for rain, snow and a caustic breeze they hit the jackpot. The Wheelers were out in force again, with at least seven riders capable of a top ten placing. Whilst Williams had a point to prove, and a fifth of a second to find, Gareth Armitage was also hoping for a better ride than his catastrophic last encounter

---

* Keith Bingham, *ibid.*

with the course. Spectators began filing up the course from Llangollen, heading for the higher slopes above the slate banks with easy access to the Ponderosa Café for a comfort break.

Early rain had given way and tempted riders out into the open, warming up in the car park and getting ready for the last 10 minutes of the season. As the 10am start neared, the heavens opened again, but with additional reports that it was snowing at the top. At 417 metres elevation, the pass is frequently closed in winter. The start was delayed on account of the conditions – a horrible mixture of snow, sleet and slush on the road. By 11am nerves were frayed and it fell to the RTTC officials and the local constabulary to assess whether the race could run. At 11.30 the snow abated and the race was on.

Darryl Webster set the early mark with a 9'-32", immediately putting the Wheelers at the top of the leaderboard, and no doubt pleasing Jack Fletcher in the process. Williams was off in the middle of the field, riding a new bike with super tight clearances and silky lightweight tyres, perhaps not ideal for the conditions, and his only anxieties stemmed from the eternal fear of an unscheduled deflation. Any form of preparation that didn't involve physical injury would be an improvement on the previous year and he stayed calm and collected, chatting away with John Herety, who was excited to have signed for Mercier. Williams dug in and floated to the top in 9'-17" dead, setting the mark for the rest to topple. No-one came close. Elliot was ten seconds back, Callum Gough the surprise package at a further five seconds, and Armitage back in eighth.

1982 was a Commonwealth Games year, but more importantly, the 40th anniversary of the birth of Robert Dover, the organiser of the 'Cotswold Olympicks', a rural games first held in 1612. Dover was a strong advocate of physical exercise, seeing it as integral to the defence of the realm, but also a source of social harmony. I'm not sure how useful 120 stick-thin, reedy cyclists might be in a serious scrap, but they could at least ride away quickly if needed. Hill climbs could be added, at least in spirit, to the list of games taking place in the natural amphitheatre at Dover's Hill. Competitors were called forwards by the shrill toot of a hunting horn and events included 'jingling, bowling, leaping and running in sacks', along with 'shin kicking' and 'handsome prizes to be danced for'.

The former presented a minor logistical challenge for Jeff Williams, fresh (or not fresh at all) from the road race and a 30-hour flight home from Brisbane. He had come home from the Antipodes empty handed, but team member Malcolm Elliot had taken two gold medals: in the road race and the team time trial. Seventeen years after he organised the first event on Dover's Hill in 1965, Vic Clark embodied the spirit of Robert Dover and was on hand to watch over proceedings and help present the prizes – on this auspicious occasion an inscribed cut-glass goblet from the Dover's Games Society.

Elliot was absent for the climb, but other riders had emerged over the course of the season, including Keith Reynolds, who was starting out on a career that would encompass Commonwealth Gold, stage wins in the Tour of Britain and significant domestic success. He started well, but as if to confirm the adage that hill climbs can't be won in the first 300 yards but they can be lost there, he cracked over the last 400 yards. Gear choices were big, with 66.9" for Dave Jarvis – too big, but even a smaller gear wouldn't have helped. Williams opted for a 64.5" and rode the climb perfectly, setting a new course record to take the win. Pete Longbottom came fourth, commenting concisely, 'I thought I was a climber until I rode with Jeff.'*

It was Jeff Williams' third and last title in a year when he managed a unique double, winning the National Road title alongside the Hill Climb. Will Mansfield in ninth was the third counter of the Wheelers – and the first schoolboy to win a gold medal at a national level.

---

* Keith Bingham, 'Hill Climb Championship', *Cycling*, 6/11/1982

The Wheelers had tapped into a rich seam of talent. They were a bulldozer, a powerhouse, and it's questionable how fair or appropriate the buying of talent is in terms of the amateur roots of the sport. These are quibbles, because it also acted as a home for the top talent of the day, providing them with some remuneration. It was never a huge amount, but it was enough to subsidise training and equipment costs. In the absence of a structured national programme, it became a proto-British Cycling. The successes experienced by the club accelerated exponentially as more riders joined and the strength in depth broadened. It was simply too much for any other club in the country to cope with. On occasions another talented amateur, or someone with one of the other sponsored clubs, Joe Waugh for example, might threaten their monopoly, but only briefly. Their stranglehold on UK bike racing only became more asphyxiating with the emergence of Darryl Webster.

9

The Enigmatic Darryl Webster

(1983–1986)

'I don't like hills at all. They are so hard. There is nothing to love or like. I'm not into masochism.'

Most people who follow cycling with any degree of interest view Webster as one of the most talented riders of the 1980s to emerge from the UK, if not the best. It's worth searching out footage of his 101-mile solo breakaway in the Nissan Classic, finishing in Limerick.* It's a ride that saw him signed up by Teka, who won the subsequent battle for his signature. At the point where everything should have gone right, it went horribly wrong. He didn't move to Spain and didn't speak a word of Spanish. Instead he headed out for the races and then returned home again. At the end of the season he came home for good, and at the age of 27 he never rode professionally again.

---

* For example, https://youtube.com/watch?v=JiWc4FyccFY

At best Webster had an ambivalent relationship with the National Hill Climb. At worst, it was quite provocative and dismissive. Nevertheless, he kept coming back for more. There is a form of logic underpinning his arguments and his outspoken comments, but it's hard to discern where exactly. He is forthcoming and blunt, with a refreshing candour. However, it's hard not to discern the feeling of bitterness – perhaps of talent and hard work that wasn't fully rewarded. The big leap to Teka transpired to be nothing of the sort. When asked about regrets, he is unambiguous: 'Possibly not turning pro earlier, but on the other hand, turning pro at all. The pro game is full of disgusting, small-minded , ego-driven people. Decent, moral and ethical individuals are the rarity. There are some good people; most are not.'

After a year at Teka his contract wasn't renewed. Webster puts it down, at least in part, to comments he made regarding drugs in cycling at the PCA (Professional Cyclists Association) AGM. He then saw a 'plethora of second-rate riders gain pro contracts for 1990'. Cycling was hurtling into the EPO era, as the great Colombian climber, Luis Herrera, later commented: 'When I saw riders with fat arses climbing cols like aeroplanes, I understood what was happening.'

Webster also speaks accusingly of doping practices in UK domestic races when riding for PMS Dawes at the Kellogg's Tour of Britain in 1987: 'I saw injecting of dope on that team for the first time and was pretty pissed off about it, because no one asked me if I minded; they just went ahead and did it. I thought it was pathetic as the racing didn't warrant it.'* He finished eighth after using his hill climbing legs to good effect, making the split across the Rosedale Chimney on the second day.

The easy option is to position Webster as another rider whose career was blighted by the systematic pharmacological

---

* Edmond Hood, 'The Tale of Darryl Webster', (21/3/2011)
http://www.pezcyclingnews.com/interviews/pez-talk-the-tale-of-darryl-webster#

quagmire that was continental cycling in the 1980s and 1990s. There is clearly truth in this, but it doesn't completely explain his fractious nature – that was evident long before a professional contract was ever on the table. Since his career ended, and more latterly with the advent of internet forums, Darryl Webster has openly challenged the accepted narrative of events in cycling, both on the continent and also in the UK: 'I have on many occasions been moved to tears of frustration and anger about the issue of doping in cycling and the level of personal abuse and personal loss I've taken simply for speaking my truth.'

Webster came into the 1983 championship as another of the Manchester Wheelers' hit squad of elite domestic riders. He looks back fondly on the 1983 season and in particular, his win in the Isle of Man mountain time trial that year:

'It was one of my best ever rides. The organiser of the Circuit of Windermere had put me last off, behind Dave Lloyd where I broke Dave's course record. He was the defending winner and had been upset at the start order, so due to that I specifically asked the IOM organiser to put Dave off behind me. Dave believed time checks had given me an advantage at Windermere. Truth is I never had any. I was very motivated for the IOM record. I had a brand new pair of Wolber 20mm silk pista tyres, about 4oz each and the wheels were Mavic CX18, 28 hole – radial front, tied and soldered rear. Gearing was 53:42 with a Suntour Alloy 12-18 straight through block. I stripped everything I could off my bike. It was a 753 Raleigh, no bottle cage, no bottle cage bolts, half bar tape. I started very fast and was up at every time check. As far as I know two of my timed sections remain the fastest ever. On the mountain the lowest gear I used was 42:15. The descent was very scary, probably touching 60mph in places and I tried to pedal almost every yard, though it was very hard to catch up at those speeds. I finished in tears from the effort and took about two minutes off Dave's record.

Dave went straight through the finish area and didn't stop. He was very dejected. Again, I never had any time checks on him or anyone else, my rationale being that if you're riding as hard as you can that's all you can do and time checks aren't going to help. If anything they'd be off-putting. Dave never spoke about his ride, but I know he used time checks and it's very possible I crushed his concentration from the first check.'

The record stood until a heady combination of aero-equipment and Chris Boardman rewrote the books somewhat. By the season's end Webster was unbeaten in all hill climbs and the hot favourite for the title. The race had returned to the south west, on a steep incline on the edge of Bath. At barely a thousand yards, the winning time was going to be below three minutes. After not riding the year before, it's questionable whether Webster wanted to ride the event at all, but was under team orders from the oligarch himself, who wanted a third straight Wheelers win from either of his two 'marquee' riders – Williams or Webster.

In the bigger scheme of things, Webster saw Jack Fletcher in both a pragmatic and paternal light: 'Without him I'd most likely have packed in by the end of 1983. I'd decided before 1983 that if I couldn't make it pay, have a bit of money in my pocket as opposed to none, I would pack it in. Jack's support meant I made it pay. Not a fortune, far from it, but enough to get by. He was a legend of a man and I've never forgotten how he and Nora, his wife, gave me the chance.'

Like Gareth Armitage before him, Darryl Webster had found the means to train and ride. The link between success and training is not complicated; but even at the bare minimum, of perhaps 15 hours a week, the subsequent demands on full-time work make it very hard to sustain success in cycling with the other demands of life. Those taken under the umbrella of Jack Fletcher were able to make time to train and to ride; it was a financial lifeline. In stark terms, then and now, hill climbs can appear some way down the list of priorities for the amateur chasing a professional contract and then further success; they have their merits and some riders like them for what they are, but for most it's a series of nasty races too far after a season of road racing and time trials.

Webster is more honest than most about this: 'It's true that my main motive for riding them was my sponsor. I got a small bonus, £25 for everyone I won, and when I won four in a weekend that was, for me, a nice bit of income. Jack paid my entry fee and petrol. I'm proud to have won them but they really don't mean much. I guess I came to realise that to others they do and that adds a bit of pleasure. I never trained for hill climbs. I raced from the first weekend of February and by October I was sick to death of training. I'd ride two or three times during the week, couple of hours at tempo, and rely on the fitness of a full season.'

At the time he was more concise in his attitude: 'It means nowt – it's unfair on heavier riders; anyone over ten stone stands no chance. I'll say this now before we know the result; this shouldn't be a national title, it's purely for those fortunate enough to be built for hill-climbing. You've got to be nine stone or just over. Anyone over 10 stone stands no chance.'* Webster was 10 stone 4lbs.

On the day several riders were absent. Malcolm Elliott, Keith Reynolds and Joey McLoughlin were racing in Australia, leaving it a straight shoot-out between Williams and Webster for the title. First to make his mark was the 19-year-old Phil Mason, winner of the Cat and Bec, troubling the timekeepers with 2'-57.2". It was a significant leap on his performance from the year before, where he squeaked inside the top fifty. He was the first rider to break the three minute barrier. Despite the brevity of the course, competitors had to get to grips with the subtle changes in gradient and a false flat at the top. Equipment

---

* Keith Bingham, 'Webster: the Reluctant Champion', *Cycling*, 5/11/1983

choices were typically esoteric; Webster opted for a Reynolds 753 Ray Inkley frame, a Lincoln framebuilder also favoured by Joey McLoughlin. He used a narrow section rim on the front and different weight tyres – a four ounce front and six ounce rear.

Martin Webster, Darryl's brother, was Mason's minuteman. He crept inside the top ten. Darryl Webster was off at 95 and was the favourite, despite Williams being the incumbent. He looked smooth and remorseless, turning the gear with rhythm and panache, coping with the gradient. At the line he had taken nearly seven seconds out of Mason's time. With Mark Noble five seconds down, only Jeff Williams could upset the podium places and challenge for the win. The cognoscenti knew otherwise: Williams had been struggling for form all year and was unable to hold the wheel in the Tour of the Peak, being dropped out of the back on the climbs. But it was Jack Fletcher who called the shots. Despite not starting the National Road Race championships, Williams was told that he must start the hill climb. Visibly disappointed, he came in seventh fastest. Pete Longbottom was the third counter for the Wheelers in fifth place, continuing his record of top ten placings.

With Webster's comments and some noted absenteeism, it was hard to escape the view that somehow the championship was not what it should be or had been devalued publically. Despite his stance, 'the reluctant champion' lined up again the following year to defend his title. Dave Lloyd was a notable 'DNS'.

Be it a change in heart or simply being a year older, a more sanguine Webster emerged from the long road season, seeming to recognise that 'to others they [hill climbs] meant so much more and I guess I felt I should respect that.' The 1984 climb was much longer, clocking in at over two and half miles with a steady gradient. The ascent out of Stanhope was reminiscent of the Horseshoe. What the longer climbs make up for in challenge, they often lose in atmosphere. Many riders welcome the chance, especially the rangier beanpoles, who make their power to weight count as the clock marches onwards and the gradient remains steady, but for spectators, it lacks the tunnel, the wall of sound and the packed banks of a thousand-yard snorter.

Callum Gough had put down the marker two weeks beforehand in the test event, recording a 9'-51" for the course record. He also unwittingly put pressure on himself to 'do a ride' in the big one. A tailwind on the day made it highly likely that the record would go, and most likely to one of the roadmen with their musette full of endurance and a season's base. The smart money was on Webster. He'd perfected his approach and was winning hill climbs all over the place: 'They were all about pace. I'd carefully and very slowly ride the courses, work out how far in I'd be making the transition from anaerobic to aerobic effort and take great care to ensure I didn't over-cook the first minute or so and could make the transition with the minimum of red lining. Over-cook it too early on a climb and you're finished. Once the line was in sight I'd give everything I had left and used to say to myself, "It doesn't matter if I black out after the line, it won't kill me." In a short climb there's little room for error, get it wrong, choose the wrong gear, start too fast, there's no recovery possible. Pacing was everything.'

On the day the early time was set by the Kirkby rider, Roy Chamberlain. He had the honour of holding the lead with 10'-03.2". Half an hour later Steve Marchant got ready to do battle. He had low expectations, being a master of the short, steep and nasty stuff, but flew up the climb as though propelled by an invisible hand, in the process smashing Gough's record into tiny pieces by a margin of 23 seconds. No-one was more surprised than Marchant himself. However, Pete Longbottom was confident. The Manchester Wheeler and international roadman was an outside prospect for a medal; he exuded confidence at the start and felt the conditions would lead to a strong ride. He faded badly and finished off the pace in eleventh. Several other riders tried and failed to dislodge

Marchant from the top, with Karl Smith coming closest, an agonising four seconds outside.

The effort of the longer climb, the sustained pace and force needed to climb at speed for ten minutes was taking its toll on the field. Rider after rider rolled across the line in a state of exhaustion, tongue lolling, eyes sunken, arms tensed and taut, legs convulsing in lactate agony. It fell to Webster to ride through the pain and the near catastrophe of a slipping set of gears; the chain slipped at the start and at 1.65 miles he was a second down. The last mile of the course was a demonstration of unabated power, turning over the biggest gear he could and charging towards the line, somehow finding a remarkable 21 seconds to finish in 9'-08.8". Both the course record and championship field had been bagged. Webster was pleased because it was a longer climb, 'proving I could win on either type'.

Ultimately, he was in a different race, something he agreed with in 2013 when I asked him if he had any rivals. 'None. It was me against the hill.' The results confirm his singular vision. Unfortunately for Steve Marchant, it left him always one small step from the top, an eternal second, initially as bridesmaid to Webster, but later reduced to looking upwards by a bloke from the Wirral called Chris Boardman, who in 1984 was busy rewriting the schoolboy record books.

For someone who ostensibly and vocally didn't like hill climbs, Webster kept coming back for more. When pressed on the love-hate relationship he had with the Championship, he gave nothing away: 'I don't have any favourite hills. In fact I don't like hills at all and always preferred to train on flattish roads. Hills kill your speed. They are so hard. There is nothing to love or like. I'm not into masochism.'

Even if you like nothing better than the metallic taste of blood in the mouth and the lacerating pain in the lungs from a savage hill effort, the climb at Challacombe in 1985 was an exercise in masochism. The Championship hadn't visited this particular bit of North Devon before and has not been remotely near it since. This is probably because it's one of the nastiest bits of uphill road there is and racing up it is a horrible experience. Nearly all those involved in the day, either riding or spectating, described it as possibly the hardest course yet. Even the normally serene Webster was left struggling for breath and unable to conceal the pain and suffering. Some thirty years later, Webster remembers it as 'a fearsome hill, positively dangerous!' which had many competitors looking for dinner-plate sized rear sprockets to take them below 50". Beyond that, many of the riders felt mentally and physically cowed by the ordeal that lay ahead. It was rendered more awkward by the extreme contrast between an initial false flat and then almost downhill section of 200 yards or so, followed by the severe and unrelenting ramp of 25%. It made it hugely technical, but also left most in a quandary as to how to ride it; a 50" gear on the flat is not much fun – 25mph would require a cadence of 176rpm! As a result, most soft-pedalled to the start of the hill, saving every ounce of energy for the challenge ahead. 'I had to spin in the saddle to the ramp with high cadence, but not get out of breath, then once on the ramp remain out of the saddle all the way to the very last bit, where it flattened out a bit. If I'd sat down on the ramp I'd have slowed.'

The knowledge that there is nowhere to hide on a hill weighed heavily on the starters; you can't slow down, you just have to keep on pushing all the way to the top, and if it hurts, it's tough; you have to ignore it. You can't hide in the bunch or contemplate something else, or even have a dislocated monologue about how things aren't going too well; the mind and body are consumed with the pain of the effort. Contemplating what is about to happen is a recipe for disaster and usually a sign that your days as a hill climber are numbered – if you begin to recognise what it actually is you're doing then it's time to stop doing it.

In this case, though, contemplating the hill ahead was inescapable for Webster: 'Psychologically it was very tough. I was fighting back tears on the line, dreading what was to come as I knew it was going to be totally shit or bust with no margin at all for error, and was going to be one where you really were close to blacking out from lack of oxygen.'

Phil Mason, the scourge of Catford, surged up the hill and tracked his minuteman with a remorseless acceleration, the catch was on and his baying supporters knew it, until suddenly and violently, everything caved in and he died a thousand deaths. The minuteman escaped his clutches as Mason pedalled through treacle, turning squares and fighting to keep moving. He laboured across the line, ashen and unwell, nearly two minutes down on the leaders. The Red Cross were on hand to administer oxygen and an ambulance was called to take him to sanctuary.

Pete Longbottom rode better than the previous year, coming in sixth on a 51.5" gear. He described it to the press: 'As you got further up the hill you felt as though elastic was pulling you back, getting stronger and stronger, like in a Tom and Jerry cartoon.'* Callum Gough went even lighter, opting for a 49", but finished just outside Longbottom's time. Number 75 on the card was Darryl Webster's younger brother, the second of two, Alex. He stole the top spot with a 4'-40.6". Webster senior had complained that in preparation for the climb over the weekend Alex had given him a kicking. He was fearful the practice run might be repeated in the headline event.

The first of the big guns, Karl Smith of Clayton Velo, then obliterated the younger Webster's time by twelve seconds and looked good enough for the win – but it depended on two men. Steve Marchant was the first to go. He had been struggling with illness, bouncing between one virus and another, with short sharp bursts of training in between. Anything below the neck is anathema to hill climbs or any kind of competitive cycling. Riding with a snotty cold is permissable, but once it

---

* Keith Bingham, 'Webster Wins for a Third Year', *Cycling*, 31/10/1985

hits the lungs the race is up. Nonetheless, Marchant was on form and felt relaxed, knowing he was outside the reckoning beforehand, and he did a ride, sneaking past Smith by a couple of bits of a second. In between times Tim Norman of the Dursley Road Club experienced the full horror of the climb. Earlier in the week he'd had his bike stolen. After struggling up most of Challacombe he suffered the indignity of being felled by a Red Cross nurse walking down the hill. At least medical attention was on hand.

It left only Webster to come. He was using lightweight track tyres and had stripped the bike right down, ditching the bar tape completely and running a stubby right hand lever. He settled for a smaller margin of victory than he might have liked, a scant five seconds over Marchant, citing the significance of power to weight as the main reason why others had run him closer, and the toughness of the climb.

The cover of *Cycling* magazine shows Webster moments after the finish. Someone has kindly draped a blanket over his shoulders. His eyes are screwed tightly closed, unable to climb off, perched on the top tube and searching for breath. Recalling the event, Webster said: 'My legs hurt like they did after a GP.' It was a fifth successive team prize, with the two Websters abetted by Longbottom. In the process Webster became the first rider to equal the consecutive hat trick set by Vic Clark in the 1940s.

It's hard to know what Steve Marchant thought when he saw the start sheet for the championship on the Riber in 1986. He would again have to beat the three-time champion to win the coveted title.

For Webster, though, other things were on his mind. His brother Alex, fourth at Challacombe the year before, had been hit by a drunk driver on the A50 at Leicester: 'He was hit from behind. He suffered multiple skull fractures, broken ribs and a broken leg and lost five pints of blood by the time he reached hospital. He was in surgery through the night as they battled, firstly to save his life and then to save his leg. He wasn't expected to live. I spent the first three days at his bedside with my mother. This happened just before the hill climb season and as a result I barely did any training that month. I mostly used the rollers to loosen off. He was kept in an induced coma for a week or so due to swelling on his brain. When he was brought out of that he couldn't speak properly; he would wake briefly and sit up, make a few noises, then fall back asleep. The doctors had no idea to what extent he might recover. It was only the week before the National that I put in a day reconnaissance of Riber Hill and planned the ride. Afterwards I went straight to the Hospital in Nottingham to see him.'

Considering his mental turmoil, it's surprising Darryl Webster rode at all. Although from within a cycling family there's arguably a sense that it was expected. Nevertheless, it made it very difficult to attain the requisite level of focus to compete and win the championship. Webster was chasing a fourth straight success – something no-one had managed before. Even the great Granville Sydney's wins came in pairs. It was because of the rotating nature of the event: a three-minute eyeballs-on-stalks horror show one year; the next a quasi-Alpine rhythm effort. It suits different riders and is the enemy of consistency.

Riber Hill, near Matlock, is still a popular climb, although the National hasn't yet been back. Matlock CC started using the climb in 1976, and like many club events, it carries the name of a rider who died too young. George Higton was just 27 when he was thrown from his bike whilst riding through Rowsley. Riber Hill is the hardest way to climb out of Matlock Bath. The easiest is via the tourist gondola up to the Heights of Abraham. It's much more sedate, yet climbs more quickly, and beyond a slight popping of the ears, contains none of the pain and suffering of the alternative route. If you're feeling even more adventurous you can walk through the woods in search of Tinker's Shaft.

All-round hill acolyte and regular National rider, Simon Warren, describes it as a 'legendary challenge' and waxes lyrical about the climb, coining the phrase, 'a bonsai Alpine pass'.* The fickle gradient chops and changes, from an extreme 1-in-4, to false flats, then back up again in vindictive ramps, all interrupted by five sweeping bends to contend with on the journey to the top. The form rider for many was Paul Curran; he had achieved a double gold at the Commonwealth Games and a hatful of other wins, including the Lincoln GP and the overall Premier Calendar. Most knew that Webster was riding in difficult circumstances. He wasn't discounted, it was more that with Curran on the up and up, Webster would have to be on form and riding hard to win.

When Curran crept inside the course record, it became clear that a special kind of ride was needed to win. Curran was unambiguous: 'I expect Darryl will romp up it.'** Phil Longbottom and Karl Smith did their usual rides, sitting in the top ten and ending up just outside the medals. The eternal hope of the south, Steve Marchant of '34 Nomads, turned in a course record ride, inside Curran's mark by two seconds, to nail down his usual place at the top, where the crowd waited, breathlessly, for Webster's arrival. In between times Chris Walker pushed Karl Smith into third place and became the third rider to break the hill record. It was typically tight at the top.

The rows of leaning onlookers crowded the timekeeper, awaiting the noise rolling up the hill that would signal the progress of the scratch rider. Webster was a picture of determination; rhythm and brute force were the order of the day – in sharp contrast to the battle of survival on Challacombe twelve months earlier. He rode through the line and waited. It can only ever have been a battle of the minor placings, Webster finished in 4'-48.8", a good six seconds up on Marchant, who cemented his Poulidor status, albeit in an insular and slightly

---

* Simon Warren, *100 Greatest Climbs*, 2010

** Keith Bingham, 'It's Webster Again – In Record Time', *Cycling*, 30/10/1986

parochial manner. Webster views this title win as his best, 'because of the circumstances of my brother being in intensive care and barely riding my bike between events.'

Alex Webster made a recovery and raced again, only to experience another serious crash in a criterium at Market Harborough, that left him deaf in one ear. He was then knocked off his bike whilst training and broke a leg. After that he felt that maybe, just maybe, it might be time to call it quits and he took up running, opting for high impact on the knees as opposed to the rest of the body. He now runs marathons with a PB of around two hours 40 minutes, making him one of the fastest in his age group.

Webster seemed poised to tackle Granville Sydney's record, not that it was uppermost in his mind: 'I don't even know how many times he won it and never have known.' However, he failed to return the following year due to a knee injury, before turning pro in 1988, and never rode another hill climb. After his abortive year on the continent insofar as he rode some races on the continent but returned home after each one, he all but retired and spent his late twenties driving a taxi cab. He returned to amateur racing in 1991 'for fun'.

To achieve a spread of victories across everything the topography has to offer arguably makes Webster one of the strongest hill climbers the sport has ever seen – although he'd bridle at that definition: 'I never thought of myself as a specialist hill climber; they were something tagged on the end of the season. It doesn't count for much and isn't any basis for a career.'

Of course, he's right. He was a roadman and a tester, an international rider and the hill climbs represent a footnote in his career. It's a footnote he came to appreciate, despite his initial reticence, but even now it's the Isle of Man TT that has him glowing with pride, or the Nissan Classic. As for the National? 'It's nice to be able to say I was champion four years running but they don't count for much in my career.' If the one thing that seems to be missing from Webster's career, or at the least, from his account of his career – his happiness and enjoyment – then it's good to see that he's found some equanimity of late. It's a curious reversal of Gareth Armitage's trajectory: 'I had 17 years off until three years ago. Since then I've ridden Land's End to John O' Groats touring solo, over two weeks using the CTC scenic route. It was the most enjoyable cycling I've ever done.'

10

The Professor

(1987–1991)

'I never considered myself particularly gifted, but I managed to stretch and mould the ability that I have and found a niche for myself.'

Chris Boardman is one of the busiest men in the universe. I know this because I spent a very long time trying to get hold of him to talk about the majestic, if insular glory of the hill climb. He was more than willing to help but our schedules were a perpetual source of conflict. Minor events like the Tour or the London Olympics kept getting in the way. Eventually I managed to ask him some questions, but it transpired that he'd forgotten the key details. He was the only rider I came across who couldn't remember anything about the individual races he rode. In hindsight, I had given him a list of fairly obscure details from fairly obscure bike races from the decade that time and fashion had largely forgotten, the late 1980s. He went on to win Olympic gold and a yellow jersey in the Tour de France, not to mention recording the fastest time ever for a prologue. It's no surprise that the specificities of a two or three minute blast up a hill in the Shropshire badlands might pale into insignificance and become overshadowed by the startling technicolour memories of a hallucinatory time trial waltz through the outskirts of Lille astride a Mike Burrows Lotus monocoque.

In 1991 Boardman was National Hill Climb Champion, having defeated all-comers with a savage assault on Park Rash, at Kettlewell. In 1992 he became the Olympic pursuit champion. In 1993 he took the World Hour Record. In 1994 he rode the 7.2 kilometres from the centre of Lille to the new 'Eurolille' retail and TGV station at 55.142kph. In English money it's 34.3mph, which would roughly work out at 17'-30" for a 10-mile time trial.* He caught and overpowered Luc Leblanc, who looked utterly startled and confused by the young Rosbif hurtling past, a vision of infinite souplesse and speed, not even out of the saddle or moving, until he crossed the line, only then letting his head drop from the aerodynamic straitjacket, gasping for oxygen. He became the first British rider to don the *maillot jaune* since Tom Simpson in 1962. He remains the fastest rider in Tour Prologue history. If you haven't watched it, go and watch it now, it's on the same site where you watch all the vintage cycling videos for hours and hours when you should be working or doing other things.

There is a wealth of 'vintage Boardman' out there, with perhaps the best being Gary Imlach's documentary on the hour record attempt. Boardman is visited by the camera crew at a Rudy Project race in the national circuit championships. It sees the Olympian return to the TT scene – at Astley and Dunham – a setting no different from that of his youth, perched on the car boot, chatting to his Dad, with the only difference

---

* The '10' record at the time was 18'-37".

being the gentle queue for signatures. The time trial, in all its grassroots glory, is clearly something loved by Boardman, much in the same way Alex Dowsett professes to hold a love for the sport, even if he did manage to open a chasm between himself and everyone else by shading a marginal 25 seconds from the competition record at 10 miles in 2014. Boardman's Dad speaks to the camera: 'If he could have done time trials as a professional, he'd have stayed with that.' He is wearing the colours of the North Wirral Velo. The staple elements remain the same: the village hall, cakes, dogs, a noticeable superfluity of veterans and the disorientating sight of the aforementioned veterans getting changed in the car park. Rule number one for attending a time trial: never glance inside a parked car at the HQ; you will see things you will never be able to unsee.*

Watching the documentary succinctly demonstrates the overwhelming singularity that the master time triallist brings to the discipline: the silence of the individual contest, the battle with the self, the control of external reality, the internal reality of control and pain management. Yet pain is visible as a narrative on the face, in the eyes, the mouth, the contortions and creases, the lines and forks of veins on the arms. And at the end everything is spent, the rider is lifted off the bike. This is the time trial, this is the hill climb, a finality of effort: here is your task, do it as fast as possible, do not play a tactical game, defeat only the external corporeality of your body.

It's easy to think that if any of us were just that bit more single-minded, or had a bit more time, more ambition, we'd be somewhere near Boardman, or at the least somewhere further on than we are at the moment, lodged in the realms of amateur sport. Watching the documentary dispelled any lingering ideas that I might have had. Chris Boardman turned his son George's bedroom into a hypoxic chamber, sealing up the doors and

---

* At a cyclo-cross race at the new Odd Down circuit near Bath one of the Bristol South contingent stated sagely, 'Never look, and if you do, for some awful reason, look, beware the sight of unkempt gooches.'

windows with tape. For the record, George wasn't in there at the time – he had to lodge in another room. From the outside there are three tubes coming and going, linked to generators in the workshop outside, pumping in a lower oxygen content. Normal air content is just under 21%, in George's bedroom it was a lowly 16%, or the equivalent of being at 16,000 feet. If George had been sleeping in his room I suspect he might have cleaned up at Sports Day that year, with raised eyebrows and sinister accusations of 'two speed' children's running.

Commitment consists of a remorseless desire to prove that at one specific discipline – whatever discipline that was – he was the best in the world. If it meant training for six hours a day and breathing oxygen-starved air in the house… so it goes. It's no surprise then that he proved a bit handy in amongst the British time trial circuit, breaking records and paving the way for a successful career as an Olympian and ultimately, a continental professional.

In 1987 the promoting duties for the National Hill Climb fell to the Yorkshirte District of the CTT. They duly set out to claim the title of 'toughest national ever', and plumped for the Rosedale Chimney. It's a mythical slice of road, used in several premier calendar events over the years; a 1-in-3 tarmac strip up the side of a wall which is closed to caravans and other assorted charabancs. I went to look for this climb on a day trip from my Dad's house in Withernsea. It's a beautiful and sparse part of the country (North Yorkshire, not Withernsea), with desolate, unpopulated moorland and some long and challenging climbs. I enjoyed Blakey Bank and others, but knew that the headliner at this particular bike festival, the heavy metal monster, was the Chimney. Maybe I built it up in my head after hearing rumours of the excessive steepness, but it wasn't as bad as I feared. Climbs often aren't as bad as one might expect, until you have to race up them. The Rake is a good example: I had a great time in the warm-up; nearly died in the race proper. The Rosedale Chimney can lay good claim to being the steepest national course ever used, at least for the short section in the middle where it pitches up like a startled colt.

In the absence of Webster, the field was open. Steve Marchant, after three second places, was itching to go one better and finally sit on the throne, whilst Paul Curran, the National Road Race Champion that year, was looking to grab his first title. He had ridden strongly throughout the season, winning in March at the GP of Essex, then taking the Star Trophy overall. In amongst the established roadmen and hill climbers, including Phil Sheard and Pete Longbottom, lurked a young, fresh-faced time triallist. At 21 years old, Boardman was just beginning to make his mark in his first season in the senior ranks, having taken the bronze in the team pursuit at the Commonwealth Games a year earlier. Curran had taken the gold medal in the road race. There was no doubting the senior partner in the Wheelers, and whilst Marchant was favourite, Curran was also the name on most people's lips. For a select few, the young tester from the Wirral was the dark horse.

Marchant's preparations were interrupted by the Great Storm of 1987. It tore through the south of England, laying waste to everything in its path with gusts in excess of 120mph. This included a not inconsiderable number of trees. The internet says fifteen million in total, so it must be true. A secondary victim was the world's oldest competitive cycle race at Catford, and not unsurprisingly, the Bec. Yorks Hill and the surrounding area of the North Downs Ridge collided with the full force of the storm and the roads were impassable. The following year the aspect of the climb had changed markedly, with the steep embankments denuded of foliage. For Marchant, it took away a key element of his preparation. At one point he considered not riding, but news of Webster's injury tipped the balance and he became enthusiastic at the prospect of taking a first title. Curran lived locally and knew the road well, and despite a self-confessed loathing for the pain of the hill climb, decided to compete.

Gear choices were very light, sub-50", with both Boardman and Curran opting for a freewheel and close ratio block. Marchant went for fixed, with a rear cog almost as big as the front chainring, to give 51.8". The gradient did for more than a handful of the middle markers; several ground to a halt, some were unlucky enough to be pushed onwards by the encroaching crowd, whilst others collapsed into the grass verge or were caught by the spectators. It was a gladiatorial contest in the best traditions of the event, a roaring crowd and a Thanatos-like urge for death or glory from the competitors.

Regardless of any ambivalence towards the climb, Curran was in peak condition. He tore up the hill and assaulted the steepest section, pushing all the way to record 5'-22.8", a full eight seconds up on Marchant, who would miss out on the prize yet again. Boardman was using a block on the back, but had stripped it that morning and had to use a mountain bike block as a spare. He was stuck in the 42:24, unable to change up when it levelled out. At halfway he was a second down, provoking a charge for the line to claw back time and overhaul the leader. He came perilously close, falling just outside by a fifth of a second. After the event, he expressed his plans for the future: 'For the first time I am going to train through the winter, about two hours a day.'

The steep section of road did for most people: Steve Hulme dropped thirteen seconds to slip from fourth at halfway to an eighth placed finish; the aptly-named T. Pain came home in 6'-36". With Webster now out of the picture, a changing of the guard had occurred, and for many, it was Chris Boardman who was the revelation of the event.

In 1988 the climb returned to the Nick O' Pendle, a favourite course and for many, a true test. Oddly enough, it hasn't been back since. The course is still used, but it hasn't been used in the National for 26 years. It's a shame. I'm not sure why this is – possibly because Peter Graham's promotion on the Rake has become the 'go to' Lancashire climb. Either way, the Pendle

Moorland, with its natural amphitheatre at the top, is now a neglected part of the sport.

Times on the Nick can vary wildly, as much as thirty seconds up or down depending on the wind direction. It reverberates down into Sabden and roars up the other side, blowing cyclists up the climb, or halting their progress with an invisible wall of stubbornness. It began as a still and clear autumnal day. The sunshine gently warmed the spectators and all was calm; the early starters limbered up and performed their effort, dispelling the gentle crystallised remnants of the night's subtle frost, lying in the shadows at the side of the road and in the stalks of amber moorland grass.

Jeff Wright was the first to go fastest, and if it was the first time his name featured at the business end of things, it certainly wasn't going to be the last. He had won stage eight of the Rás Tailteann that year and was getting a reputation as a bit of a whippet. Riding for Tyne Velo, Wright did enough to sneak ahead of Longbottom and set the fastest mark at 3'-47.4". At this point it was breezy, but nothing overly strenuous.

After twenty minutes Wright was deposed and the new incumbent was Rob Langley of Solihull CC, who forced his way up the climb on a 63" gear, commenting that it was 'just right'. In the next twenty minutes the first potent breaths of wind emerged, with Phil Sheard the first to capitalise, spinning a 59.4" gear with languid insouciance to nail the top spot by three seconds. There were only two more riders to go who were capable of wresting it back. With each middle marker the wind increased by a degree.

Next to go was Boardman, tense and wiry, fearful of the waiting Curran and the effort ahead. He turned the 60.1" gear with muscular clarity, hurtling upwards at a pace that seemed quicker to the eye than anyone else. Up and over the cattle grid, before putting in the final burst, around the bend and amongst the watching spectators, his face was a picture of exertion; forehead furrowed in corrugations of pain, mouth wide open, desperately inhaling insufficient oxygen, gloveless hands grasping track-taped bars, out of the saddle and pushing the gear round in savage circles of angst, over the line and into the arms of helpers, spent and exhausted, everything left on the road in 3 minutes and 29 seconds. It was a full fourteen seconds quicker than Langley, a yawning chasm of time for a short climb like the Nick. Rumour had it that Boardman had been dieting for the first time. His weight had dropped from 11 stone 1 to 10 stone 4: 'I have never dieted in my life. I have eaten chips every day for a long while, and now I am on an all-protein diet. I used to eat four sandwiches for lunch, now only one.'*

Not only that, but he had made some extreme decisions in the name of reconnaissance: 'I got married to my wife Sally-Anne then got up at 6am the next morning to ride an event on The Nick, not because it was the National Championship, just it was the only opportunity to race the course before the title race!' Commitment has several meanings in the Boardman household.

Curran had his work cut out and knew that nothing less than physical oblivion would do in the pursuit of glory. Boardman waited at the top amongst the crowd, shepherded by the Rossendale Road Club and an army of helpers, necks craned down the viscous strip of tarmac to catch a glimpse of the international roadman heading up the hill. He rode through the line and was initially clocked at 3'-33", just outside Boardman's mark for second place. It was then confirmed as 3'-43.6", putting him 'only third'. Boardman had broken Malcolm Elliot's record from the 1980 National by four seconds. It still stands. After taking the title he acknowledged that he had some decisions to make: 'After the Commonwealth Games I will seriously consider what I am going to do in the sport. It is a question of whether I am going to treat it as a hobby or whether to earn my living at it. Now that I am married I need the money.'

---

* Dennis Donovan, 'Boardman Wins Title, Curran Only Third', *Cycling*, 3/11/1988

In 1989 the Championship moved to Shropshire and the Burway out of Church Stretton. It's a single-track road sketched in pencil on the side of the Long Mynd, a precarious and precipitous ascent above the Carding Mill Valley. The area is a fingerprint of whorled contours, double arrows and loops on a map dotted by the gothic script of 'tumulus'. All of which makes it the ideal place for a hill climb, even though it hadn't been ridden in anger since 1947, the year of Vic Clark's win on Winnats. The climb features the welcoming 'Devil's Mouth', a momentary respite between two punishing ramps, swallowing the riders whole before vomiting them up the road.

In keeping with the tradition of returning champions having calamitous experiences (see Armitage, Williams), Boardman's gears were slipping in the immediate warm-up, with no time for a repair. He had to lump it with a 59.7" instead of his favoured 56.7" at the bottom end, using the 19 when he favoured the 20. It's quite a big step up and had the potential to unpick any carefully stitched preparations. Boardman had opted against riding fixed, more through pragmatism than any ideological conviction. He hadn't had time to set it up. He rode a carbon Graham Weigh, only removing the large plate. Added to his mechanical woes was an increase in racing weight – he was a stone heavier. The Manchester Wheeler was down to ride the Tour of Mexico the following week so had bulked up, at least partly in fear of the 'continental cuisine' and the likelihood of a tummy bug. The final component of this unsavoury triple-whammy was a vindictive headwind. The end result was one word: overgeared. It's nice to know it can happen to superheroes like Chris Boardman, as well as rank amateurs like myself. I feel like I'm in loftier company.

As riders came and went, and in the case of Tim Warriner, were blown off the course into the barriers, it became apparent that a negative split was the key to this particular course. Riders who had the wherewithal to save themselves for the second half found the seconds easier to come by. Boardman's methodical and scientific approach seemed tailor-made for the

Salop parcours: 'I used to find that most hill climbs were lost by others rather than won by me. I would find myself in third or fourth position at half distance. Most people, especially under pressure, ride flat out from the start and hang on. You can't free wheel in a hill climb so speed drops dramatically when you die, making the second half much more than fifty percent of the race. Good hill climb riders have the self-discipline to manage their effort with intellect and keep their instinct to push harder under control.'

Which makes it all the more improbable that he contrived to 'blow up' and yet still somehow take the win. His Dad, Keith, was watching: 'He looked terrible. I knew he had done something wrong.' A tricky start, compounded by no minutemen to chase (ahead were three DNS) led to confusion and an existential struggle. After a mile he cracked violently and it became a race to limit his losses, limping over the line. He was immediately pessimistic about his chances of victory. It was a new experience for the talented international rider, and not one he wanted to repeat. The perfect storm of mechanical problems, a head wind, a savage climb and extra weight had undone the relentless specificity of preparation. Nevertheless, just because it's hard it doesn't mean you haven't done well. Given the circumstances, Boardman's class and strength shone through. He still managed to steal eleven seconds from Scott O'Brien in second place and a huge seventeen seconds from the perennial nearly-man, Steve Marchant. Two riders stood out in the first half of the field, a crestfallen and annoyed Pete Longbottom finishing in tenth, but cross at being seeded at 55, and the junior BBAR winner Stuart Dangerfield, finishing in 5'-38.9" for an impressive seventh place.

After the 1979 excursion to Dartmoor, the race returned in 1990. Rather than revisit the long and varying ascent of Haytor Vale, the District opted for the climb out of Widecombe-in-the-Moor. It's further into the moorland and a very tough climb. Mid-Devon CC occasionally use it as part of a double-header with Haytor, early on in September. They used to opt for Mamhead, but this clearly didn't rate highly enough on the masochism scale. The Mid-Devon CC seem to churn out ridiculously fit young turks at a rate of knots. Most people blame Colin Lewis, a *domestique* for Tom Simpson*, for showing them the ropes and making them ride over Dartmoor, day in, day out. I rode Mamhead once and Colin Lewis was stood at the side of the road, taking photos. It was enough to knock me out of my stride, Tour de France super domestique and all-round legend of cycling taking my photo on a hill near Starcross in Devon. It's on a par with the time I passed a clearly out of shape Sean Yates in a 10-mile trial. I resisted the temptation to unclip one foot, he probably would have lamped me.

Widecombe is scenic and beautiful. It's surrounded by a series of tiny tributaries flowing into the East Webburn river, which then empties into the Dart. The river rises just south of the Grimspound prehistoric hut circle before rolling down the sinuous rills to cross the main road out of Widecombe. The climb rears up in 20% increments, coming to a rest just before Bonehill Rocks, a characteristic granite outcrop in the tawny, windswept moorland. It's an eerie and desolate landscape, containing echoes of prehistory and the people that once lived on the rocky and gorse-ridden outcrops. The blinking lights of the prison are visible by night, enclosing the inmates within the solid granite walls and the moorland, a prison within a prison.

Boardman made a mockery of the triangular 20% warning signs, hurtling upwards with power and stillness in four minutes and ten seconds. He used a disc (arguing that the stiffness more than made up for the weight) with a trispoke front. He had the beating of Steve Marchant, by now surely

---

* 'On day two one of my prize possessions was my Great Britain team hat – freshly laundered cotton. I was really proud of my team hat (we didn't wear crash helmets) and about forty miles into the stage Tom came alongside me and said, "Colin, give us your hat," and he ripped it off my head. "I want to wipe my arse with this," he said. He did a dump by the roadside and wiped his bum with my hat. So that was the life of a *domestique*.' http://vimeo.com/70258445

wondering what he had to do to win the race. The answer, as is often the case when someone like Chris Boardman appears, is race in a different era. Dangerfield gave notice of both his improvement as he entered the senior ranks, and a capacity to perform on different climbs by taking the bronze medal.

With a double Commonwealth bronze in the trophy cabinet at home, Boardman was beginning to turn his attention to Barcelona, some 18 months away, and the possibility of Olympic success. In the interim he carried on riding for the Manchester Wheelers, benefitting from the patronage of Jack Fletcher: 'I enjoyed winning hill climbs; they were lucrative for someone with absolutely no money and you could fit two into a single day.'

Park Rash is a long way from Widecombe. Such is the nature of the championship. One year it's in prehistoric Devon, beyond the pale and the Anglo-Saxon hordes, practically the land of the Celts, the next it's in the Yorkshire Dales. The climb out of Kettlewell continued the recent tradition of horribly long and horribly steep ascents, with several bits pitching up at a limb-threatening 20%, and not much below that. It's also one of those climbs that looks even steeper than it actually is, just in case you didn't think it was quite steep enough in the first place. It resembles a Bridget Riley painting of wobbly optical illusion, lines of tarmac and a rough-house road surface, all leading inexorably upwards.

1991 saw a revolution in times and equipment across the season, with aerobars being permitted in CTT events. The emerging arms race in carbon bling and aero-aids saw at least a handful of riders taking to the start line with trispokes, looking to scratch out any advantage. It looks strangely anomalous now, where lightness is the defining feature of hill climb bikes.

Two riders looked capable of causing an upset – Dangerfield and Jeff Wright. On his day, which wasn't very often, Wright seemed capable of beating anyone, but had yet to take that form or willpower into the National proper. Dangerfield was simply getting faster and faster, an all-round powerhouse and prodigious time triallist. With the climb taking place in the heartlands of Yorkshire hill climb territory, it was no surprise that the great and good came to watch. Vic Clarke was watching over proceedings, as was Beryl Burton, arguably the greatest cyclist the country has ever produced. Even some of the testers made their way up to the slopes, with Gary Dighton enjoying the vicarious masochism and glad not to be riding. Kitching and Dave Rayner both cheered on the riders and helped cement the reputation, at least in the North, of the event being an end of season jolly for anyone bright enough to not put an entry in. Spectators lined the climb, especially the hairpins at the beginning, the best place to see the different gurns.

Earlier in the season Jeff Wright had scalped Boardman on the Rake, a much shorter climb, but nonetheless, the win was enough to flicker an ember of anxiety in the mind of the emerging professional. However, it wasn't to be repeated. The margins between the top three were big; Boardman took twelve seconds away from Wright, who in turn took nine seconds from Dangerfield. The pecking order was established, Boardman was cock of the walk. Again. With his attention for the following season firmly on the Catalan capital, the next year promised to be a battle royale. Ultimately, the hill climbs suited Boardman's attention to detail and his methodical approach to racing: 'I enjoyed the intellectual challenge of understanding what it took to do it well. This covered diet, bike set up, gear selection, warm-up strategy, pacing strategy, specialist training and dealing with pressure – a whole host of parameters to be blended and mastered. Do I look back on them fondly? I almost never look back at all. It could be a psychological flaw, I suppose, but unless there is something to learn that I can apply going forward, I just have zero interest in my own past. I am fascinated by the present and the future; so as soon as one challenge is over, I'm on to immersing myself in the next. Does that sound cold and dispassionate? I suppose it does, but I certainly wasn't, at that particular moment.'

He articulates the status of the hill climb within cycling and his career in a way reminiscent of Darryl Webster, albeit more politely: 'Hill climbs were a fun exercise and satisfying to tackle at that particular time, but I was always aware that being good at them was a very specialised ability of little value in any other arena. If there was a power to weight ratio uphill pursuit event, then this skill set would be similar!'

Secretly, I'm sure the golden shiny cap awarded to the Hill Climb Champion sits comfortably next to the Olympic gold medal on a groaning trophy shelf in the Wirral.

11

The Hill Climb Bicycle

With all due respect to Mr. Bidlake, I feel I cannot let some of his remarks about the fixed wheel pass without protest. I have found that in all conditions the fixed wheel is far superior. Anyhow, I have found the fixed wheel a great help in hill-climbing.*

For over 60 years there were two key elements to the hill climb season: the pain of racing uphill and the use of fixed wheel bicycles for this purpose. Only the first of these has remained constant: the pain of racing uphill. If one thing encapsulates the change in equipment and approach, it's Matt Clinton's choice of bike for the 2014 championship on Pea Royd Lane. In the 2009 Championship on the same climb he opted for a fixed wheel, in 2014 he plumped for a Trek Emonda with an 11 speed cassette.

The bike of choice for the specialist has historically been fixed wheel. For many years it was unusual to find anything different. Some would even argue that the use of variable gears

---

* W. J. Mountain, *Cycling*, 5 October, 1922

implied that a hill was not suitable for a hill climb event. In the other time trial events the change towards variable gears came much earlier. Ray Booty's 1956 landmark sub four-hour '100' was ridden on an 84" gear. Five years later, John Woodburn won the blue riband 25-mile championship on gears, creating a sudden rush away from the fixed cog and eroding any lingering certainty that fixed was quicker. This transformation took much longer for hill climbs, primarily because of an ongoing preoccupation with weight, a factor not affecting the flatland rider.

Chris Boardman was a devotee of the single cog, setting competition records on fixed at multiple distances, but was keenly aware of the additional benefits when riding uphill: 'The bike was a third lighter than a geared machine; the drive was direct and without frictional losses; taking load off the pedals to change gear loses speed and when highly fatigued, it is extremely unlikely that speed will be recovered. It's impossible to slip a gear or miss a change when you only have one. Psychologically, decision making under pressure is stripped to the minimum; using fixed made it all about focusing on pace judgment. On the downside, most courses varied in gradient to some degree, so fixed meant I had to feel confident that I could work effectively over a wide cadence range. This was a training focus running up to the events.'

Up until 2003 nearly all of the winners of the title race rode fixed. Stuart Dangerfield and Jim Henderson wouldn't have thought of riding anything else unless there had been a compelling reason, where either the length of the course (the apocryphal 'roadman's climb') or significant variations in gradient had posed distinct problems – the Horseshoe Pass and Haytor being two examples; both climbs are long with substantial sections of different gradient. In 1976 Joe Waugh opted for a three speed block and won on the Horseshoe. Five years previously both John Clewarth and Dave Lloyd chose multiple cogs on the same climb. Clewarth turned over a 108" gear on the last section up to the Ponderosa Café, leaving

Granville Sydney, the specialist's specialist, twiddling on a 72".

Twenty years later, a 'Boardman technique masterclass' in *Cycling Plus* magazine had Jim Henderson salivating over the possible advantages to riding fixed. The article insisted that a fixed wheel would always be quicker unless there was a large amount of downhill. The central argument rested on the potential weight saving. In recent years bike weights have plummeted to the extent that it's relatively easy to bring a bike in below the UCI limit of 6.8kg, and no longer prohibitively expensive to do so. Nevertheless, whilst riding fixed has other subjective benefits, it's clear that the definitive marker for anyone assembling a hill climb weapon is still weight loss. In 2005 Jim Henderson lost the National on the Rake to Ben Greenwood by 0.3 seconds. He argued that this equated to 240g. Essentially, and unscientifically, a kilogramme saved is worth two seconds for a 100-metre height gain. On such margins are championships won and lost.

Jim Henderson remains a fan of the fixed drivetrain: 'I am on fixed all the time. Coming home from work on 60" – it's flat, very light – I spin like mad. It's 25 miles in total. I naturally spin and one of the things I always found interesting is that people would ask you what gear you're on, as though, you know, "He's one of the best people in the country and he's on 59", so I'll do 62", that'll be right for me." But he'll be fifty percent slower than me, so he should be on two-thirds the gear for the same kind of cadence, and for me, pedalling is preferable to grinding your way up. Sit down and keep the pedals spinning. It wasn't ever something I struggled to adapt to. The bike feels very different, very stripped down and light.'

In the post war era and throughout the next fifty years a fixed wheel bike would have been the same as a geared bike, or even the same bike but press-ganged into winter duties. A quick conversion, ditching the groupset, was possible on a lightweight frame due to the forward-facing dropouts. The switch to vertical dropouts in the 1990s made it much more difficult to tension the chain when converting road frames and effectively put an end to the practice. The development of road bikes continued apace, but with an unforeseen consequence – fixed wheel frame development became stuck in the early 1990s. Out-and-out track bikes became more aerodynamic and tighter, but not lighter. The fixed wheel bike boom, where a retro aesthetic was more important than weight, did nothing to help. All the while racing frames changed radically in terms of lightness, coming in below 800 grams. With a bit of judicious drilling, sawing and stripping, a 5-kilogram *geared* bike is achievable. I use a Bob Jackson Vigorelli for hill climbs, but I'm under no illusions that it's lighter or faster. I just prefer it for certain climbs. It's an affectation; I enjoy the experience and sense of tradition. It hasn't won me that many hill climbs.

There are occasional spikes in the competitive use of fixed wheel, with a brief resurgence on the Rake in 2012. Perceived wisdom in Ramsbottom (or what Peter Graham says) states that on the nasty climb through the town riding fixed is better: *if* you can manage it and *if* are used to it. It's steep and short, meaning that every gear change therefore has the potential for disaster. The championship in 2012 was a treasure trove of eccentricity; neatly captured by the CTT cameraman in a video entitled "Me and my hill climb bicycle". It's not quite Vittoria De Sica, but is a diverting way of spending two minutes of your time.*

The lens gazes longingly at a range of different idiosyncratic machines, from Carl Helliwell's aluminium track frame, to Paul Brierley's road conversion. Matt Pilkington, who came fifth, describes the modifications made to his standard road frame: 'I ditched the bar tape, headset cap, front mech and hanger,

---

* My Bob Jackson is also featured. The video later went a little bit viral and appeared on some sort of blokeish internet website where I was described as 'the aidsy bloke with the beard'. I was at racing weight and took it as a backhanded compliment. The dangers of riding fixed are choosing the wrong gear, and I was 'probably one cog too big. Right in the middle of that section the whole world was just caving in on me.'

removed all the padding and cut out my saddle. The stupidest thing is the rear brake that barely works – an old Weinmann I drilled out so it only weighs 65 grams.'

Without the front derailleur you run the risk of coming unshipped, but the answer is to remove eight links – an added bonus. Whilst shaving off eight grams for a headset cap might seem extreme, it's the totality of weight saving that drives people on. Four grams on bar tape, forty grams on a rear brake, a hundred grams on each tubular – cumulatively it adds up, subtracting all the way.

In recent years, Matt Clinton and Pete Tadros have been two of the last men standing when it comes to riding fixed. Tadros reputedly has some sort of dark matter 'unobtanium' machine* that is reputed to weigh less than five kilogrammes, and Matt Clinton keeps threatening to dig out a fixed weapon for another pop at the title. The last genuine fixed hill climb specialist to be winning regularly at the highest level was Jim Henderson. He had two bikes he used for his five wins, starting with a Bill Nickson which came in at 6.7 kilograms, or not that light. The second attempt (with help from Pete Matthews) was a svelte 5.6 kilograms. Pete Matthews sourced a lightweight aluminium frame for him with semi-vertical dropouts.** The rest of the specification was a custom built, hard-to-find manifest of bike erotica, from Royce Special hubs to carbon cranks and saddle. He managed an impressive ten podium placings and five championship wins between 1996 and 2009.

Outliers and traditionalists aside, it's hard to ignore the fact that the days of fixed wheel hegemony are over. Matt Clinton has a love-hate relationship with riding fixed, and at times he

---

* 'Unobtanium' – a tongue-in-cheek term for any rare and unusual frame material. Historically, titanium has been viewed as the same element as unobtanium, in part due to the mythical qualities of the metal (it never rusts, it doesn't flex, it's used for spaceships) and due to its association with high-tech industries. It's now the material of choice for the sportif bike. which cheapens the effect slightly.

** Matthews was National Road Race Champion in 1968. He is now known as a wheel builder of repute, having hand-built wheels for Robert Millar and many others.

openly regrets it. In 2014 he opted for gears: 'I hadn't got a fixed and the bend was dodgy last time, it nearly threw me into the ditch, the angle. You're going into the bend at 17mph. And it's too easy to cock up riding fixed. I might consider it next year but if there's a hint of a headwind it'll be gears.'*

It's clear he hasn't banished the fixed to the attic just yet, but the stakes are high and there is far less margin for error. Why bother when you can get a Trek Emonda down to 5.2 kilograms? The simple answer might be price: a Trek Emonda costs a whopping £11,000 in the full frontal version. It weighs 4.85 kilograms. The frame weight is 690 grams. This works out at £2,200 per kilogram. It's worth thinking how much all of this weight saving actually costs. If you wanted to change your saddle from a beefy 205-gram Fizik to a smutty 75-gram AX lightness, as ridden by Tejvan Pettinger, the price would be an additional £145, or more than £1 per gram. A conservative estimate would imply that every gram saved will set you back around two pounds. Getting an eight kilogram road bike down to six will cost you £2,000. Or, if you're Pettinger or Clinton, borrow one for the weekend, then give it back on Monday. If you're a mere mortal like me, it makes more sense to lose three kilograms around the midriff, and it's much cheaper.

On the right day, with a tailwind, with a very light bike, and with the right gear, and on the right hill, for the right rider, it's still possible that a fixed wheel will be quicker. But the paradox is that there are far more variables to riding fixed than there were twenty years ago, when it was a case of substantial weight saving, a no-brainer. In this respect, fixed is now no longer a choice, it's an affectation. I ride fixed because I enjoy it. Newer entrants to the sport, the apocryphal middle-aged-men-in-lycra, or the youngsters who aren't quite sure what a club is or why anyone would ride for a team that doesn't have

---

* The 2015 Championship will be held on Jackson Bridge, West Yorkshire. The course record of 3'-49.9" was set by Jeff Wright on a 59" fixed gear in 1994 and no-one has come remotely close to beating it.

at least three obscure sponsors in the name, look confused and wonder why you'd choose one gear over twenty-two. Maybe I'm a hopeless romantic, but it warms my heart every time I see someone lined up at the bottom of a hill on a fixed wheel hill climb bike.

A view down Winnats on race day

'Hup! Hup! Hup!" Gareth Armitage out of the saddle

Armitage on the Rake, cresting the steepest section
with just a hint of a wobble

Steve Joughlin on the Horseshoe Pass in 1981

Armitage hits it hard across the moorland on Haytor

"It bites into the memory."

Malcolm Elliott riding, and winning, for Rutland CC on the Nick O' Pendle in 1980

Darryl Webster on the Horseshoe Pass in 1981

Elliott setting the untouchable course
record on Monsal Head in 1981

The 1980 podium: Elliott, Williams, Armitage

Chris Boardman takes his first title in 1988, setting the current course record for the Nick in the process

Boardman rides the Rake in 1992, some months after
individual pursuit Gold at the Barcelona Olympics.

12

Dangerfield

(1992–1997)

'Four weeks of comfy, one-hour rides and he's back on form.'

There are few riders in the history of domestic time trialling as quick as Stuart Dangerfield. He tore across the dual carriageways and hilly circuits in the 1990s and early 2000s, only to became another of the lost riders of previous generations, those drowned by the unceasing wave of wide indifference to cyclosport and a myopic governing body. Within the current landscape, ruled with wit and formidable guile by Sir Dave Brailsford and by Sir Bradley Wiggins, it's hard to imagine a time when things might have been different, when cycling was a niche sport in which odd people wore odd clothes and the myths were written in French. Nowadays, everyone has an opinion on the Tour, or bike racing, and anything other than continuing British success seems strange. The Olympic

Development programme marches on and key clubs like the Maindy Flyers feed a conveyor belt of talented youngsters up through the ranks. Heading for the continent, like so many neo-pros, has become just one of the routes into professional cycling.

It took a while for cycling to build up to its current mainstream popularity in the wake of Chris Boardman's success and it wasn't until Athens, fifteen years later, that a causal link became evident between greater investment and greater success. There is a clear argument that the planets began to align: the congestion charge resulted in more people buying and riding bikes; Olympic success raised the profile further; the cycle-to-work scheme made it all somehow more affordable and an obsession with all things retro as somehow 'authentic' led to the resurgence of fixed wheel bikes in London. There is another book somewhere about how and why we have reached peak bike, and even how the all-consuming bike boom has resulted in plagues of wayward sportivistes clogging the landscape on any given weekend, locked into a perpetual war with the startled locals in the New Forest, but it's not this one. If Stuart Dangerfield had had the foresight to be born just a few years later it might all have been different. As it is, he fell into the gap between the continent and the nascent British road scene.

Dangerfield spent at least some of his career locked in a battle for selection with a short-sighted British Cycling Federation, wary of sending the best time triallists abroad to do battle with the frisky continentals. Early on, he cut his teeth on the National Championship Hill Climb, coming back time and time again. His name first appears in the medals in 1990 on Widecombe, where he came third to Boardman. The following year he repeated the trick on Park Rash, but in 1992 in Durham, he had grown in strength and came into form to take the title.

One of the other names that comes up at this point and throughout the later 1980s is Pete Longbottom. A clever and intelligent bike rider, he turned down the alluring promise of a pro career with Wolber in 1982 to stay in the North and continue working as a civil engineer for Ryedale Council. He had missed out on Olympic selection in the early 1980s, finally making his debut at Barcelona in 1992 in the men's team time trial. He also experienced Commonwealth success, with a bronze alongside Chris Boardman in 1990 and a silver in 1994. He finally retired in 1996, but two years later was killed by a lorry whilst riding on the A64. His sense of humour and supportive nature is evident in the interviews in the press when he was racing, and also in the sense of loss when he was killed. He was 'the heart and soul of his sport', and all the more impressive for the Corinthian and amateur ideal, of working and riding.*

The 1992 climb took in St John's Chapel in County Durham. It's in the heart of the North Pennines and a very long way from anywhere. As the aerodynamic revolution took hold many of the field had begun to dabble in exotic equipment. Dangerfield opted for a pair of four spoke Corimas weighing 650 grams each. Throughout his career he had his frames built by Arthur Needham of Argos Cycles, a bespoke Bristol framebuilder. Many of the design flourishes were ahead of their time, including recessed and hidden brake calipers, tear drop profiles and elaborate tube shapes. Dangerfield was the ideal customer for Needham. He kept rows and rows of maturing silk tubulars under the bed, each one being aged slowly until ready to race.

At County Durham Dangerfield beat Jeff Wright into second place, the second year running Wright had missed the top step. Dangerfield's margin of victory was a whopping 20 seconds, with Longbottom 45 seconds adrift in third place. Wright made it a hat trick of near misses in 1993 when the race went even further north, stopping at Newlands Pass in Cumbria. It's a tough climb and another one-hit wonder, cresting out at 1,093 feet. It's made more challenging by several eye-watering

---

* Robin Nicholl, 'Obituary', The Independent, 13/2/1998
http://www.independent.co.uk/obituaries/obituary-peter-longbottom-1144459.html

sections of steepness. It pitches up to 20% out of Buttermere, climbing steeply on the pitted road surface, easing for a time, before throwing a 25% bend in at the end, just in case you felt like you might make it up in one piece with legs and lungs intact. This time Wright had narrowed the gap to a more credible four seconds

In 1994 the Championship moved to Huddersfield and the climb out of Jackson Bridge. In the years from 1988 to 1998 the championship visited an entirely new course on each occasion. Jackson Bridge is a tough and technical ascent with undulations in gradient, the requisite amount of steepness and is long enough to pose a challenge. It's also the home event for the Huddersfield Star Wheelers, an event these days organised by Andrew Pearson. The winner takes away the Granville Sydney trophy, with the first name etched on the cup being that of Graham, in 1974. Since then it's been won by all of the great hill climbers. It forms part of a classic double-header with Holme Moss in the morning. I rode the event in 2012, opting for a 57" gear. I found myself out of the saddle for most of it. Matt Clinton won by some distance. I think I was sixth. My mediocre placings aside, I remember the road names being unusual. It starts on Staley Royd Lane, which then turns into Tenter Hill, before changing into the evocatively named Scar Hole Lane. It finishes just short of Tinker's Monument at the junction of Scar Hole and Dick Edge Lane. I looked for concrete evidence of Tinker's Monument but found none.

On paper, the climb suited Jeff Wright, but his nearly-man status counted against him. Few could see beyond Dangerfield for another title. His power, fitness and form made him the irresistible favourite. The course record was Chris Boardman's four minutes dead, which would take some beating. Jeff Wright had been riding the Japan Cup road race eight days previously and it was suggested he might be tired and jetlagged.

A stiff tailwind, the remnants of a storm in the morning, helped the riders up the hill, but the technicalities of the course made it an easy one to get wrong. The hope of the home club, Chris Giles, blasted up the first section but tailed off towards the end. Despite the changes in gradient, most riders opted for a fixed gear, with 59" being the order of the day. In new money it works out at 42:19. Steve Marchant rode well, but was unable to add to his long list of second places.

Wright was off at 110 on the card, providing the opportunity to pile the pressure on the scratch rider. He climbed with purpose and a ruthless efficiency, controlling the bike and staying on top of the gear, getting up out of the saddle to maintain the cadence then sitting back down where necessary. The clocks were stopped at 3'-49.9", hacking an enormous eleven seconds from Chris Boardman's record. It was a startling achievement and Dangerfield must have felt there and then that the game was up. He dug in, finishing a distant second, seven seconds back. It was the first championship with a tailwind for a while, favouring the lighter riders. Further down the pack, a young Dean Downing managed fourteenth and his brother Russ was in the middle somewhere in 5'-05.5".

That same year, 1994, the biggest show on earth had made its way to the South of England. It was welcomed by parachute teams and a strange pompom lady in one of those slightly dated and painfully high cut red swimsuits, as modelled by Erika Eleniak every Saturday tea time in a slow motion waltz along a beach somewhere hot with David Hasselhof.* Sean Yates, replete with earring, turned out for Motorola, whilst Boardman was looking to make good in an escape and keep the fans entertained. Three years previously he had been honking up Park Rash. Now he was wearing the yellow jersey (and losing it in the team time trial when he seemed a bit too fast for his dishevelled GAN teammates) and returning to the UK as a very different rider. The shorts were bright and helmets absent.

---

* 'Baywatch' was a very popular tea time programme in the 1990s. Saving people from drowning tended to be the dominant narrative, accompanied by a slow-motion montage of scantily-clad ladies running along a beach, bosoms heaving in time to a soft-rock soundtrack.

Crowds were big, certainly bigger than the last time it visited the UK for a blast up and down the Plympton bypass in the name of artichokes.* It lacked the hysterical excitement of bike boom Britain as seen in Yorkshire in 2014, but it is a clear part of the journey towards the current ubiquity of cycling.

At 25 kilometres to go the peloton stormed up and over the fourth category Col de Ditchling Beacon to large crowds. It was a scene repeated in 2014 when the Tour of Britain used the same roads, with Kwiatkowski (who would be crowned World Champion some three weeks later) working hard to distance Alec Dowsett. In 1995 Flavio Vanzella was first over the crest, but failed to cling on. The stage went to the Kelme rider, Francisco Cabello from Emmanuel Magnien, with Vanzella taking yellow. Boardman chased hard along the seafront to come in fourth. He gave a hearty cheer and raised his hands to salute the crowd. It looked a bit like he was celebrating the victory but I'll give him the benefit of the doubt: 'I never felt I would get emotional about this sport, but I felt I just had to do something.'

In 1995 the hill climb was held on the Beacon. The organisers, hoping to capitalise on the success of the Tour the previous year, were optimistic of a big crowd. It's not the toughest climb, rising up in a series of ramps and never really testing the rider. This was reflected in the gear choice, with most opting for the high 60s. Dangerfield had been struggling all season with diminishing returns; something wasn't right. He was chasing Olympic selection in 1996 and wanted to do everything he could to ensure he was uppermost in the selector's mind. It led to burnout; he was overtrained.

The relatively unknown High Wycobe CC coach, Gordon Wright, came in with a series of diagnostic tests and speculated that a combination of sustained overtraining, a lack of rest and viral fatigue had resulted in inconsistent results. The danger of

---

* Taking the Tour to England had been the idea of the artichoke growers of Brittany, as a way of promoting sales of their produce in the UK.

overtraining is you end up trying even harder to rescue the form you feel should be there, and so succeed only in prolonging the bout of nothingness, or making it worse.*

Despite his inconsistent season, Dangerfield was rested and ready to go. He won a hat trick of 25-mile time trials, then the hill climb on the Rake and the Knaresborough Hilly. Whatever Gordon Wright had done – and he argued it was a case of getting his different 'energy systems' to peak at the same time – it had worked. Instead, it was Jeff Wright who looked ill, having fought a losing battle with a throat infection and loading up on penicillin on the run up to the event. Time trial equipment was still proving popular and Wright opted for a Specialized trispoke on the front and back.

A 21-year-old Paul Manning** in the colours of North Wirral Velo, came 17th, a couple of places behind Jim Henderson who was riding his first championship event. Manning, Chris Newton and Julian Ramsbottom were possibly the tallest group to take the team prize and were managed by Pete Longbottom. Despite the strength in numbers, Dangerfield was unruffled, his 3'-45.2", a full nine seconds up on Jeff Wright in second place and 17 seconds ahead of Newton, was more than enough to take his third title. He headed into the winter aiming for Olympic qualification and optimistic of a breakthrough season.

About ten miles west of the Rosedale Chimney is the village of Carlton, home to the unpleasant, if scenic, Carlton Bank. The North Yorkshire Moors are particularly remote and unforgiving, making them a suitable location for hill climbs. The Bank rises out of the flood plain of the Tees. The streams and becks pour down off the Moor, nourishing the rivers, flowing into the Leven and then the Tees, and out to the North Sea and across to the continent. Carlton Bank rises up in stages, like many classic

---

* Wright had coached the young Peter Keen when he won the 'George Herbert Spencer 10' – the National Schools' 10-mile time trial championship. He later became a big influence on Keen's coaching career, especially seen in the context of the emerging discipline of Sports Science.

** Manning went on to win Olympic Gold in the team pursuit in Beijing.

hill climb courses. It's a long one, with most riders dreaming fitfully of getting under six minutes. The inevitable cattle grid breaks it up into a distinct before and after, with the first half being merely the appetiser for a series of sharp and troubling ramps. Like Challacombe in 1985, the penalty for a fast start would be certain death well before the top.

Gear choices were very light, with Dangerfield opting for a spinny 54". At some point on an undulating course a fixed wheel is going to be either overgeared or undergeared, as was the case on the Bank: 'It was a bit small for the first part of the climb, but just right for the second half – I had already decided that was where the title would be won. I knew I might be down at halfway, so I didn't panic and I didn't get carried away by the crowd's enthusiasm. I put the pressure on in the second half. It was a matter of judgement.'*

It proved more than enough, with an enormous winning margin of some 22 seconds and a course record by nearly a minute. Despite the steepness, expensive carbon time trial wheels were popular; Shaun Tyson opted for a Spinergy front, whilst Phil Marshall used a Zipp disc. It seems anathema nowadays, but at the time the shiny promise of new technology and plasticky things must have been alluring. Whilst some riders got it spot on, others died on the steep rise to the finish; the County Durham Emergency Volunteers were kept busy supplying oxygen to the prone riders.

Despite his prowess, Dangerfield again tasted disappointment in his international ambitions, not getting a ride at either the Olympics or the Worlds. Jim Henderson was delighted with his podium finish and the apparent simplicity of training for, and racing, hill climbs. He was unfailingly positive when speaking after the event: 'They are so short you get a chance to familiarise yourself with the whole course, you don't have to put in the hours of training you need for ninety mile road races and you don't need to do the scary bits, like

---

* David Taylor, 'Dangerfield Out on his Own', *Cycling Weekly*, 2/11/1996

cornering and descending... it's not every week you can be cheered by crowds lining the route. It's all a lot more healthy and less secretive than your average 6 a.m. time trial.'*

If it has the word Bar in the title, you know it's going to be a bit of a stinker and long. Rowsley Bar was the scene of Dangerfield's last hill climb before he turned his attention solely towards international qualification. Fixed wheel still held sway in 1997 as the bike of choice for the *cognoscenti*, and whilst gears were making inroads, the podium was invariably decided by those of a singular vision. Henderson was seen as the dark horse, along with the returning Jeff Wright, but not many were prepared to bet against Dangerfield. Gear choices were even lighter than at Carlton Bank, with 52" and 53" being the most popular, showing the severity of the gradient.

Dangerfield again showed his mastery of pacing to accelerate over the second half of the climb, spinning the gear in a high cadence, having trained to spin for the previous month. In contrast, Henderson struggled towards the top. The winning margin had narrowed to a more acceptable six seconds, but there could be no disputing the victor, and his fifth victory put him one behind Granville Sydney.

Tom Anderson grazed the podium for the second year, improving by one place to fourth. Jeff Wright was 'gutted' but Henderson typically chipper, vowing to head straight for the pub as soon as he made his way back to Southport, and drink to a silver medal in the National and gold in the University championship the day before. Henderson was emboldened by the narrowing gap and the incremental increase each year; he began eyeing up the top spot. But for Dangerfield it was his last title as he focused his energies on the mostly futile quest for international selection.

Dangerfield was frequently at odds with Doug Dailey, the national coach. His performances were treated with a

---

* David Taylor, *ibid.*

latent suspicion by the BCF grandees, at least in part due to the selection critieria, but also because of engrained attitudes towards the specialists, the CTT men, going back many years. Experience dictated that when the great hopes of time trialling made the pilgrimage over to the Continent, they came back chastened. Ken Joy was annihilated by Jacques Anquetil at the Grand Prix des Nations in the mid-50s, Alf Engers was treated with disdain by Mogens Frey in 1969, and Derek Cottington was taught a lesson by Gilbert Nischoff in 1971. Dangerfield got to ride at Kuala Lumpur in 1996 precisely because he made it impossible for the selectors to ignore him by meeting all of the selection criteria. He came sixth, with Newton in seventh, but admitted that he struggled in the humidity. He then went to the Worlds in 1998, hoping for a top 15 placing, but confessed that he felt daunted when warming up between Lance Armstrong and Abraham Olano, with the latter going on to win. Dangerfield was 3'-48" back.

His career subsequently became an ongoing battle with the other big beast of domestic time trialling – Hutchinson versus Dangerfield – and he professed that it was 'all quite wearying'. The British Cycling Federation's focus on medals and Dangerfield's singular focus (despite riding and winning some road races) meant selection became a more and more distant dream. Why pick a time triallist aiming for fifteenth place, and therefore no medal, when you could pick a roadman who could do both?

Ultimately, Dangerfield paid a heavy price, as had Webster some years previously, for being too good to ride domestically, but unable to make headway on the Continent. His best result was 29th place at the Olympic Games in 2004. It's impossible to escape the spectre of two-speed cycling, with Olano's 1998 Tour sample showing signs of EPO, and wonder what might have been had he started that little bit later. As it was, Dangerfield's international record represents a scant return for a rider of prodigious talent, and one whom the BCF didn't know quite what to do with.

13

Antigra

(1997–2000)

'I had a feeling that I hadn't felt before; it was surreal. I had this sensation of riding through a tunnel of people all leaning forward, with faces that you know coming past you, screaming something that you get snatches of. It's just a continuous noise, through people continuously, but different people saying different things.'

If you were a hill climber choosing where to live there are lots of places that might appeal. Perhaps the Peak District with its endlessly undulating range of tough climbs, or anywhere in the West Pennines, where you can throw a pebble in October and you'll be sure to hit a hill climber on his cotton-capped head. Maybe Devon or Cornwall might seem like a good prospect – the bane of any LEJOG rider with 200 miles of purgatory before you get out of the south west. Chances are you'd probably seek to avoid some of the low-lying flatlands, the sultry and sub-sea Fens would be out of the equation, as would the Holderness Pensinsula as it slowly slips beneath the shimmering and sultry surface of the North Sea. Vic Clark lived at the top of a huge hill. Rob Gough lives in Bath, a city surrounded by picturesque walls of suffering. Rob Hayles lives near Buxton and chose to make the National his valedictory salute. David Millar and the mighty Wiggins live in the High Peak.

Jim Henderson chose to ignore such topographic pleasures. He lives in the flattest place you could possibly imagine. It's called Downholland on account of its unremitting evenness, and because the area was drained by Dutch engineers. His house sits on the West Lancashire Coastal Plain, where the highest point is barely a few metres above sea level. In his own words, 'it's a desolate, flat and windblown place' and the most unlikely testing ground for a hill climbing legend as you are likely to find. It's not without its attractions though: there are red squirrels, holding out against the steady march of their grey cousins from North America.

Jim Henderson isn't the first climber to emerge from a resolutely flat hinterland and in this respect he has something in common with the legions of Dutch climbers to have conquered Alpe d'Huez. He's the Hennie Kuiper of Formby, sneaking in amongst the other striplings and running away with the spoils. His last competitive race was on the Rake in 2011, having been coaxed gently out of retirement by Peter Graham, who was looking to bolster the field for that year's open event. Since then he has slipped back into a gentle retirement, riding a 60" fixed wheel around the spirit-levelled landscape of East Lancashire. In the years that have passed he doesn't look any different from the compact climber who last won the National in 2003. His arms are a bundle of tensile hawsers and he has no excess weight. He seems somehow permanently paused and ready, as though waiting on the start line giving a sensation of silent strength. Henderson hasn't let it slip. After years of pursuing the unattainable heights of maximum thinness and power, hill climbers don't tend to let their weight rocket like some latter-day cycling Elvis. They continue their infatuation with the outdoors and with the violent undulations of the British Isles, but at a less violent pace. I'm struck by one thing whilst sitting opposite Jim Henderson in his dining room. If you could design a hill climber he'd look like this. Jim Henderson was carved from the initial blueprint, modelled after Harold Worthern and Vic Clark. He reminds me of Conrad's description – 'a bundle of acute angles sat with their legs drawn up'. He's spring loaded, as though there's a catch somewhere waiting to be flipped, allowing the pent-up energy to explode outwards like a bursting balloon. It's an impression of control and a specific strength.

Much of his youth was spent on a mountain bike; he was an early adopter of what later became an all-out craze. The fascination of the great outdoors exerted an influence: 'To me the attraction was that you could use it to go places and get views and see things and get away from it all. I rode up Snowdon, I rode up Skiddaw, I rode up Helvellyn. The woodland trail thing didn't appeal to me.'

The competitive road scene didn't appeal either, and for a number of years Henderson rode his mountain bike to all corners of the island, doing very long off-road rides, blissfully unaware of the tarmac-based racing scene all around. There was one exception; during an afternoon spent riding across the top of Winnats Pass his progress was stopped by the peloton in the Tour of the Peak, climbing up the col in a technicolour ribbon of rapid luminosity.

The mountain bike lasted a few months before it was stolen, never to be seen again. It was replaced with a Ribble 105 road bike, and longer rides on the tarmac became the norm. In his third year at Oxford University (of eight spent in the hallowed corridors, doing two degrees) he became a member of the University Cycling Club. A picture from the time shows Henderson in the front as club captain, and a shock of unruly blonde hair in the back row masquerading as Tejvan Pettinger;

both were club cyclists but went on to become prolific hill climb winners.

It didn't take long for Henderson to realise that he was climbing well, keeping up with the super strong time triallists, and he plotted a course towards hillier events once he started racing. The University Club provided a structure and shape over those eight years, with a steady diet of winter club runs out along the lanes into the Cotswolds and Chilterns. The key difference between a university cycling club and any other typical band of wheelmen is the narrowness of the age group; the members of the OUCC were all within five years. It made for a dynamic and evenly matched group, probably with a bit more time on their hands than the average club rider, who might be juggling work and family. In general the University club lacked the wider range of abilities to be found on the usual Sunday bun run, the pace was quicker, the effort harder – and the student hangovers probably more severe. With the same commitments on a weekly basis it made a perfect springboard to ride more, make adaptations and improve quickly.

Henderson enjoyed riding in the dark blue, and the club had a yearly influx and departure of members, with roughly a third leaving in any given year as they completed their degrees. Jim Henderson was elected club captain from autumn 1994 and found himself having to work really hard to keep the club alive and active. Essentially, this entailed riding and entering every single student championship going, including mountain bike, cyclo-cross, time trials and road races. Again, it's serendipity that brings people in, and from a standing start the bespectacled engineer suddenly found himself competing throughout the year, with one startling exception: hill climbs: 'I had no concept of hill climbs. Someone had said to me offhand, "You don't want to do hill climbs, they're too hard, too painful." I thought, "Alright, he knows".'

Eventually he went against his better judgement and rolled up to one 'for fun' in 1994 with David Ryan, a close friend.

The climb was at Kingston Blount in the Chilterns. It's a two and half minute special and the hill runs alongside the M40 cutting, where the clogged arteries of traffic slowly creep towards London. Henderson won and Ryan was second. More significantly, the winner found that he enjoyed the feeling of victory and also the general sense of pain and discomfort involved in the effort of winning. He recalls the event and Dave Ryan's companionship, with the memory slightly shaky as to whether it was 1993 or 1994. The clock ticks audibly on the wall within the silences of reminiscence; the seconds so palpably less precious now, in conversation, than they ever were in the race.

David Ryan was a physicist at the university and a keen amateur cyclist. Like Henderson, he rode every race going and loved touring, the epic and meandering days in the saddle. He was killed by a speeding motorist in 2004 whilst cycling in the United States where he lived and worked. In his memory Jim Henderson and Tom Ryan organised the Tour of the Cotswolds, taking in many of the lanes and hills they used to tackle together on training rides. It still runs, with the proceeds going towards charities in his memory.

1995 was a transition year. Henderson invested in a racing licence. It's one of those things: once you make the outlay for a licence it seems silly not to race; it turns out to be quite expensive otherwise. He purchased the RTTC handbook and adopted a more systematic approach to racing, circling the key events and planning the season ahead, this time to include a handful of Open hill climb events and the National Championship.

The BUCS (British Universities and Colleges Sport Championship) was held on the Nick O'Pendle and he won it fairly comprehensively. He then surprised himself again by winning an Open at Alton in Hampshire, embarking on a complicated journey to get there in the first place – riding fifteen miles to a station, getting a train for twenty miles, then riding for another twenty miles. His form was on the up and he made the top three at Edge Hill and then came fifth on the long drag of the Snake Pass. Henderson's goal for the National was 'to see what the thing was like'. Something had stirred, a competitive instinct harnessed to a previously dormant ability.

The 1995 national was held on Ditchling Beacon. It's a familiar climb to thousands upon thousands of leisure cyclists who make the annual trek in the British Heart Foundation London to Brighton ride. It's the hardest hill on the route and appears late on, rising up in a series of ramps around the side of the escarpment, before cutting into the chalk and providing sweeping views down to the sea. It has provided the downfall for many an inappropriately clad Bromptonaut straying far from the city with the other 27,000 riders each year. The year before, a slightly more athletic peloton tackled the fabled slopes of the 'Col de Ditchling Beacon' with the Tour de France, taking in two days on the south coast before dashing back across the Channel.

For Henderson, the hill climb was an eye-opener. He turned up on his Ribble, taking the pump and bottle cage off as the only concession to lightness. There were no fancy racing hoops, just a stock wheelset and some high pressure clinchers. The bike weighed in at a fairly stocky 23 pounds, but it didn't lose a huge amount to the lighter bikes. There wasn't quite the same focus at that point, with many riders still experimenting with relatively heavy time trial wheels or trispokes for the climbs. The top three – Dangerfield, Jeff Wright and Chris Newton – were riding fixed and it remained the bike choice for the out-and-out specialist. The combination of light weight and simplicity still made it the best choice on most hills.

Henderson was off early on the card with no expectations or a particular grasp of how it worked. He rode well to take 15th place, without setting the world ablaze. The fixed wheel podium gave Henderson food for thought for the following year, even if he had no real intention of getting rid of the gears. All that changed in the winter of 1995 when *Cycling*

Plus ran an article written by Chris Boardman about his hill climb bike. The technical details and gearing choices appealed to the graduate student and suddenly his peer group became fascinated with the idea of riding fixed hill climbs. It's quite a captivating concept; building a highly specific bike for a highly specific purpose. One of the chaps in Henderson's local bike shop was from the North East and knew Carlton Bank, the venue for the following year's contest. He'd also been at Sheffield Poly at the time and shared a house with Simon Bray, UK Road Race Champion in 1992. His knowledge of hill climbing proved to be a catalyst and Henderson acquired a second-hand track bike with the intention of building it up as a hill climb weapon.

In 1996 on Carlton Bank he was ready to join the contenders and saddle up on the single gear. It didn't quite work out that way. He had a set of large flange Hope hub track wheels built up by the Oxford shop and rode up the climb to have a look, picking up tips and tricks, but also a large flint which worked its way into the front tubular. Rather than chance it, he pulled the road bike out of the car, which was at least an improvement on the Ribble, with a new Chorus groupset, and attacked it on that. Whilst he was hoping to improve, the level of improvement was surprising. Henderson took his first medal by squeaking into third place behind Dangerfield and Steve Hulme.

It aligned with his other results though, having ridden Premier Calendar events and the Tour of the Peak, finally joining the peloton he'd seen from the top of Winnats some five years previously: 'In 1995 Stuart Dangerfield was some guy you saw on the cover of *Cycling Weekly*; he was going to the Olympics and was at a totally different level from where I was. By the following year he was only twenty seconds in front on a five or six-minute climb. All of a sudden I was thinking what I might do to close that gap. I beat Chris Newton, who was one of the favourites. I beat Mark Kay, who'd won the Tour of the Cotswolds. I was improving even as the season went on.'

The Chesterfield Coureurs' Event on Rowsley in 1997 was a 1700-metre fixed-wheel special. The second half of the course jerks backwards and forwards in steep hairpins through dense woods, providing some lovely mulchy leaf matter to test traction in the wet. The club extended the course up over a false flat and another rise to make it more challenging. Henderson was chasing his third title at the BUCS championship the day before, which had now moved to its current home at Curbar. It was the season's goal and very important to him to win in the OUCC colours. He didn't see winning the National as a target, at least partly because Dangerfield still stalked the inclines like a latter-day colossus. After tackling Curbar on the Saturday he went across to Rowsley and walked up it to prepare. The two hills are cheek by jowl on the edge of the Peak District. By the following morning a sense of soreness from the previous exertions made itself felt, but despite that he more than halved the previous year's time gap to seven seconds and climbed up to second place on the podium. The crowd provided their customary level of raucous support, but it wasn't quite enough: 'I pressed on, was starting to hurt at the false flat and could feel the burn. It's going to hurt whatever, so it became about survival. I tried to limit the suffering to the present, what I'm going through now. Afterwards I thought I shouldn't have done Curbar.'

It's an easy decision to make in hindsight, but at the time the response was rational. With the continued improvement Jim Henderson decided that further assistance was required if he was to close the gap. Over the winter he rang round as many bike shops in the North East as he could, asking for help with equipment. Bill Nickson came up with a lighter steel frame – not earth-shatteringly light by today's featherweight carbon standards, but certainly a pound lighter than anything he'd ridden previously.

The National moved back to Dover's for the first time since 1982. The absence of Stuart Dangerfield due to illness meant the Championship race was suddenly wide open. Jeff Wright was chasing his second title and Milk Race stage-winner, Gary Baker of Condor Cycles, was also hoping for the title. At a shade under four minutes, it was just long enough to shake out the heavier sprinters, but short enough to damage the roadmen, making it the preserve of the specialist, and a climb hewn from the bedrock of the Cotswolds almost solely for Henderson.

For the first time Henderson was the fancied rider on the day, which led to an uncharacteristic outbreak of nerves and hypertension until a fellow rider, Andy Brennan, quietly said, 'Relax, it's your day.' It did the trick of settling the nerves, but the complexities of the morning hadn't yet finished. The entourage had made its way to Weston Sub Edge in a hired minibus, in order to accommodate two bikes – the brand new hill machine with chopped handlebars and finest 'drillium', and the more mundane road bike to warm up on.*

Whilst out warming up, the hill climb bike was locked firmly to the seats in the back of the minibus, keeping it safe until the moment came to ride it in anger. The keys were held safely by a university colleague who was off chatting and making the most of the highlight of the hill climb and time trialling season, catching up with old acquaintances and chewing the cud. With no-one in sight and the bike clearly visible inside the locked van and locked to the seat, Henderson began to panic, contemplating riding the reserve bike for the second time in three years. At the last minute the lackadaisical student sauntered around the corner. He grabbed the bike and ran alongside Henderson to the start, shouldering the top tube to avoid a puncture over the mile or so, making it just in time for the off.

Just like the Sydney brothers, the OUCC had a man on the climb giving the split times. With a helpful tailwind it was clear times were going to be rapid and he yelled out 'Minus three!'

---

* 'Drillium' reached its zenith in the late 1960s and early 1970s. Almost all components were drilled for lightness.

once he saw the club colours cross the imaginary line. The split was longer than that; Henderson conceded five seconds at the halfway point: 'I thought well, I've got to go now, and I just buried myself and had this kind of thing that I hadn't felt before; it was surreal. You're trying so hard, looking ahead, people are right in thick and I was riding at people to smooth out the bend and you know they'll get out the way, but I had this sensation of riding through a tunnel of people all leaning forward. Faces that you know are coming past you, screaming something that you get snatches of and you're gone, and there's all this stuff going on and you can't concentrate on it because you're concentrating on your ride, turning the pedals – push, push, push, push – and I think I just felt like I was trying more that time than previously.'

Dangerfield was renowned for riding hill climbs with a 'negative split', hitting the second half of the climb harder than the first; it's the holy grail of a perfectly paced effort. A year previously Henderson had been some way off, but this year he was determined to flip things around. Over the second half of the climb he somehow made up eight seconds on Jeff Wright to take the win and obliterate the existing course record by eleven seconds. Every other rider rode the first half quicker than the second. It is clear that something had shifted, either the level of effort, or the mindset, or the psychology of the race; the experience had changed: 'There is an awareness of something outside the race, but you are in the race and seeing through peripheral vision all the time – a face is beside you but it's close, and because you're going slower it's not like a road race or the track, you might be the fastest person in the national hill climb but you're still only going 15mph. So when someone is really close to you it takes a couple of seconds in hearing range. It's just a continuous noise, through people continuously and of different people saying different things.'

1998 was also the first year the championship became 'open' and accepted women competitors, although there was, as yet, no title or medals for them. The women's race was won by a fifteen-year-old Nicole Cooke in the colours of Cardiff Ajax CC in 4'-37.5" – the start of an unmatched racing career that also featured the Olympic Gold Medal at Beijing. At the other end of the field, Joe Waugh carded a 5'-05", smiling wryly at 'a great weekend away with the lads, which is what cycling's all about'.

After eight years of successful and atmospheric races in Ramsbottom, the Rake hosted the National for the first time in 1999. Peter Graham took the helm in his inimitable style and an enormous crowd lined the narrow streets from the gentle start of a minor 10% outside the library, before clinging on, three deep, to the 25% wall at the top of the course. The location in the heartland of hill climbing country, with cycling clubs located all around, makes it the ideal place for the final race of the season. Winners past and present turn out to watch the litany of suffering, most relieved that their day has passed. Peter Graham pitched his commentary tent on Rake Fold, providing an elevated view of the nastiest part of the road, allowing him to comment pithily on the efforts of the racing men and women caught in the eternal struggle to maintain rhythm and shape and make it to the finish. The height gain and final savagery of this short and steep climb makes it a true test. The course record stood at a frightening 2'-14" by Jeff Wright, who had won five of the previous seven promotions. It was very much seen as 'Jeff's climb' and Henderson was under no illusions about his chances of victory. He had never got anywhere near Wright's time and couldn't see how it might even be gettable, having never gone under 2'-20". He wasn't confident.

Wright's equipment choices on the day were bizarre. Photos show a low profile time trial bike with Cinelli Spinacci aero extensions and a Hed 3 trispoke on the front. On a steep hill weight is proportionally more of an issue and the Rake is a very steep hill. It's hard to escape the thought that Wright must have been giving away a lot of weight. The low-profile bike might have been relatively light, but the adornments seemed superfluous. Having ridden the Rake it's completely inconceivable that there would be any part of the climb where the TT extensions might prove to be anything other than excess baggage. It was noticed by Henderson, who felt that he would have been closer if he'd ridden his normal hill climb bike.

The margin for error on the Rake is extremely tight and it's possible to lose handfuls of time over the last 200 metres where the incline assaults the rider in the most unpleasant and visceral manner. If your legs are starting to buckle by the time you round the corner then it's over, there and then.

Henderson opted for a different gear from his previous attempts: 'I applied some logic: it's the National; you've got to go faster, so go down a cog to 42:19. It felt like I was riding through treacle. I thought, this is the course record gear, that was what Jeff had ridden. Subsequently I found out he was on 180 cranks, which compensates for the bigger gear. Effectively, I wasn't on the same gear and I just felt very slow on the steep bit.'

He clung on for the final section, desperately trying to minimise any time loss and just keep turning it over. A season spent riding Premier Calendar events meant he had the legs to just about cope with the error, but he was startled to find out he'd done enough to win. Detailed preparation paid a huge part in the victory. Henderson had ridden the Rake over twenty times beforehand. One afternoon in early October he'd headed over after work and ridden a triangular circuit 7 times, alternately hard and easy, mapping the incline and gradient in his mind, every contour and undulation, which line to take through the pockmarked surface.

The team prize stayed in Lancashire, as the Blackburn CTC outfit of Carl Helliwell, Ian Stott and Dave Ebrell began to etch their names into the history of the event with a resounding team success, cheered on by the rest of the club. They won return ferry tickets to the Isle of Man and spent a fun filled weekend at the festival of cycling, vowing to return and have another crack at the team title on Westclose, in Somerset in 2000.

Westclose Hill is on my doorstep. The first choice hill was Draycott, a close relative. For the record, Draycott is one of the nastiest and most unrelenting climbs I've ever ridden and had it made the National in 2000 it would probably have entered the annals of fame, along with Challacombe. Mendip CC opted in the end for Westclose for practical reasons. It's a challenging climb that pitches and rises in uneven steps. The contours on the OS map wobble together in tightly packed parallels of pain and the openness of the summit can cause havoc for riders in the event of a headwind, where grasping talons claw at fatigued riders and shove them back down the hill from whence they came. On the morning of the National, conditions were favourable with a roaring tailwind taking the sting out of the climb.

Henderson took his hat trick and, in hindsight, what he views as the easiest of his wins, or as he puts it succinctly: 'It was like Chris Boardman's day at the office.' He still rolled around the grass verge at the top, had to be helped from the bike and needed time to recover sufficient energy to talk and breathe, but the margin of the victory was eleven seconds. Paradoxically, until that point the season had been a bit of a disaster, including coming to a dead halt on Matlock because of some 'crummy' Wellgo pedals, and then following it up with a puncture on the Rake. Things were also changing; student life was a distant memory, replaced with the stability of family and work – those areas that expand exponentially, like a retired cyclist's waistline, taking up energy and effort that was previously diverted into racing and training. The reward for his efforts was a meeting with Eddy Merckx at the Champion's Dinner, but he wasn't that much fun and wasn't all that well. Seeing the Cannibal at his chubbiest and out of breath is slightly anticlimactic. At least it was in keeping with the Championship the following year, with a distinctly underwhelming choice of hill. Even in his slightly overweight dotage, it's probable that Merckx could have 'done a ride' at the 2001 Championship.

14

The Roadman's Climb

(2001–2006)

'There can't be many hill climbs where you can get in the big ring and the 13 sprocket and clock up 40mph.'

Over time, the tone and tenor of an event can change. There are a number of reasons why this might be, but one of the more noticeable trends in recent years has been towards shallower and longer courses. There are several schools of thought about this. Some see it as a shame, moving away from those uniquely testing courses that are emblematic of the British hill climb. Others see it as a step towards a more inclusive and accessible event. I side with the former. Hill climbs are supposed to be ridiculously hard; it's their raison d'être. Some variety from time to time is perhaps a good thing, but five of the seven events between 2001 and 2007 were on shallower, easier gradients.

2001 was initially pencilled in for a return to the Horseshoe, but a landslip put paid to that and they opted instead to use the Bwlch. At the time the organising District (Liverpool) had concerns regarding parking and how the riders might get back down the Bwlch after their effort. The toughness or level of challenge involved became of secondary importance to the practical considerations in hosting a big event. The *old* Bwlch is a savage climb, taking in the archetypal cattle grid and offering beautiful views out over the Vale of Ruthin. The first section peaks at a 1-in-4, climbs 853 feet in 1.4 miles and is a testing destination for many Liverpool based riders. It also forms a key part of the Dave Lloyd Megachallenge, one of the more difficult UK sportifs. It would have been a superb and suitable venue for the yearly painfest. The hill moved Nigel Blackwell, of the cult 80s indie rockers Half Man Half Biscuit, to declare that, 'the biggest achievement for me is creating a situation for myself whereby I can get up of a morning and decide to go and tackle Bwlch Pen Barras on the bike'.*

However, the committee made the strange and misguided decision to opt instead for the shallower and less challenging side. It's a steady ramp along a main road and was not subject to a road closure For many enthusiasts this is antithetical to the spirit of the event. A closed road is a 'must'; it's an important part of what marks out the Championship Hill Climb as different.

On the day, the lack of a full road closure meant that traffic became a problem, with the seeding contributing towards hold ups. Middle and back markers created an embouteillage of vehicles and in turn slowed the faster riders spaced throughout the field. Henderson was baulked by a tractor and trailer and had to resort to veering around the outside, overtaking near the finish and running the risk of not being seen by the timekeeper. An indication of the shallowness of the gradient can be seen

---

* http://www.thevpme.com/2012/03/08/risk-it-for-a-biscuit-half-man-half-biscuit-interview/

by the choice of gear ratio, he opted for a 50 tooth dinner plate on the front and a 20 on the back. Probably a wise choice, given the acceleration needed to escape the John Deere. It was an eminently forgettable event, run off in sunny conditions without a breath of wind. Henderson rode away from the field and described it as 'the easiest of my five wins'. Tom Anderson grabbed the silver medal from Chris Myhill.

As if one meagre and shallow climb wasn't enough, the following year saw an excursion to the Cat and Fiddle in an attempt to replicate the 'experience' of Bwlch. It can be summarised by Michael Hutchinson's comment: 'There can't be many hill climbs where you can get in the big ring and the 13 sprocket and clock up 40mph.' That's 105" for those in the know, in contrast to a typical hill climb gear ratio of between 50" and 65". The *cognoscenti* raised an eyebrow at Hutchinson's presence on the startsheet, surely a sign that this was more of a time trial course for the big-boned flatlanders than one for the mountain goats. It certainly suited one rider perhaps more than any other – Mark Lovatt. In fairness, Lovatt is committed to the hill climb cause and in recent years has returned to ride some of the famous climbs in the colours of the Planet-X Racing Team. In 2002 he was at his strongest, having won the Premier Calendar in 2000, the Tour of the Peak in 2002 and represented Great Britain at the UCI World Championships in 2001, and England in the 2002 Commonwealth Games. Undoubted pedigree aside, the Cat and Fiddle happened to be his commute to work from Leek to Macclesfield.

One person the climb definitely didn't suit was Jim Henderson: 'I never really thought I could win it from when I knew it was on that hill. When I rode it I just thought, "This is bad, this is ridiculous." On principle I just refused to consider putting tribars on.'

On the day of the championship the weather gods chortled and hurled a bagful of horrible storms at the Peak District. The downhill section of the hill had filled with standing water and the conditions were brutal. The organisers had no choice but to postpone for three weeks. All the finely-honed form and preparation had come to nothing and the challenge suddenly became how to sustain form, fitness and racing weight for three weeks, but without having any racing to keep things ticking over. The season is a classic exercise in build, peak and taper and at eight weeks long allows for a perfect process of periodisation and specificity. With the event shifted back, the clocks changed, disrupting evening rides. Henderson resorted to riding the track leagues at Manchester and trying to simulate the effort of the hill climb at the weekend, but his form ebbed away. Lovatt, somewhat fortuitously, went on holiday to Tenerife and rode up and down mountains in the sunshine all day, returning fitter and with even more sharply defined tan lines. He stormed up the 6.35 miles in 19'-33.6" to take almost half a minute from the existing course record. Hutchinson came second, a minute down, to be the first BBAR winner to take a medal in the National Hill Climb. Ian Stott continued from where he had left off at Westclose Hill with an impressive third place, somewhat shocked to edge out the defending champion by a second and a half. They brought the team prize back to Blackburn again, with more Isle of Man ferry boat tickets and a burgeoning reputation as the dominant club team. Henderson vowed to return a year later and make good his challenge for a fifth title.

In 2003 the race returned to a 'true hill climber's course'. Luddenden is a small village near Halifax, resting quietly in the bottom of a steep-sided Calderdale valley. I visited it the day after speaking to Jim Henderson, ostensibly to see what the fuss was about. I'd been out on the West Yorkshire Moors, taking in Scar Top, Wycoller, Trawden and Heptonstall. It was June, but it felt distinctly like early spring: the mercury refused to rise and a pedantic headwind picked holes in my riding all afternoon.

It's horribly, unrelentingly steep at the bottom with a series of hairpins scarred by the corpulent underbellies of cars and wagons dragging themselves up the hill. The organiser in

2003 came from the tiny Halifax Racing Club and decided to lengthen the course to enhance the level of challenge. It's entirely possible he was inspired by the flaccid nature of the previous year's outing in his desire to come up with a much more tumescent monster. He succeeded on every count. The road rises and turns into the aptly named 'Raw End', where both sides of the tarmac are lined with ominous dry-stone walls. It pitches up and over to the finish, offering a height gain of 190 metres in an imperial 1766 yards, providing a 12% average gradient. In short, it's one of the toughest climbs I've ridden.

Henderson scouted the course three weeks prior to the event with Chris Myhill, assessing the gradient and preparing a plan of attack.* He relished the climb and knew that things this year would be different. He was fired up with self-belief and had overcome the doubts that bedevilled his ride on the Cat and Fiddle. In addition, the technical guru, Pete Matthews, had been furtively working away on a new überbike. It wasn't a straightforward process and some of Matthews' ideas were distinctly wacky; at one point he suggested a bike with two chains and the same gear on either side because he was convinced that the flex of the frame was one of the biggest inefficiencies. Aside from the obvious – it was a crazy idea – the engineer in Henderson talked the mad scientist away from his eureka moment by highlighting some of the minor flaws: wrong handed threads on different sides, the need for a specially constructed rear hub and the changes in force at different points in the pedal stroke.

The completed bike incorporated a set of Weinmann 500s; even now these are a favourite amongst the fraternity because of their low weight. They have all the stopping power of a

---

* Chris Myhill fits the description of 'evergreen'. One of the first riders to break the 20-minute barrier for the '10' without aero equipment in 1992, he won a bronze in 2001. In 2014 he rode the National on Pea Royd Lane, coming 18th and winning the Veteran B title.

Jamaican skid,* but that's neither here nor there when you're heading upwards. They made some fantastic modifications: the locknut on the brake was a valve cap from a tyre; there was a gear cable for the brake; the brake blocks were cut in half. The finished bike came in at 5.6 kilograms.

The Pianni wheels had a low spoke count and were piano-string tight. On the day Pete Matthews – known for his opinions on a number of things – held forth on the topic of tyre pressure. Henderson recounts: 'I was pumping up my tyres to 11 bar; they were a set of new Tufo tubeless which say on them inflate to 15 bar, something absolutely absurd. Pete suddenly says (cue Henderson's impression of Pete Matthews, a slightly high-pitched and angry sounding Scouse voice) "WHAT ARE YOU DOING?! WHAT ARE YOU DOING?! WHAT PRESSURE? 11 BAR?! 11 BAR?! ROBERT MILLAR USED 7 BAR IN THE TOUR DE FRANCE!"'

He enunciates each word of the most famous race in the world for added emphasis, and adds volume. Pete Matthews built the wheels for the best in the world, for Millar and Yates. The prevalence of the machined wheelset has now eroded the dark arts and mystical craft of the wheelbuilder. And yet, there's something comforting and reassuring in riding a hand built set with spokes tightened and then backed off, just so.

The technology and outright desire to win worked for Henderson on Halifax Lane. The state of the finishers was a clear indication of the severity of the course, with several collapsing into the arms of the catchers and some needing treatment from the St John's Ambulance. Dave Clarke set a fast time early on, but Henderson was six seconds up at halfway. From that point on he surged up the straight and over the line, collapsing in an awkward heap by the side of the road, desperate for breath, to take Blackburn CTC rider Ian Stott's course record with a 5'-19.2".

---

* A method of stopping a brakeless fixed gear bike whereby you place one foot under the leading pedal and pull up. It's arguably as stupid as riding brakeless on the road in the first place.

Defending champion Lovatt fought hard for second place, somehow finding the strength to use the big ring over the last section of the course. Henderson's margin of victory was a gigantic nineteen seconds. The Mayor of Calderdale, Geraldine Carter, had the last word: 'I can't understand what pleasure you get out of going up that hill.'* Looking at the pallid faces and sunken eyes of the competitors, it would be hard to disagree. It was Henderson's fifth win, placing him within one title of Granville Sydney's record.

In 2004 the race headed northwards, to the village of Elsdon on the edge of the Northumberland National Park. The climb is known as 'Winter's Gibbet' and the gibbet still stands at the top of Steng Cross with a plaque inscribed with the grisly narrative of William Winter who 'murdered old Margaret Crozier of the Raw, Elsdon' in 1791. The enduring connection between hill climbs and a miserable and brutal death seems to have risen up at various points over the years. A stone head swings ominously from the chain, with the cross silhouetted moodily against the grey Northern skies. In reality the savagery of the tale was not quite reflected in the gradient of the climb, unlike for example, the Barber of Llangollen, or the Pendle Witches. There are plenty of hills in the immediate area, but the District again opted for a lesser challenge. Jon Dayus took the win with James Dobbin confirming his potential in second place. Henderson finished outside the medals in fourth place, missing out on the elusive sixth title.

The Rake reappeared in 2005 after a six year absence, gradually cementing its place in the folklore of hill climbing. It was widely seen as Henderson's for the taking – it was his climb, just as it had been Jeff Wright's some years earlier. In a new and hitherto untested strategy, Henderson opted to go flat out from the beginning. A couple of weeks previously he'd turned up late to Rowsley in a bit of a rush, grabbed the number and then blitzed the hill in a rush of adrenalin,

---

* David Taylor, 'Henderson Recrowned', *Cycling Weekly*, 6/11/2003

nailing Dangerfield's course record along the way by fifteen seconds. Impressed with this new tactic, he decided to take the opportunity to disprove the adage by showing that a new trick could indeed be foisted upon an old dog.

It was an abysmal Lancashire day, hosing it down with rain. The Rake is a short climb; it's all over in two and a bit minutes if you're one of the super-fast men. The lesser mortals come in at around the 2'-45" mark. If you're an even lesser mortal like me and opt for one tooth too many on the back you might dribble home in about 2'-51" in a state of considerable distress.

The sting in the tail is the savagery of the last 200 metres; Henderson faded at the top to hand the victory to Ben Greenwood by 0.3 of a second. The Rake is seen as a young man's climb, and Greenwood, the Under-23 National Road Race Champion, was a young man and a worthy winner. For Henderson it was disappointing, and hard to escape the feeling that a decline had set in. It's as much mental as physical, having to cope with the demands of a life outside of the sport, and it's the eternal paradigm of cycling; it never gets easier, you just go faster… or slower. 'Plainly I'm not going as fast, but I'm not trying less hard.'

The scene was changing, with a flush of younger road talent coming into the end of season anti-gravity events. Peak Hill in Sidmouth in 2006 confirmed the trend, with James Dobbin saddling up to take his first win, Clarke in second and Dayus in third. Also lined up near the shingle beach on the south coast were Alec Dowsett and Luke Rowe, with the former in the Junior National Champion's jersey. Good friends Dobbin and Clarke squared up to do battle along the coast road, with form and the type of climb favouring Dobbin, the thin Westcountry wunderkind.

Jim Henderson's previous experiences on the Cat and Fiddle suggested it might be a bit long. What's more, Dobbin knew he was riding bang into form: 'I remember going there on the Monday before it for a test day, on my first flying run up the hill I went half a minute inside the course record, so I decided no more tests were needed and put my bike back in the car and went home. On the day of the National I'd never felt stronger and as I got to the half-way point, where the climb leans right and steepens, I just felt that I wanted to ride harder and harder. It was such a great memory.'

But with an arrival comes a gradual leaving. When things are simple and going well, a racing cyclist will turn up and race at the drop of a hat. There is no additional motivation needed. It feels as though there will never be a time when that motivation might slip, and yet by increments it does, and it's never the racing that slips, it's always the context behind it. Changes in life, the things that happens outside of cycling. Marginal gains of one per-cent make the difference, and yet even a tiny increase in performance requires an additional six months of effort, a change in routine and in the daily calendar. Jim Henderson's gentle argument is not dissimilar to Boardman's: 'I feel that with hill climbs I wasn't massively gifted, but I applied myself well to the task in hand: got the bike right, did specific training, made sure the weight was ok, worked hard. There were other people who just didn't have anything quite click right on the day.'

He cites Jeff Wright as an example of one of those riders who didn't quite hit the same heights in the Championship. Henderson rode Jackson Bridge and won the Granville Sydney trophy many times, writing his name underneath Boardman's. But each season when he headed for Halifax the course record was inked alarmingly on the startsheet, a 3'-49" from Wright, some twenty seconds or so up on Henderson's best effort. And it wasn't the only one he had; over a five-year period Jeff Wright annihilated course records up and down the country, and some of them – The Rake for example – still stand.

Henderson is disarmingly honest on this count: 'Those records were always a reminder: Mr Bigshot, you're doing ok, but there're other people. To my mind, Jeff Wright was a much better hill climber than me. And he only won it once, and I've won it five times. That's the way of these things, the way the courses go from year to year.'

To be a multiple winner you have to be able to tackle the full range of gradients. However, even with five wins, it's arguable that Henderson was robbed of a few more by particularly injudicious choices.

As we talk, in Henderson's living room in Southport, with a view of a garden where the red squirrels fight a similar battle of diminishing returns, struggling against the new wave of harder, faster, younger, more aggressive greys, our talk veers away from the hill climb and into other aspects of cycling, just as it did when I spoke with Gareth Armitage, Vic Clark and Graham Sydney. The fellowship of the road extends its comforting arms around us and we are no longer talking solely about bikes, or racing, or hill climbs, but the unifying and singular joy that comes from riding a bicycle. It's something I feel strongly and try to articulate. I've left the house at seven in the morning, wending my way through the sleepy outskirts of Bristol, down across the Mendips and the Blackdowns, before finally, some 12 hours later, climbing Haytor and crawling into a crepuscular Youth Hostel at Bellever after 127 miles in the saddle. Time and space became suspended and only the journey and the moment became real, the gradual unfolding of the landscape and the utter serendipity of the world around me.

This is the profound and realising capacity the bike has. In a world where we become steadily more insular and introverted, more virtual, and in some bizarre paradox, ever less connected and not more so, cycling provokes a real and telling experience with the here and now. It provides the opportunity to see amazing things that you wouldn't have seen if you were doing anything else apart from riding your bike at that precise moment in time, moving through the continuous landscape of flux and change. Being on the bike for that long, getting further and further from home, creates a space in time where all of the things, the world of work and the petty worries you have, begin to melt away in layers until you are suddenly there in the landscape. Just don't expect to be able to explain the profound nature of the experience to someone who hasn't left the house. I rode to Lynmouth after work one afternoon – got on my bike, eighty miles later I was heading up Porlock hill, over Countisbury. It was a fantastic experience, and when you arrive people are baffled – it's inconceivable. The two facets of existence and experience rub against themselves like continental faultlines. We ruminate, slowly chewing the cud, sharing stories of rides and adventures.

Henderson continues: 'It puzzles me why people think it's unusual or are surprised that I might ride twenty five miles to work and back. I do it three times a week and I see animals, I see owls swooping down out of hedgerows. When was the last time you ever saw an owl? I see them. Or there was the time that I was riding to work and I saw a Shetland pony in the middle of the road. Cars were stopping and carefully driving round it. So I led it into someone's garden to stop it being run down. I got into work and said, "I put a pony in someone's garden this morning". And they look at you like you're not on the same planet; they got up, got in the car, drove to work.'

The Shetland pony is simply an obstacle to the car driver, rather than another part of the fullness of life to be experienced and embraced, along with the curious sound that a deer's hooves make on tarmac, because it's a sound that only early morning cyclists experience, startling woodland creatures out of their reverie by just being there at that time, and making silent incursions into another space.

'I have better memories of touring and doing big, long rides on the road than winning races. I rode to Newcastle. I just did quite a few things like that. My brother had a stag do in Newcastle and I rode from here to there in a day, and I picked a route that went up Park Rash in Kettlewell, went up Crawleyside, the Stang and some other ones. These are really big, monstrous climbs. Then you go over the Wear and the Tyne, really brilliant country. And then I turned up and they all looked a bit baffled.'

His words echo round the living room, spoken recollections hanging silently for a moment in the air, before disolving back into memory. Winning a race, a hill climb, even a National Championship, is a very compressed and finite memory. It's the longer, continuous experiences that steadily unfold as we drift through life that seem to leave a rippling across our wider consciousness.

15

Equal Opportunities

'It's amazing what it can do to you. You can have two days when you're nervy about something then you're exhausted for days afterwards.'

Never let it be said that the Cycling Time Trials Council (CTT) is slow to adapt to change. As recently as 2012 they opened up the Pandora's box known as 'internet entry', much to the chagrin of their target audience, who remain happier paying in shekels and pfennigs, delivered by carrier pigeon. Another comparatively recent innovation involved opening up the National Hill Climb to women in 1998. Better late than never, I guess. It took a further five years for them to recognise an outright women's Champion and it wasn't until 2012 that medals were awarded for second and third place. You can't accuse the CTT of not celebrating the feats of female riders. After all, Eileen Sheridan, Beryl Burton, Yvonne McGregor, Lynn Taylor, Lisa Brambani and Bridget Boon have all been justly lauded, but it seems a bit strange that women were not able to contest the Championship until the cusp of the twenty-first century.

The omission was ended in style by a super-fast junior called Nicole Cooke on Dover's Hill in 1998. She finished in 4'-37.5", going slightly quicker than she had two hours previously when she took the Schools' Championship. There is a picture in the press of Cooke in the colours of Cardiff Ajax. She doesn't look all that different from the rider who went on to become one of the greatest cyclists the UK has ever seen. Cooke then disappeared on to the continent to garner a glittering palmarès – including victories in the Classics as well as the *Giro Donne* and the *Grande Boucle Féminine* – culminating in the Olympic and Worlds titles in 2008, the only rider (male or female) to achieve this last feat.

The recent history of the Hill Climb Championship has seen the women's title keenly contested between two very different riders from opposite ends of the country – the powerful and relatively stocky Ann Bowditch, and the tiny, bird-like Lynn Hamel. More recently, Hamel's stranglehold over the event has been interrupted by the expatriate Canadian, Maryka Sennema.

The years following Nicole Cooke's win saw a number of different riders take the title. Helen Dawson won on the Rake in 1999, finishing a long way down in 4'-05.2". Tracy Maund won at Westclose in 2000, whilst the following year Ann Wooldridge came in nearly eight minutes behind Mark Lovatt on the Cat and Fiddle. Ruth Dorrington became the first officially recognised champion in 2003. Arguably, the (belated) recognition given to the women's winner began to raise the number and standard of the entries. Things changed markedly with the arrival of Ann Bowditch and Lynn Hamel. Their rivalry altered the complexion of women's hill climbing: large time gaps and paltry fields became less and less common.

Ann Bowditch is from the Bailiwick of Guernsey, where it's generally quite tricky to build up a head of steam. The island's '25' course is twisty and slow, especially in comparison to the traffic-assisted motorway courses beloved of the mainland testerati. It's not uncommon to see Guernsey cyclists at the superfast R25 course in Wales, aiming to shave eight minutes from their '25' times.* Bowditch started out mountain biking, before switching to the road in order to take part in the 1997 Island Games. It's an event which includes all of the tiny islands in the world, gathering them together for a mini-Olympiad, where the Isle of Man is the resident superpower.

In 2004 Bowditch took the women's title on the Gibbet in Northumberland. She managed the effort on the steeper section at the start, before putting out the watts on the drag to the finish and making up time on her nearest rival, Lynn Hamel. As Hamel puts it: 'She really picked it up over the last bit. It did help that they had a stonking tailwind towards the second half. It's quite exposed. She probably would have won anyway.'

It was Hamel's first National and very much a learning curve: 'I didn't have the light wheels and I wore baggy stuff, and I wore sunshades, which again is extra weight. I don't know why. I was still doing a bit of running at the time, a bit of time trialling in the club, but not really seriously. I didn't know how to train; if anything, I was overtrained.' She opted for a helmet with a clip on visor, big glasses, big socks, a jersey like a sail and three-quarter length bibs.

It was back to the shorter stuff and The Rake in 2005, on a climb that Hamel particularly likes: 'It's my favourite hill, I got the women's record on there. It's a bit of a dip in the middle, but because you know it's such a short effort, when you get to the first corner you go all out from there. Some people say

* The R25/3L is the code for a course that runs near Resolven. It's extremely quick on the right day and the current competition record of 45'-43" was set there by Matt Bottrill in 2014.

you shouldn't ride it like that but I'm used to it. Peter Graham reckons I should do it fixed – it'll be better – but I'm a bit nervous about it. I haven't ridden a fixed on a hill climb before. I'm a geared person, I like my gears. I go between two or three gears.' In the end, Hamel didn't ride, leaving the way open for Bowditch to take her second title on the bounce, utilising her 'power to weight, mental strength and pain threshold' – in short, the hill climber's armoury.

Lynn Hamel writes children's books in her spare time; she is engaging and open, with the uncanny ability to spring up a hill at a savage pace. It's ironic that the creator of gentle children's literature is capable of such a violent explosion of effort. She is quietly spoken and welcoming, but once on a hill her calm demeanour slips away to be replaced with something a bit more scary. She seems at war with the bicycle, her face contorts and mouth hangs open in the desperate battle to get in more oxygen. It's an impressive sight. Again, there's something obsessional in the eye, a steely determination, a willingness to do strange things in slightly strange ways.

She's also a self-confessed nervy character and our conversation was punctuated with references to being 'nervy', or 'my nerves', or 'I'm nervous in groups': 'I don't think it helps knowing someone is breathing down my neck. I'm a panicker. I can get a bit too worried, a bit too much anxiety, and then get really worried and then go like jelly and then the power disappears.'

Bowditch is the polar opposite, an expert in 'sports psychology, neuro-linguistic programming, emotional freedom techniques and matrix reimprinting'. I really don't know what the last one is, but I'm sure that if you combined Bowditch with Hamel you'd have some sort of utterly calm, killer hill climbing android.

The event alternated, and it was on Peak Hill in 2006 that Hamel and Bowditch battled again, with Jane Kilmartin looking to grab a share of the spoils. On a longer, draggy climb Bowditch again came out on top, edging it by twenty seconds. Hamel saw enough to know that there was space for improvement and resolved to come back the following year at Cheddar and aim for the top step. The run of longer hills from 2000 to 2007, the Rake notwithstanding, was doing her no favours. The South Devon climb, up and away from the shingle beach, required careful pace and judgement: 'It was very flat, actually, more of a roadman's climb, but still a hillclimb. It was like Cheddar Gorge: it had a steep bit and then it was a drag.'

Bowditch found the climb to her liking. The flat start with steeper sections, followed by a level finish, played into her hands. She had made the trek over with James McLaughlin, a young Guernsey Velo rider who was benefitting from her coaching.* Bowditch became only the fifth rider after Clark, Webster, Boardman and Henderson to secure a consecutive hat trick.

On Cheddar Gorge in 2007 the diminutive Hamel finally hit her stride, beating Bowditch by some distance, only to come second to Caroline Kloiber, a continental professional hailing from Bristol. Kloiber hurtled up the steep-sided gorge with a rapid time of eight minutes dead. Like the men's champion, James Dobbin, she was recovering from injuries, although they were sustained in an early-season crash rather than a skiing holiday. In a common strategy shared by most of the field, Kloiber attacked the steep bend as quick as she could, using the small ring quite far across the block, before sticking it in the big ring for the time trialling section of the climb and pushing on to the finish.

Lynn Hamel was second fastest, some 23 seconds down: 'I came second on Cheddar Gorge; it was the first time I'd beaten Ann Bowditch. Caroline Kloiber, who we thought would win it, just disappeared after that, but she'd beaten Rebecca Romero

---

* McLaughlin came fifth in the National TT Championships, behind Wiggins, Rowe, Bottrill and Thomas.

in the National Time Trial Championships.* We thought, "Eh up, she's going to do something in the hill climb," and sure enough, she won it.'

At Matlock the following year, Hamel won her first championship, by a not insignificant 25 seconds over Claire Thomas – another international rider having a dig at the season-ender. Her time of 2'-59" saw her just graze the top fifty, a fantastic achievement deserving of wider recognition. It was a climb that suited her – short and horribly steep. In chasing her second title, things came unstuck. The climb was Pea Royd Lane, scene of the 2014 Championship. Most hill climbers ride through September and October in a state of permanent hypochondria, anxious to avoid any cough or cold as winter edges in. Hamel didn't escape the curse, and came up against the in form Anna Fischer.

Anna Fischer was a German based near Bristol. She rode a few climbs that year, including Burrington Combe. Incidentally, this was my first hill climb and she was off a minute before me. I only just caught her at the top. After her win in the National she went across to ride in Belgium, won her first big race and competed in the women's pro tour. She is small and powerfully built and rode with strength and control on the climb. She seemed unfazed by the abrasive tunes from the resident bagpiper near the top and managed to beat Hamel by half a second – or a gear change – or next to nothing. Sandwiched between the two on the results sheet was Paul Kippax. Paul isn't likely to win a prize in a big event, unless they begin handing them out for most spectacular collapse into oxygen debt, in which case he's a shoo-in. At the top of Pea Royd he crashed off the bike, limbs of jelly, eyes on stalks and rolling back inside his head, before assuming the foetal position on a slightly damp grass verge on the wild and windy Sheffield moorland.

---

* Kloiber came second to Wendy Houvenaghel in the 2007 National Time Trial Championships, with Romero in third.

Hamel acknowledges that Anna Fischer was 'a superb rider', but the winning margin left her wondering what might have been: 'I had a bad year, I caught something before. If I hadn't had the chesty cough and had my head in a bucket before, I'd have liked to have known what I could have done. I got to the end of that hill climb and my chest hurt for ages, and I knew that it would have made a difference, oxygen wise. I was gutted, because I wanted a good result against a good rider. And it would have been four times in a row. But stuff happens, you know. Everyone has shit that happens to them. There are always other years. It was hard and I was upset, I have to admit.'

Hamel set things straight at Dover's. In 2010 her competition took the form of Chrissy Radon, a fearsome triathlete, straying far away from her normal proving ground by opting firstly to ride uphill, and secondly to neither precede nor follow a bike ride with another sporting activity.

Hemel was anxious and unsure: 'I wasn't keen on it at all. I'd had a really bad year: I'd burnt out; I got tired. Road racing had mentally knocked me and I found myself going backwards through the season, so I just disappeared and rode round with a few friends and didn't do anything until the Rake. I only did two races that year – the Rake and the National. I did three efforts in total, one training effort. I think because I was fresh and looking forward to doing a race it made a difference. In a short effort you can do well on not much training, if you're light. Your V02 max is better. It's funny to think that I won a national off two efforts.'

I'd like to be in her shoes. If I did two efforts and tried the National I'd be chewing the stem to bits and pedalling in squares. Such are the vagaries of form and fitness. Freshness and form aside, Hamel made the right choices: 'I was pleased because I thought I was going to get beaten. The winning margin was eleven seconds or something, not much. I was pleased with that, and Michelle King rode it and I was pleased with the gap there as well. It was steep and it wasn't. Any hill is hard; a pursuit is hard. It doesn't matter if it's seated or if it's upright, or you're standing, a hard effort is a hard effort.'

On the start sheet Hamel was up immediately after me. I thought I had put in a bit of an effort, I certainly tried quite hard and was more than usually out of breath at the finish, but Hamel's effort as she came through the tunnel took me back a bit. There was a level of determination that I couldn't entirely comprehend, a willingness to put mind, body and spirit on the line in search of the victory. I've never been in a position to chase a victory in a big event, it's always been about doing my best and riding home with my dignity intact. There is perhaps a difference when you know it comes down to the tightest of margins, a tension and a pressure, an unceasingly physical and mental quest for success. I sensed it in Hamel at the end and it seemed alien to me. Eleven seconds was a significant margin of victory over Michelle King, and also Maryka Sennema. As if hill climbs aren't hard enough, Sennema revealed that she was 'already two months pregnant by the time it rolled around, so didn't do very well'. She vowed to return and challenge again for the title.

A year later, on Long Hill at Buxton, Lynn Hamel proved her aptitude for a very different course, perhaps through foresight and prior preparation, but it's also posible that she benefitted from being fresh: 'It felt flat, it was more about aerodynamics, and everyone was saying that after. I rode it three times, predominantly in a headwind, and I didn't use my Zipps either, I would waste power, mental energy and torque by using light wheels. I needed to be solid and it worked, and my wheels weren't actually that light. I did a lot of research: the three times I did it I learnt something every time. I was overgeared the first time, I tried to ride it like a pursuit. It was like a '10' effort in terms of time. Power-wise I didn't do much more than a '10', and I knew if I did the numbers I might win it. In training; I was 10 watts down. I managed it on the day, but not in training.'

A dry run in the Open event served notice of where it might go wrong: 'I usually set out hard. On the open event on Long Hill I was 20 watts over, bars too close together and blew up spectacularly.' It was one of the strongest fields seen for a National, with the fast time triallists lured out of the woodwork for a rare go at the anti-gravity stuff, but they were all put to the sword. Hamel distanced Rebecca Slack by 21 seconds. A fastidious attention to detail saw her take the title and set up a tilt for a third successive crown, an elusive hat trick of wins.

After the trials and tribulations of Long Hill, in 2012 it was back to more comfortable terrain, at least metaphorically, on the Rake. Lynn Hamel loves the Rake: 'I think I like the idea that I know it's a short, hard effort, and it's how long you can hold that effort for. You get people cheering you on – it's more of an event than a time trial. They usually have an atmosphere. Peter [Graham] has been a mentor, he's always keen for me to do the Rake. He tells me a lot about his hill climbing days.'

Graham tried to get her to ride fixed in 2012 – he swears blind that it's quicker – but to no avail: 'I'd have to practise all year because of my nerves.' Watching alongside Peter Graham on the climb was the 93-year-old Vic Clarke, cheering her on through horizontal sheets of rain, 68 years after he first took the title. Hamel smashed the course record with 3'-08", beating second placed Joanne Clay by over ten seconds. Ann Bowditch made a return to the event and finished in third with 3'-23". The margin of victory is compelling on such a short course.

A year later the Championship visited the horribly hilly and long climb of the Stang, in some of the nastiest weather ever, although Teesiders will doubtless argue that they've had far worse. Hamel just missed out on a fifth title to the Kingston Wheeler, Maryka Senemma, who beat her by seventeen seconds on the two-mile climb. Senemma's time trialling power did the damage on a day when the weather was violent and uncompromising.

In 2014 the National returned to Pea Royd, with Hamel looking to atone for her near miss in 2009, and Senemma out to prove a point: 'Last year nobody knew who I was, but I won it. And yet I still felt the underdog this year, because everyone seemed to be talking about who might win it, but I never heard myself mentioned.'* Hamel went quite a bit quicker than she had done last time out, but Senemma was quicker still, winning by several seconds from Lou Collins and Hamel.

A sense of vindication was evident in her comments after the event: 'To come out here and win, and win convincingly, was important to me.' Senemma is in her forties and, along with the 48-year-old Chris Myhill, offers hope to the legions of veterans still aiming to compete at the highest level in the hill climbs – raging against the dying of the light and the stark truth that it's the ability to ride uphill quickly that disappears first.

It's clear that the women's event has grown in stature and competitiveness, and that it can only expand further with the growth in both leisure and racing cycling. But the progress has been painfully slow. It's almost impossible to fathom why it took until 2012 – fourteen years after the inauguration of the women's championship – before medals for second and third place were finally awarded. The winner that year, Lynn Hamel, is deeply critical at the reluctance of both organisers and the media to be more proactive: 'It's still crap on the women's front – why didn't they write more about Ann Bowditch? She won it three times. And then last year there was nothing, like there were no women or juniors. Rebecca Slack was second: she had won lots of things, including the National 100-mile Time Trial. There was one prize in the hill climb – not three – and no coverage. They should encourage more women and do more.'

She was right: after Long Hill in 2011 the report in *Cycling Weekly* was so blinkered towards the men's event that you

---

* http://www.cyclingweekly.co.uk/news/latest-news/dan-evans-wins-hill-climb-national-championship-141321 [November 2014]

would have been hard pushed to identify any of the women who rode. It hasn't improved that much since. Any number of self-serving arguments are used, but ultimately, it's coverage that creates interest, and then more coverage. There have been some steps in the right direction, with allocated field placings, but the differences in prize money and the awards are still painfully apparent.

Yet the strength of truly consummate hill climbers is their capacity to ride any of the hills, long or short, with similar levels of success. Lynn Hamel and Maryka Senemma display that capability every bit as much as a Jim Henderson or a Granville Sydney. There is an obsessive edge to Hamel, an unspoken sense and awareness of what it takes to achieve at this most challenging and specific of sports. There is also a similar drive and determination bristling beneath the surface of Senemma, a sense of unfinished business and a desire to prove people wrong. It's this that drives them onwards and upwards. And it is the same latent force within all successful hill climbers – men or women.

Henderson hurtles up the side of the Mendips in 2000

Ann Bowditch on the Rake in 2012

The author being cheered on by a five-times Champion on the Rake

…90 seconds later on the point of collapse –
"definitely a bit over-geared."

Vic Clark and Lynn Hamel, two champions 60 years apart

Sarah Helliwell shows just how hurty the Nick O' Pendle can be

Michael Hutchinson and a drainage van, riding
downhill on a time trial bike, in a hill climb

Rob Hales gives a valedictory salute at Long Hill

The Stang – lovely there this time of year

Rob Gough, King of Catford, at Hinton Hill near Bath

The Bec Hill Climb

David Millar signs off at the Bec Hill Climb

Evergreen Chris Myhill at
Pea Royd Lane in 2014

Lynn Hamel gasps for
air on Pea Royd

Maryka Sennema

Some gentle encouragement from the
University of Bristol cheerleaders

Matt Clinton takes another medal at Pea Royd 2014

Dan Evans caps an astounding 2014
season with the top prize

The Scratch Rider

The catch

16

Contemporaneity

(2007–2010)

'In 2006 and 2007 I cancelled everything else in my life for three months. I would just sleep, eat, go to work and train and go to hill climbs. In those two years I think I forgot about girls entirely.'

In particularly spiteful winter months Cheddar Gorge is closed to traffic. The surface run-off wreaks havoc to the cambered edges of the road, forging rivulets of cascading water that run across the road and dislodge gravel, soil and boulders. It makes for treacherous driving conditions. Paradoxically, it makes it a cyclists' paradise. The wide main road has more than enough room in between the eroded edges to allow riders the full closed road experience. There are other more violent climbs in and around the gorge; the escarpment leading up to the Mendips pitches up aggressively just two miles further down the road with the ascent of Draycott Steep, the intended location for the 2000 National before a last minute switch to Westclose, the neighbouring climb in a run of four. Deer Leap and Old Bristol Hill are the remaining two; each one is a savage and uncompromising ascent from the tiny villages overlooking the prehistory of the Levels to the unkempt beauty of the Mendips. The hills are lined with hidden valleys, tumbling down the verdant slopes and offering views across to Wales, and then down towards Glastonbury Tor.

A solitary ride up Cheddar Gorge in the heart of winter can be an unnerving experience. The temporary barriers prevent any traffic and lead to a solipsistic experience through a normally busy tourist attraction. It's reminiscent of the scene in "Close Encounters of the Third Kind", where an increasingly deranged Richard Dreyfuss heads towards the Devil's Tower in search of the aliens: barriers and road closures stop people from driving on, and there are dead and bloated cattle by the side of the road. There are no dead cattle in the gorge, only the hardy goats, perched on shifting scree and straying out into the road to startle descending cyclists. The sound of the winter wind funnelling down the gorge reverberates around the 140-metre cliff face, and up above a white and rolling coverlet of clouds breaks across the top in a ceaseless occlusion. The silence is shattered by the harking scream and whirr of the pairs of peregrines that nest in the very highest battlements, terrorising rooks and ravens by swooping against the mottled darkness of the rock face.

The unnerving sense of darker forces at work within the isolated setting is deepened by knowledge of Cheddar's paleolithic secrets. Several caves adjoin the gorge, porous tunnels leading to caverns measureless to man. The largest of these, Gough's Cave, contained the oldest complete human skeleton found in the UK, dating back to 7150 BC. A puncture wound in the skull suggested a violent death, with hypotheses of cannibalism and ritual slaughter doing the rounds. After 9,000 years, mitochondrial testing revealed that some direct descendants still live in the town. This strikes me as both utterly outlandish and completely believable.

In 2007 a motley assortment of West country cycling clubs came together to organise the National on an entirely new hill. They opted for scenic and beautiful, as opposed to harsh and unforgiving, and succeeded in advertising the natural beauty of the limestone gorge to all those who made the trek southwards. Local trike legend Dave Keene of Bristol South CC took time out from polishing his Longstaff to take up the organiser's duties.*

It was a beautiful setting for the event, but the lack of challenge was not unnoticed, especially by arch-curmudgeon Peter Graham: 'The winning time was six minutes! That's for a two mile climb! That's twenty mile an hour!'

Hot favourite for the title and a back-to-back victory was James Dobbin, riding for Arctic Shorter Rochford. Earlier on in the year it looked like all might be lost; a brief skiing holiday exacerbated a knee problem. Dobbin spent significant sums on physio in an attempt to get back on the bike, with no success. In the end, a £15 foam massage roller did the trick. It wasn't until August that he was riding again and, come September, celebrating with a course record on Snake Pass. Maybe the rest and steadier build-up worked well, for by the time the hilly stuff came around he was lean and ready to race. Most of Dobbin's training was spent indoors with a simple maxim: 'The benchmark I'd aim for was to be able to hold 420 watts for ten minutes. If I could do that I knew I'd be in with a chance of winning the National. I always thought that if it hurt enough it must be good.'

At 6ft-2ins and weighing 67 kilos, rain or shine, Dobbin's power to weight was a clear strength over the longer distances. Dobbin had been aiming for Dangerfield's course record on the

---

* Dave Keene holds the current 100-mile competition record at four hours and one second. He was baulked by a tractor on the last roundabout, costing him his 25mph ride.

Horseshoe Pass for a couple of years, missing it by a second in 2006. In 2007 he returned to Llangollen for another go:

'I had tried several times before for the record and got closer each time. It was the 25th anniversary of the Fibrax Wrexham Roads Club event and a lot of people had turned out to remember Terry Smith, the founder, who had died the month before after a long illness. My brothers and one of their girlfriends had come along; the weather was calm and ideal for an attempt at the record. I parked at the bottom and rode up the climb to warm up and met my brothers in the layby at the summit, the views were amazing as early morning mist was still in the valley. I was more determined than ever. The ride itself was as good as I could have done. I remember seeing my time on my speedometer as I rounded the last right hand bend before the last section to the finish, and I knew it was going to be close as I'd remembered what time I got to that point in the previous year. To hear I'd got it by a single second (9'-03") was such a relief and I'm still very proud of that course record. I also felt proud to have done it on a day that was special for the history of the event; people were commemorating Terry Smith.'

The record stood for a further seven years, when reigning National Champion, Tejvan Pettinger, took another second off, sealing a long held ambition, only to be well and truly scalped by a lean and fearsome looking Dan Evans, who somehow managed to card an 8'-52", kicking the record well and truly into the long grass by the slate quarry.

At Cheddar, in 2007, the battle between James Dobbin and Dave Clarke had become the headline event. The lower section of the climb features a sharp turn up through the towering walls of rock, pitching up to around 20%, but only for a short time. After that the road levels and the gradient is negligible. At the 0.6 mile mark, once over the initial ramps, Dobbin had taken 1.5 seconds from Clarke. At halfway they were dead level, the time check provided by Dobbin's Dad. He turned on the afterburners over the flatter final sections to carve out a six second win. Clarke was philosophical and magnanimous in defeat. Matt Clinton made an appearance on the podium for the first time, capitalising on a season's racing at elite level in Brittany, to fall just outside of the seven minute mark and snatch the bronze from Jim Henderson.

Henderson was characteristically upbeat in his recollections of the day, despite coming fourth: 'I surprised myself on Cheddar and did a lot better than I thought I would. I took it way too easy in the first half. For the time trial bit I was on the big ring, put a bit of thought into it – 48/50 rings – knew what I was doing. Got in the big ring, never thought like that for the Cat and Fiddle. But through 2007 I'd been saying, "I'm not going to do brilliantly so don't worry," but when I got to the end I thought I should have done a bit more, training-wise. It certainly meant I carried on for Matlock the following year and then Pea Royd.'

The excursion to an untested course was a success of sorts. The scenery and support from the local clubs was impressive, but it lacked drama and pain. The steep-sided valley may have borne a cursory resemblance to Winnats Pass, but it missed out on the level of challenge. Several riders opted for time trial bikes, leaving the purists weeping silently into their drilled, fixed-gear weaponry.

The return to the North for the next two years saw the Championship reacquainted with the short, nasty and violent climbs that perhaps honoured more closely its history and traditions – first at Matlock and then at Pea Royd Lane in Stocksbridge.

One look at the parcours for Matlock and Dobbin must have known the game was all but up. Matlock is a classic town centre climb situated on the edge of the Peak District. It produces a fantastic atmosphere and a baying crowd, eager to see the pain and suffering etched upon the corrugated brows of the hardy competitors, particularly when hitting the steeper sections. Bank Road climbs up away from the River Derwent in a straight line, giving the anxious rider plenty to think about. It's up front about the pain and suffering to follow, there are no gentle curves hiding the true nature of the climb. It does not flatter to deceive. The road bends near the Gate Hotel where the crowd lingers several deep, one on top of the other, inching up the hill to create several vertical tiers of people. The council had kindly resurfaced the road with a glassy strip of new tarmacadam to help riders contend with the average gradient of 14%.

The most carefully planned of pre-race rituals and warm-ups can be derailed in an instant. Reigning champion James Dobbin snapped a carbon crank practising his 'jump', moments before his slot. He had to take team-mate Danny Axford's bike and shoes and could only manage 21st place on the day: 'I lost quite a bit of time on the climb, but in truth I'd never have won there anyway; the broken chainset was a convenient excuse!'

Matt Clinton was on a red hot streak of form, the kind of run that comes once in a career. He had won eleven from eleven in the build-up to the championship, and the final course was to his liking. Not only that, it was suitable for fixed, and Matt is one of the few riders at the top end of the sport to still use fixed wheel for hill climbs. He doesn't do it always, and admittedly uses it less and less, but opted for the single cog in 2008. A gear ratio of 42:20 gave 54", although the bike wasn't overwhelmingly light, at 6.3 kilograms. 'As light as I could cobble together at that point. We later found the rear wheel fairing was 150grams'.

It was enough though. The crowd rolled inwards, making the most of the short course to gather in numbers and press at the riders, creating the archetypal tunnel of noise that makes for an amazing event. It was a course for the strong men, not the winnowy, sallow beanpoles. Step forward the king of the Midlands courses, a superlative rider over most climbs but a master of anything between two and five minutes. Clinton was the out-and-out favourite, but Jim Henderson was also looking to grab his elusive sixth title, putting him on a par with Granville Sydney, and a strong Bill Bell threatened an upset. Clinton completed the course in 2'-24.2", beating Bell by a second and Henderson by two. He wasn't overly modest in his appraisal of his performance: 'I'm not sure it's such a surprise: I've been going really well recently', and to be fair, he had a point.* There's little to be said for being self-deprecating when you've won eleven races on the bounce.

The following season he was confident of victory at the nastier climb of Pea Royd Lane in Stocksbridge. Earlier in the season Clinton had twice been beaten by Daniel Shand, but only on the longer climbs of Holme Moss and Cragg Vale. Pea Royd Lane was shorter and more savage, with several unrelenting sections topping out at 20%. It's a real snorter of a hill and it hurts to ride it at pace. There is no rhythm or sensibility or dignity, unlike the Tour of Lombardy, which has all three of those things in spades. All of which makes it seem strange that Dan Fleeman, riding in the colours of Cervelo Test Team, should hurry back from the traditional end-of-season Monument to have a crack at a four minute climb in a post-industrial town on the edge of Sheffield. With just six days between the Ride of the Falling Leaves and the Ride of the Slipping Wheels, Fleeman was in luck: a week of sofa was the extent of the training he put in. He shot out of the blocks like he'd stolen his bicycle, pedalled ridiculously hard and then clung on all the way up.

It was clear to the spectators and those competitors coming down the hill that he was ascending at a faster rate than anyone else. His style on the bike looked ragged, arms and legs moving, the bike swaying from side to side, none of the steady and controlled force of Henderson or the consistent, inexorable power of Clinton, just strength and physicality. He

---

*http://www.cyclingweekly.co.uk/news/latest-news/clinton-wins-national-hill-climb-championship-92179

didn't dispel this perception: 'Before the start I was going to pace it evenly, but at the line I shot off like a mad man, and at the end I felt like I was dying. I was going to work on 600 watts average and hold it the whole way. Then at the start a few people told me not to bother. Anyway, off I go. I had about 700 watts for the first bit and then at the end I almost came to a standstill and dropped to about 550 watts and I didn't think I'd done that well.'*

Matt Clinton was hit by rain which came down five minutes before his start. He also opted for a cog too big, going for the 20 instead of the 21. I'm not sure it would have changed the result. Fleeman staggered across the line, bike and rider a contorted mass of limbs and brutal gurn, tongue hanging out, at 3'-17.8", more than fourteen seconds up on Clinton and a further twenty two seconds ahead of Henderson. It was an enormous margin on a short climb and left more than a few of the riders feeling chastened. The winner did have form though – he'd ridden two hill climbs before, in 2007, the Cat and Bec, and won both.

Fleeman's victory called time on the distinguished career of one of the strongest hill climbers in the history of the event, Jim Henderson: 'The week before I'd done the Nick O' Pendle. The week before he'd done the Tour of Lombardy and come thirtieth. He'd done the Tour of Britain. I could see that he wasn't going away. I've a good sense of realism of what's possible. If you want to come back and keep doing them you've got to be like Malcolm Elliott. He's still going. It's got to be your job though.'

Dobbin never rescaled the heights he had achieved in 2006 and 2007. His powers and motivation waned. He continued racing and had some notable successes in Open events, but when it came to the big one he never recaptured the form. He's sanguine about it in retrospect: 'When I wasn't exactly flying, it was sort of frustrating, but at the same time I knew I'd just not trained enough and I could just live on my memories. In

---

* http://www.cyclingweekly.co.uk/news/latest-news/fleeman-wins-national-hill-climb-65372

2006 and 2007 I'd managed to just about cancel everything else in my life for three months, so I would just sleep, eat, go to work and train and go to hill climbs. In those two years I think I forgot about girls entirely! I would enter as many hill climbs as I could and normally did two or three each weekend. That was it.'

A thread seemed to be emerging: no matter what the distance or the severity, or how well or badly he appeared to be going in the build-up, Matt Clinton was a good bet for the podium. He rode fixed at Pea Royd in 2009 and again at Dover's in 2010, where Fleeman returned for another bite of the apple. And, as is always the case, riders creep out of the woodwork, find form, come from nowhere, interrupting any calculations of success.

The new gun in town was a quiet Buddhist who might object to being called a 'new gun', for reasons of zen and mindfulness. Tejvan Pettinger was getting stronger with each season, even though it's questionable how anyone can ride strongly uphill with an apparent lack of muscle mass or anything above 0.3% body fat. Nevertheless, after a couple of merely 'good' rides, Pettinger had made several changes which contributed towards a sudden improvement: he worked less, opting for part-time hours teaching, supplementing his income with a second 'job' blogging. Pettinger's blog is a popular read; it's erudite, funny and honest.* Several things shine through: a commitment to riding the bike in beautiful scenery and a celebration of the feelings that this entails; a wider enjoyment of cycling in all its forms, from the student on a utilitarian sit up and beg, wending through the streets of Oxford, to the blingtastic bike porn of the Tour de France; and a recurring theme of spiritual enlightenment.

Pettinger had won seven out of ten climbs over the season; beating Dobbin, Richard Handley, Mike Cuming, Clinton on Saintbury, whilst just missing out to Cuming and Clinton on Dover's. It was a premonition of later results: the longer climb

---

* www.cyclinguphill.com

played into Pettinger's hands, but the shorter one was trickier. The field for the September double-header* promoted by the Warwickshire RC was getting warmed up for the National four weeks later and it boasted a big entry; organiser Alex Laycock treated it as a dry run for the blue riband event. The only person missing was the defending champion, Dan Fleeman, who kept his powder dry for the National.

Four weeks later Fleeman turned up to ride the same race plan he had succeeded with on Pea Royd: explode out of the blocks, max out on an absurd power figure, cling on to the top, win by some distance. Clinton was second, just ahead of Mike Smith, with Pettinger exiled to fourth place: 'It was bang on what I expected, just one second off the podium. Had it been on Saintbury I might just have had that extra advantage. I was neither over pleased nor unhappy, it was just what I expected. I was excited to get so close to a medal, I came away happy, thinking, "Wow, you're one second off a medal. Next year..."'

It was Fleeman's last race before he retired, and his hill climb *palmarès* is surprisingly short. It consists of five Opens: the Cat (twice), Bec and the National (twice). Rob Gough at Catford and a fourteen year old Germain Burton at the Bec were the only riders to beat him.

---

* The two-stage hill climb on Saintbury and then on Dover's.

17

When is a Hill not a Hill?

Over the years the championship has visited some spectacular climbs and parts of the country; the event has become synonymous with beautiful scenery. It's also made a few slightly duff choices. Exactly what qualifies as a 'hill' is a tricky matter of definition, especially when you consider that different types of hill suit different riders. Most cyclists recognise a couple of truisms; that the classic length is between three and four minutes, and a nice bit of steepness is the best way to ensure that you get a real 'gurnfest'. Outside of those parameters things get a bit woolly. The Horseshoe Pass is seen as a test, but also as a roadman's climb: it's long and has a steady gradient, meaning it's a 'rhythm' climb, rewarding a steady, paced effort. It draws the spectators and is a longstanding fixture in the calendar, but it's not particularly steep. In contrast, The Rake is on the short side, but the utterly revolting last ramp, combined with the town centre setting, make it a shoo-in for classic status.

Although it's not that simple when it comes to defining what makes a super climb, it's fairly easy to state what makes a rubbish climb, and it is typically when the event works against the things people cherish about the National. It's the great get together, but string it out over a four mile road and people don't really get together and it's not great. It should be run on a closed road, allowing spectators to encroach on the course and galvanise the efforts of the competitors. An open road causes traffic problems and other difficulties. Riders should be digging out their hill climb bikes and making absurd modifications for no real gain, but optimistic that the totality will see them ascend quicker. And lastly, each competitor needs to be left flailing on a grass bank like a dying goldfish.

On several occasions the event has worked against this, either through bad choices or an error of judgement. Exhibit one is Long Hill in 2011. It's almost surreal in retrospect that the top four riders used a full time trial set up. You can also tell if it's not much of a hill if Michael Hutchinson fancies his chances.

Jim Henderson went along to watch: 'I feel bad to criticise the National Hill Climb, but it was just shocking. I was appalled. It was so easy, the gradient so gentle, the bikes that people were riding, the level of traffic. It was terrible. I'm really pleased that a climber won it at the end and not a tester. One day I will get myself motivated to do something about that; they need some kind of rule, some understanding of RTTC politics and some way of ruling out hills that are less than 1-in-20 average.'

The oracle and bona fide hill climb legend Peter Graham, scourge of over-geared riders everywhere also waded in: 'Long Hill. What a farce. There was every opportunity for skulduggery. Team cars were following riders, building up traffic, then drawing past.'

There is a jarring disconnect between the traditions and topographical history of the Hill Climb and an event that favours a time trial machine. Most people welcome the variation in gradient and the use of longer, shallower climbs in the Championship race. However, the gradient and length of Long Hill make it particularly unsuited and possibly the most ill-judged course in the history of the event. I rode the course the day before to try and get a feel for it. This involved locating the start. I checked the course description carefully and eventually located what had to have been the postbox indicated, but was utterly baffled by the absence of any gradient. It can't have been more than 1% at that point.

I can sense why it might have been chosen; there was a possibility that the many professional riders who are based in and around High Peak might have put an entry in, and this would have been nice to see. It's a shame though, that the dozens of fantastic and challenging climbs in the immediate area were ignored, including some absolute belters used by the promoting club in their Mountain Time Trial. I'll accept fully that the organisers' intentions were good; they also did a fantastic job on the day with some lovely musettes for the riders and they managed to unblock the toilets of the Bowling club at the end.

Tejvan Pettinger is diplomatic: 'If I was organising a national I wouldn't want to put it on Long Hill, but I still see it as a hill climb. The organiser really wants to run the National on Peaslows, which is 10% for one mile and by far the better choice. I feel sorry for him because he put his heart and soul into it, but it wasn't the National experience that it could have been and I think he wants another chance to put on a real, classic National.'

The best hill climbs are a gladiatorial bloodbath, and Long Hill was not gladiatorial, nor was it a bloodbath. In the end it came down to judgement over which time trial bike was best and who had the best threshold effort. The danger inherent in a gentler or 'different' championship is that you throw it open to riders who might not ordinarily classify themselves as hill climbers. A midway meeting point is worth aiming for, hence the success of the Horseshoe and also the acceptable term 'roadman's hill'. It's when it goes too far the other way that things get muddied. The Cat and Fiddle in 2002 saw Mark Lovatt ascend fastest. There is no doubting his pedigree; winner of the Premier Calendar six times and riding at the

World Championships and Commonwealth Games are lofty achievements. He's also an accomplished climber, but not a hill climber per se. Once the gradient levelled slightly, he was able to narrow the gap, winning on the Peak District climb by over a minute. Dangerfield was due to ride, referring to it as a 'six mile time trial' and most riders opted for TT extensions. Illness put paid to Dangerfield's last attempt at a sixth title.

Since 2002, the course record has been lowered by Tejvan Pettinger and stands at 18'-14". Regardless of his pedigree, he set it on a time trial bike and it's a 22mph average speed. A year later the climb visited Luddenden Lane. Lovatt was still on the crest of a wave, yet Jim Henderson beat him by nineteen seconds over five minutes. The balance was redressed.

On Cheddar Gorge in 2007 Michael Hutchinson didn't ride, but he probably could have done. Aside from a short ramp at the beginning, it's a long and gentle perambulation up the limestone gorge. It's not difficult and it's not that challenging. Riders pitched up on aero-weaponry and the winning speed was heading up towards 19mph. These are speeds most people have trouble sustaining on the flat.

It would be interesting to see what would happen if the national '25' took in Luddenden Lane or included 2,000 feet of climbing. It's important that the Championship retains its identity, staying true to the classic courses and finding new ones, but not diluting the most important elements through inadvisable or subjective choices of what makes a cracking climb, no matter how well-meaning.

18

The Stang

(2011–2014)

'You're trying to get away from your mind and the everyday world. It's torture physically but you get some kind of joy from it, you look back and think, "Wow, that was a real three minutes; I really lived in that three minutes. I don't quite know what went on but I was on the edge and experiencing something different.'

Successful hill climbers are thin. Don't let anyone ever suggest otherwise. If a corpulent chap comes up to you and says they can climb with the best of them, laugh in their plump face; it's not possible. In the jagged, linear ranks of the thin men, Tejvan Pettinger is the tallest, thinnest man I've met for quite some time. In fact, I'm not sure I've ever met anyone as thin and tall. His wrists are dwarfed by the thickness of the oversize handlebars; ankles are rounded pieces of dowel. It's almost impossible to see where the power comes from and how such force and torque can be exerted through each pedal stroke.

He's the embodiment of the received wisdom that power to weight is everything.

He says he eats a lot of cake: 'I find it impossible to put on weight. I've tried, but can't do it. I almost feel guilty.' Vast quantities of carrot cake are the sugary confection of choice; but at 6ft 3ins and 61kilos he's pushing the edges of the body mass index. The smallest of skinsuits drapes baggily across his shoulders and the leg grippers struggle to reach the slim circumference of his thighs. From the back, his spine dapples up the middle of the white jersey in a series of pronounced peaks, like the scaly ridges of a stegosaurus.

Pettinger is a specialist at the long and just-so-steep incline; at a particular pitch he moves into a remorseless hill-conquering rhythm, and an extra 200 yards can make all the difference. If the National had been on Saintbury in 2010 instead of on Dovers, he'd probably have opened his account. In the years since 2004 he's turned in a series of astounding rides. It took him ten years to work up to the big one by winning the title on The Stang in 2013. Like Jeff Wright before him, Pettinger is the hill climber's hill climber.

He started riding with the Otley CC, pitching up to super-long club runs on a 501 Raleigh frame with an agricultural Shimano groupset: 'It was fantastic, just riding your bike all day. I was intimidated going with the faster guys. I thought they'd be too fast for me, and I was happy just doing the miles.'

His first hill climb gave no indication of any hidden talent. A two-stage on East Chevin and Norwood Edge asked some difficult questions and he came close to last. It signalled the end of any nascent ambitions at racing. Later, at university, he joined the OUCC, then led by Jim Henderson, who had just won the first of his National titles: 'I remember seeing him shoot off up a few hills on the club runs and thinking, "Wow, that's pretty impressive".'

Pettinger didn't race though; any intentions were scuppered by illness or injury. A further hiatus followed, before he began pedalling in anger at the ripe old age of 28. I can empathise with this: I'm an even later starter and didn't start racing until I was 33. As a result I've always had a sense that I'm chasing time itself; making up for the lost races of my youth with an ascetic and rigorous regime. Richard Pettinger, as he was then known, immediately began winning or finishing in the top three.

He attempted a handful more, starting with the Cardiff Byways triple. This is an event I'm always desperately keen to avoid. My clubmate, Glyndwr Griffiths, a master of the short stuff, loves it. Each climb takes about a minute and there are three of them. The disappointment felt by Pettinger at the shortness of the event and his lack of success was ameliorated slightly by a trip to Burrington Combe. It winds up through a limestone gorge to the top of the Mendips – a steady two-mile ascent at around 7% with the fastest rides coming out at a shade over 16mph. It became a favourite for Pettinger: 'It's a beautiful hill climb. I did really well; I did 7'-10" and it took me many years to beat that time. I was second behind Danny Axford, who set the course record that day. I regret not doing the National; it was on Winter's Gibbet. I think I would have done quite well.'

It's feasible that he might have bagged a result on the Northumberland moorland back in 2004; maybe not winning but within a shout of the podium. These are the eternal 'what-ifs' that plague anyone who has looked at a start sheet without his or her name on it and seen a missed opportunity. The subsequent season saw a continued upturn in form and fortune, coming third in a Rudy Project behind Michael Hutchinson and the much missed Zak Carr.* He finished fourth in the National 100, then rounded out the season with eleventh at the Hill Climb Championship on the violent wall of Rawson's Rake: 'The climb was on a hill that didn't really suit me. I was pretty pleased with that, which was despite having

---

* Zak Carr was a multiple national champion and accomplished tester. He was killed in 2005 whilst cycling to work.

tremendous wheel slip. I rode and did really well – beginner's luck. When I rode it again seven years later, after doing loads of training and practice runs, I messed it up.'

At this point Pettinger was ectomorphing into an accomplished hill climber. It became the goal for the season, everything else sidelined as a prelude to the main events in September and October. This singular focus is the preserve of the specialist. 2005 saw a further significant leap forwards following on from a hard winter. He knocked seven minutes from his '25' time: 'At the end of that season I thought I was going to end up on the Olympic team because my progress was so rapid; I thought it was easy.' He said it tongue in cheek, but progress is never linear. Three years of stagnation, injuries and illnesses led to doubt and difficulty.

It's hard to know where to find that little bit extra. Cycling is a difficult sport; in many ways it's viewed as forgiving – it's gentle on the knees and there is the joyous benefit of the freewheel – but this belies the sacrifices and time needed in order to find a few seconds here and there. Runners flock to cycling in a last-ditch attempt to save their knees before they turn to dust; drawn in by the fateful words 'low impact', but ignorant of the demands on time: fifteen hours a week, five-hour rides, and so on. Over the years a steady accumulation of base miles and the onset of 'seasoned' fitness can help, but there is always a bigger gorilla, and those that train smarter or harder, with coaches, on power, who work less and cycle more. The amateur sport looks on those who combine the worlds of work with elite cycling as heroic figures: Matt Bottrill, the fastest postman in the world, or Pete Longbottom, Ryedale surveyor and international roadman, both mixing it with the professionals and grand tour winners. Hard-bitten reality means that at some point something has to give. For most of us, it's cycling. We need to work to pay the bills, we have family, children, other commitments. It becomes harder and harder to justify the inexorable pull on time and the relentless demands of a sport that offers so much, but takes so much time. Even when we get near the top, our whispering and conspiratorial self-esteem stops us from making it, from believing in ourselves. We can't all be Mark Cavendish, utterly prepossessed by a confidence that is unerring and unnerving in its acuity; we are inspired by others and keen to try and sit on their wheel, maybe in the hope that one day we might get a brief and flickering moment in the sun.

Pettinger seemed to lack confidence: 'I was really inspired by the sport and motivated to do better; I knew I would do better at longer hills. Even in the initial years the idea of winning was like a dream. I don't have this winning mentality. I underplay my chances, I look at the people winning and think they're extra special. When I came seventh in 2006 and 2007 I thought the natural progression would be to get on the podium. I thought there was a small chance of winning if I made progress.'

Even when we nearly get there, the capriciousness of the sport can slap us back down, below where we started: 'At Matlock I went backwards; it didn't suit me. In 2009 I only did one or two Open events. I wasn't on particularly great form. I was twelfth on Pea Royd.'

After making a few changes, Pettinger suddenly leapt forwards again, coming fourth in 2010 on Dover's whilst winning another seven climbs over the course of the season.

The following year, 2011, was full of promise and the tempting carrot at the end of the season was the aptly named 'Long Hill', an eight minute climb that looked ideal for Pettinger. Over the course of the season he won everything, crushing the competition and standing on the top step of the podium in eleven races. Even sceptics had him marked down as the favourite. Richard Handley, riding well for Rapha Condor, Clinton, the perennial podiumist, and Gunnar Gronlund – the season's new arrival – had all been put to the sword. But beneath the optimism lurked some potential pitfalls. Long Hill's peculiarities and a significant groundswell of opinion suggested it wasn't an appropriate course for the

National. There was disquiet over the lack of a closed road. In the run up to the big event there was a sudden outbreak of a new malaise: equipment anxiety. Typically, preparation for a hillclimb includes two key questions: can I get my bike lighter? And to a lesser extent, is it a course suitable for fixed? A third question suddenly appeared: are aerodynamics more important than power to weight? As a competitor, I wrestled with the same questions.

I arrived early at the Bowling Club in Whaley Bridge on the morning of the race. To the untrained eye, it looked uncannily like the National 10-mile Championship. A substantial majority were pulling full-blown time trial machines out of the boot, including disc wheels, with little or no concessions to weight. It was a carbon bongofest of the highest order. The smattering of lonely road bikes were adorned with tribars. It was apparent that of the top 20 or so, most had gone 'full aero'.

Prior to the event Pettinger canvassed opinion; Mark Lovatt advised a road bike with extensions. A trial run in the Open hill climb the previous year had yielded the course record, bagged with the help of a lusty tailwind. Six weeks before the National a headwind had complicated matters, but he took the win from Gronlund and went away with a sense of confidence which was only dented on the morning of the Championship:

'The contenders were on time trial bikes, disc wheels, aero helmets. But I was content to do my thing. I was a lot quicker than the Open, and I was pleased with how that went. I was disappointed that it was a headwind because I knew that lighter riders benefit from a tailwind. I came fifth and it was disappointing. It was really the next year when I realised how much quicker a time trial bike is into a headwind. This is hard to quantify but it's the perception that I have. Maybe it's a perception that I want to have because of Long Hill. In 2012 I did the Cat and Fiddle into a headwind and I was on a time trial bike, and Gunnar, for some reason, was on his road bike. I beat him by more than a minute. It was a big gap. It was always a sore point because I felt my preparations were good but I made the wrong choice. For hill climbs it's all about choosing your equipment. That's part of the sport, but you can't help but think, "If only I'd used a TT bike, maybe it could have been different, maybe that was my best chance to win." It was an opportunity to win or at least get a medal, but perhaps I made the wrong choice. I felt like I missed out.'

Hindsight is a wonderful thing. In the end, the pocket sized climber, Gunnar Gronlund, a 57-kilogram Swede riding in the colours of RST Trigon, edged out Richard Handley, with the irrepressible Matt Clinton completing the podium.

Time marches on and there is never any guarantee that the climb will be on a similar profile again anytime soon; it seemed as though Pettinger's best chance to win had slipped away. There was no chance of a win the following year on the Rake, even with the most optimistic of outlooks. Pettinger researched things thoroughly and spoke to Jim Henderson in his quest to turn in a good ride. He even considered going fixed, but Henderson's advice counselled against it. In training he was going well; turning in a 2'-35" with a tailwind.

The morning of the race was sullen and overcast. It gave way to steady sheets of horizontal rain and a headwind. In my own amateurish and shoddy preparations I opted for a 57" gear for a couple of slightly wrong reasons. Apparently it was what Jeff Wright rode. I always forget that I'm not actually Jeff Wright and seem to feel that I can push the same gear, neglecting the slight difference between club rider and Olympian. I also stuck with the 17 teeth on the back because, although I had an 18, it would have meant getting the chainwhip out. For this reason I left it as it was. I came to regret this decision. I even spoke to Matt Clinton beforehand; he'd geared down to something much smaller. I still thought I'd be alright on a 57".

I wasn't the only one having difficulty though. Pettinger had Henderson's words of wisdom rattling around in his brain, no doubt competing for space with a mantra: 'I remembered this piece of advice – "Be strict, don't change down". I set off really fast, got to the steep bit, changed down once, and before I knew it I was treading treacle, into the headwind, cold and wet, and I was doing such low cadence because I've got this mental idea not to change down, but also it's difficult to change down when you're on a 25%. I remember the commentator saying, "And here comes Pettinger and… he's overgeared!" And eventually on the steepest bit, 25%, I had to change down, because otherwise I was going to fall off the bike. And I was exhausted at the end, that buzz from going into the red, but it wasn't quite the intensity that I've had before, so I knew I was a few seconds off my best and I couldn't believe it: I'd messed up the gears. A specialist hillclimber, how embarrassing is that?' It's no doubt reassuring to know that if you do mess up in a National Championship event, Peter Graham will be sure to let you and every one else know.

The Rake is a noisy climb: there is no rhythmic quality; unkempt changes in gradient and savagery rule the day. Pettinger's failings on the Rake were framed and ameliorated by the knowledge that the following year the event was back on a long and difficult climb – The Stang in Teesdale, one tailor-made for emaciated Buddhists. 'It sounded perfect. At last a climb where at least I had no excuses about the wrong type of hill. A tough challenge, 18% at the bottom, two miles long, it wasn't going to be straightforward and I'd have preferred the Horseshoe Pass or Burrington. But I also felt that it was one of my strongest chances.'

Once the Rake was done, it was as though the genuine preparation for the following year could start, free from the desire to do as well as possible in an event where it wasn't possible to do well. He took a day off, then on the Tuesday did a 60-mile training ride, following it up with 1,250 miles in November and then 1,000 miles a month until February.

A fortuitous conversation at a time trial near High Wycombe was the beginning of the end for the long years of idiosyncratic training. It began at the Chris Hart Memorial '10' on June 17th. Chris Hart was the District secretary and instrumental in developing new courses and supporting cycling in the region; he was also a close friend of Gordon Wright, who was presenting the prizes. Wright was instrumental in Dangerfield's dominance of the UK time trial scene, and he is also known as the dark alchemist responsible for fine-tuning the revolting 'pyramid interval'.*

Gordon Wright was generous in his assessment of Pettinger's chance of success ('It was his to lose') and offered some informal guidance on how to ensure he won. Pettinger shared his plans for the season with the cycling svengali. Things were shaping up nicely and he had all kinds of irons in all kinds of fires. There were big plans to ride a first 12-hour time trial. He was also booting around a grandiose idea to beat the world record for the most vertical metres climbed in 24 hours. And at some point in October he hoped to do well in the National. Wright's initial responses seemed to stem from the prosaic coaching manual known as 'common sense':

1.   It's probably not a good idea to try and do a 12-hour time trial in the same season that you're aiming for a National title in an 8-minute event.

2.   You should have an unrelenting focus on the event you are aiming to win above all others, to the exclusion of all other goals. Don't compromise.

3.   You must ride the course many times beforehand. Not just the morning before, but in the weeks leading up to it.

If this all sounds a bit wayward, it's probably worth looking at the way Tejvan Pettinger approached previous target events:

---

* A highly structured form of training alternating between extremely hard efforts and short periods of recovery – 'not recommended for older cyclists without a 'complete medical check', according to the Association of British Cycling Coaches.

1. In 2009 he turned up late.
2. In 2010 on Dover's he didn't know where the finish was.
3. In 2011 on Long Hill he rode the wrong bicycle.
4. In 2012, in the race proper, he tried something completely different for the first time.

And he wears funny socks. Wright's words had a galvanising effect. Everything else was shelved. Pettinger headed up North two weeks before to assault the climb in race conditions. Out went the the old-school (nay, purist) approach to training of 'find some hills and ride up them as fast as you can, repeat', to be replaced by the dark science of the pyramid interval throughout the season. Six minute threshold hill climbs were jettisoned in favour of repetitive sets of savagery.

However, any focus on the proven benefits of training, the narrative of success and failure, the balance between work and cycling, the choices of equipment, the variables of bike racing, is to ignore the single most important aspect of Tejvan Pettinger's life: the spiritual existence. For many of us cycling provides a form of spiritual existence. I ascribe to this view; I bore people with my endless descriptions of the liminality of bike riding, how ascending through the clouds on a mountain peak is a sublime and irreducible experience that transcends the complexities of life. I go cycling religiously on a Sunday morning. I've done it in this book and doubtless I'll do it again tomorrow: prattle on to some unsuspecting non-bike rider about how there comes a point where those trappings of life and existence and work dissipate. You gradually become divested of material elements and enter a space away from the concrete reality of life itself. At which point the hapless victim on the other side of the conversation looks at me like I'm doorstepping him with a copy of *The Watchtower* and the disarming smile of the true, possessed believer.

That level of spirituality is completely in tune with the construction of myth in the world of cycling, the heroism and elevation of feats and the names of the sanctified riders like Hippolyte Aucouturier, Henri Desgranges, Sean Kelly. It's consuming. I don't doubt that Tejvan Pettinger is a devotee and disciple of the sport; we spoke in hushed and reverent tones of the mythic achievements of Frank Colden and the sacrifices needed in his season of transcendent form.* I find cycling to be a transcendent experience; I don't frame it in a meta-narrative of a specific something, but I understand it in my frame of reference which is atheistic. And yet, there is another layer of spirituality to Pettinger.

He doesn't hide it; it's emblazoned across the jersey of the 'club' he rides for, Sri Chinmoy CC:

'The spiritual life has to come first, but fortunately cycling is very complimentary. I never race Wednesday evenings because of meditation. I could never be a professional, couldn't live and work in a team. I'd have to be an amateur doing my only thing. I'm not the kind of person who needs to win for my self-esteem. I just enjoy cycling and I enjoy cycling hard. The motivation to try to win the Championship – it's more than an ego thing, it's an opportunity to achieve something; there is an inner element to it. Sri Chinmoy's philosophy is that a big thing is self-transcendence, trying to go beyond your limits, spiritually, mentally, physically. Trying to go faster is part of spirituality, of meditation. If you can be happy, in a good consciousness, you can bring a lot of energy to the fore. When you're about to race it can be easy to

---

* Frank Colden was an average time triallist in the early 1960s who set out to improve by creating a training regime forged in the devil's own smithy. It consisted of 400 miles per week, with anything up to 80 miles done after work on a regular basis. He got up ridiculously early and went to bed extremely late. He didn't tell a soul what he was doing, not even his club mates. He also had a full-time job. By the time spring came round he had fairly good legs. He won the blue riband event, the '25', with a competition record, slashing two minutes from the existing time. He went on to win the National '100' with a new competition record, four minutes inside Ray Booty's time. He then set a new competition record for the '50' with 1:52:38.

be nervous or think about your competitors. That's an important challenge: to be in a better consciousness.'

I suddenly feel slightly silly for getting angry about the weather conditions (amongst other things), when it's been glorious for two weeks prior, then on the Sunday it's abysmal, that unchannelled frustration at being unable to control the weather. I should be more zen. I also suspect that much of what Pettinger is on about is echoed and analogous to the work of people like Steve Peters, with his modish ideas of the Chimp Paradox. And I wonder if it's really that different; it's just the codification of the experience, but placed in a different frame. We're talking about the same experiences, but with different vocabulary; and I limit my lived experience to express things relating to cycling, within the confines of cycling. I don't see it as linked to something outside of myself, whereas for Pettinger, it's part of the whole thing.

'Often when I'm doing a race,' he says, 'I'm trying to keep my mind quiet and not think. To help that I repeat a mantra, like "supreme". It's just a mantra I use in meditation. I don't want any thoughts going through my mind, only the mantra, inwardly. The best experience is when you're in the zone, you've not got that "did I go off too hard, too early, the spectator's looking at me funny". You're absorbed in the effort. That's the real buzz of hill climbs: you can get into this state which you very rarely get into; you're so beyond the limit, you're way beyond your ordinary experience and it has some small parallels to meditation, because in meditation you're trying to get away from your mind and the thought, everyday world, and here you're doing it in a very real way because you're pushing yourself so much. And it's torture physically, but you get some kind of joy from it, and you look back and you think, "Wow, that was a real three minutes. I really lived in that three minutes. I don't quite know what went on but I was on the edge and experiencing something different." I wouldn't say it's addictive, but it's an experience I like to have and it's hard to get there.'

I don't have Buddhism or Sri Chinmoy. All I have is cycling, the landscape and my thoughts. It means I'm always fighting the atheist's battle against the passing of time and mortality, decrepitude and raging against the dying of the light: not racing means not racing.

It's different for Pettinger:

'I believe we have thousands of incarnations. In this incarnation I'm doing exactly what I wanted to do. In my twenties the spiritual life was very important for me and if I'd got into professional cycling it would have been a missed opportunity. I'm not sure whether I want to be a pro-cyclist in a future life but I might be. But if I was a pro-cyclist I would have been more unhappy. It's a lot of pressure; it's all-consuming; it leaves little for other aspects of life. I'd have had to compromise lots on other things, and I don't have that motivation. I don't particularly want to ride the Tour and race 10,000 kilometres a year. Being an amateur time triallist and hill climber is perfect: I can get the joy from cycling and pushing myself a lot, but it's not the only thing in my life, so there is an element of balance. I definitely see it as a possibility that in another lifetime I will be a professional cyclist, rather than an amateur. I am used to thinking about it and forget other people don't share that belief system.'

And our paths diverge, from my atheism, to the endless reincarnation and immortality of Pettinger, before we suddenly come back on course, to the shared bit of the Venn Diagram; about spirituality and cycling. 'Cycling springs from different beliefs and life experiences I have. There are 180 people on the start line, but so many different ways people got there. We're all doing a cycle race, but what's going on behind it is very different. On the outer plane, some are roadmen, some are testers, but there's different motivation. In one sense it doesn't matter, but it is interesting. It is a slightly quirky thing, maybe the attraction of the National Championship.'

And so to the Stang, with the power of meditation. On the day we weren't that far apart on the start sheet. I'd been set off near the end, unusually, in a horrible sandwich between one of the Rapha Condor riders and Pete Tadros. I was warming up on the road. I use the phrase lightly. It was the worst day I've experienced for a hill climb and a prelude to the violent rain and wind of winter. An elemental and furious tailwind hurtled up the climb. A headwind of the same force might well have led to a cancellation. Riders were huddled under tailgates of cars, helpers clutching inverted brollies trying to offer protection from the rain. I rode to the start and back a few times and heard a strangled sound of rubber on plastic, a squeaking and abrasion; the sound of wheels slipping on rollers. There was doubt beforehand about Pettinger's chances; the armchair critics cited previous failures as the reason. It's easy for me to say this now, but I always thought he would win. It just seemed like the right climb, day, year and even conditions. I had hopes that I might achieve a top twenty finish, but it was not to be. I rode like a bag of spanners. I didn't cope well with the wind, rain and cold. I had no sense of how I was going, or what I was likely to achieve, or what a good time might be, or how to ride the complex and technical course, with a steep first section, then a super-fast, nay frightening in the tailwind, descent, before a long climb up to the finish.

In marked contrast, Pettinger was serene: 'I'd gone beyond trying to think about the result because that gets you in the tangle, I just wanted to get to the top and know I'd done a good ride. The funny thing is I didn't mind it raining. At the start I felt it was really quite beautiful in its own way. It felt good.'

Pettinger ended up racing with a lop-sided number. This isn't the first time I've seen this. Even the mighty Aero-King,

Michael Hutchinson, had a wonky pinned number when setting the 10-mile competition record. Pettinger's number came to be wonky through a comedy of errors. The National events require extra numbers, one on each arm. This means extra pins, lots of pins, and pinning your number is all about timing. It's more complicated than people realise. You can't do the arm numbers by yourself. You can do the back one if you're practised. The only thing that gets in the way of an otherwise serene progress towards the start of the race is the unfortunate need to go to the toilet. Racing makes you nervous, being nervous makes you want to pee. There's also the unspoken understanding that shedding any weight means faster times, or as a friend once memorably put it before disappearing into the toilet for half an hour on a trip to Provence, 'I don't want to be riding up Ventoux with half a foot of cable in the pipe.' On such scatological matters are races won and lost.

On the way back from the pub toilet, the favourite stopped to get help to repin the various fluorescent numbers. An army of helpers descended, each one keen to aid and assist. Confusion reigned; a kindly lady began taking the numbers off, assuming he had finished. As soon as one pin was fastened tight, another elsewhere was swiftly removed. It was 'a slight drama'. All the while it was raining thick shifting sheets of real rain on the isolated slopes of the Stang. The top of the climb was a terrible place to be: the CTT cameraman struggled manfully in the wind and rain; hardy onlookers crested the climb, looking traumatised by the conditions. It was a classic race where the experience seemed harder and somehow more savage for the spectators; it was a proper day for the National Hill Climb. On the climb and during the race, old habits die hard. Several competitors found themselves adhering to the left-hand side, despite the closed road; it's hard to undo the accumulated habits of safe riding in a moment of competition.

The Rapha Condor team had turned out *en masse*, with Hugh Carthy riding well, alongside many people's favourite, Richard Handley, who had been cresting the climbs of the Tour of Britain a week or so beforehand with Nairo Quintana and finishing a creditable sixteenth. Mike Cuming, winner of the Tour of Korea, rounded out a crack outfit, whilst James Gullen had been putting all-comers to the sword in the colours of the Hope Factory team and seemed to have timed his form to perfection. In amongst them all lurked Matt Clinton, eager to engrave his name onto the trophy for a second time. Cuming may have been hampered slightly by a post-season interrail splurge around Europe. Jack Pullar also expressed fatigue after a long season as the cause of a slower time; in reality, there were few that picked him for the longer climb, despite his success over Gullen on Jubilee Tower. If anything gives the hill climb specialists the edge, it's the ability and determination to arrive in form on the last Sunday in October, often free of the idea that it's an extra bit to an already finished season. It is the target event.

After his ride Pettinger couldn't quite get to the results board; the small public house was packed to the gills, the windows steamed up with the exhausted exhalations of 180 hill climbers and their assorted supporters. He didn't need to see it; the upswell of feeling in the room was directed toward the new champion, who had bested Gullen by two seconds with a 7'-57.7". Rounding out the podium was Matt Clinton, a further ten seconds back. It's a small margin to win by, but it's the win that counts.

'It's a really great experience to win. I've won so many Opens and broken so many course records, it would have been a shame for the sport for me not to win. It struck me when I did Huddersfield and I saw all the names on the trophy, all National Champions.* Adding my name to the list was nice. People would be seeing my name on all these trophies and wondering why I hadn't won it. I was happy because I'd been trying for a long time and knew I had the capacity to win. If

---

* The Granville Sydney Memorial Trophy for the Huddersfield Star Wheelers event on Jackson Bridge.

things had been different I might have won before. I can forget about 2011 and the wrong bike. It's a surprisingly nice feeling.'

And Tejvan Pettinger's comments echoed those of Vic Clark, some 59 years previously: 'I was glad for Harold because there was nobody who could ride hills like him. It wouldn't have been right for his name not to have been on that trophy.'

And in a way, he's right. It wouldn't have seemed right if he hadn't won it: he's one of the pre-eminent riders of this era; he has beaten all of the contenders over the long stuff. He may lack the all-round capacity to excel at the shorter stuff, but over the longer, steeper climbs, he's imperious. His list of favourite climbs gives the game away, they're all over four minutes. As a late developer, and now a relatively old champion at 36, it's hard to avoid wondering what comes next. 'I'm definitely at that age when the physical side starts to slowly deteriorate, but because I started late, I've got a lot of enthusiasm for it and I can see myself competing, like Pete Tadros, trying to transcend age. I like Open hill climbs. Just being National Champion once changes a lot of things: winning it once would have been enough, but once you've got it once it would be a shame not to win it again, and it would also be nice to be able to win it on a hill which wasn't perfect for me.'

In 2014 the race returned to Pea Royd Lane, providing just such an opportunity.

Clinton finally put the fixed weapon in the cupboard and opted for the very new Trek Emonda, as ridden by the reigning champion, Pettinger. Both had managed to get their bike weight down to around 5.2 kilos. Any lingering arguments that fixed is lighter had been spectacularly quashed. The year's new contender was the Welshman, Dan Evans. He is one of those slightly annoying riders who seems capable of almost anything – winning elite level cross-country mountain bike races, smashing a peloton to pieces in a divisional road championship, or clinging on with the professionals in the Eddie Soens.

Evans had undergone a fairly rapid transition from weighty powerman, bullying his way up Dover's in 27th place (I beat him), into a svelte hill climbing machine, coming sixth on the Stang. In 2014 he improved significantly (losing four kilograms in weight) and began scalping the quicks on their favourite courses. He beat Pettinger on Jackson Bridge, then again on the Horseshoe Pass, with a remarkable course record. The time of 8'-52" is an eye-opening achievement, streets ahead of anyone else who has ridden the climb. He was at least an outside bet for the title on Pea Royd lane, with the former winner last time out, Dan Fleeman, giving him the nod in the build-up. He rode it on power and paced it perfectly, accelerating smoothly over the upper slopes, past the motorway bridge, to win by 2.3 seconds from Clinton.

Pettinger was back in fourth, but it was a creditable performance from the specialist: 'I thought I rode a good race; it was all a bit of a blur really. This distance isn't really my forte and I think I did as well as I could. I couldn't have won it against the guys who finished above me with their times.'*

Matt Clinton was left contemplating an eighth medal in eight years. I don't know if he's annoyed or happy. I think the latter. If he hadn't won in 2008 I suspect he'd be really annoyed. As it is, he's the most consistent rider in the history of the event. He's also an impressive rider regardless of the discipline, finishing third in the National Time Trial Championship in 2012 and winning the Isle of Man end-to-end mountain bike race. 'It comes as a shock each year when I medal. The past few years I haven't gone as well into the build-up, but always manage to step up on the day. It was tough on that climb and I had to give myself a talking to on a couple of occasions to keep going. In the end it was worth it.'**

---

* http://www.cyclingweekly.co.uk/news/latest-news/dan-evans-wins-hill-climb-national-championship-141321

** www.velouk.net/2014/10/28/news-8th-medal-clinton/

In fact you'd have to go back to 2004 to find the last time he finished below sixth. That's over a ten year period, or eleven championships. It's quite a record. Outside of the medals, Paul Brierley also can stake a claim to being Mr Consistent, solely by dint of riding the past 29 championships in a row. Brierley's feat deserves at least 29 medals.

Whilst Pettinger didn't manage to win on the shorter climb there were other plans. At one point he was looking to attempt the world record for the most metres climbed in 24 hours and casting round for a suitable hill. I expect he was emailing everyone – Sam Clark at Buxton, Jim Henderson, anyone who might be similarly deranged and have made a habit of seeking out hills and riding them. It requires a particular type of hill; the one that he was asking me about was Draycott Steep, in the Mendips. I laughed out loud. Draycott Steep is a climb that destroys perfectly decent cyclists. The idea of going up it repeatedly in a twenty four hour period is antithetical to Orpheus' descent into the Underworld, but with the same outcome: misery, pain, death. I counselled against it. The current record is 21,000 metres, which equates to nineteen ascents of Alpe D'Huez.

'Every now and then it captures my imagination completely, it's like a mania. On Burrington Combe you'd have to go up and down in nine minutes for 24 hours. If you did it on the Rake you'd have to do it 225 times in 24 hours, in about 6'-24" up and down – 4 minutes up; 2'-24" down.'

And it strikes me suddenly, and with finality. Hill climbers are utterly bonkers.

Coda

'To say that the race is the metaphor for life is to miss the point. The race is everything. It obliterates whatever isn't racing. Life is the metaphor for the race.' *

The National Hill Climb is an event which has seen beginnings and endings. It has borne witness to career-starting rides by Brian Robinson, Malcolm Elliott, Chris Boardman, Paul Curran, Alec Dowsett, Nicole Cooke, Luke Rowe, Adam Blythe and Russell Downing. It's been the curtain closer for Rob Hayles on Long Hill and David Millar at the Bec. For Millar and Hayles it represented an unbroken link back to club life and their origins in the sport, providing memories of the avuncular figures who got them started, and offering the chance to close the circle by revisiting the place where it began – a CTT event with one minute intervals. It also serves to highlight the extent to which cycling in the UK has changed.

Millar explains this change: 'The irony is I no longer fit in. The team has become an identity for a rider; before, a rider would transcend the team. It's become robotic. I liked the dysfunctionality, the cult-ness, the randomness.'**

He's right and wrong at the same time. Before the Rake in 2012 I was talking with Carl Helliwell, a member (along with

---

* Tim Krabbe, *The Rider*

** http://www.theguardian.com/sport/2014/oct/10/david-millar-cycling

Ian Stott) of the all-conquering Blackburn CTC team, and we mused on how many 'teams' appeared on the startsheet, linked to shops or small businesses, divorced from time and space, whereas cycling clubs have a clear identity, rooted in geography and the past, which last far longer than the individual cyclist or the team. As a member of Bristol South Cycling Club I know the club emerged from the working class leisure movement in the 1890s. It's a key part of Bristol's identity, regardless of cycling, and I'm proud both to be a member and to know that in years to come, when my ashes are shaken out to the ringing of a cowbell on Burrington Combe, the club will continue. I'd venture to suggest that it's this paradigm that Millar is referring to in the context of amateur racing.

The team at a professional level has become the Borg, a remorseless and controlling entity with a singular goal, sacrificing the whims of individual riders in the pursuit of victory.* It's borne of the obsessive focus on medals that led to no women being sent to Pontferrada in 2014 for the individual time trial. The embracing and grassroots stature of the cycling club has been marginalised by a press that buys into the idea of success and the materialism of cycling, in league with a bike industry that wants to sell an £11,000 bike and entries into a sportif series at £50 a pop; a world where every amateur rider has a power meter and waxes more lyrical about a power PB or Strava KOM than about any achievement in a race on the road.

There has also been a gradual change in the role and significance of cycling clubs to the sport in the UK, despite the current bike boom. People drift into the sport but bypass clubs, not knowing the depth and strength of the community and the cohesiveness that welds the members together. Who needs a cycling club when you can join the ever-growing, pulsating virtual world, uploading each ride to Strava and participating vicariously in an online community? The outdoors has become

---

* 'Borg' – a "Star Trek" species similar to an insect hive; perfection is the shared and only ideal, achieved through violent and forced technological and human assimilation.

digitalised and commodified, rides are real only if they have been rendered in virtual form and uploaded to the high score table. It's part of the gamification of cycling and the emergence of bragging rights beyond sprinting for lampposts or the café stop, where the key feature of the ride becomes the segment, not the lived experience.

The National Championship Hill Climb seems somehow at odds with all of these things. It's even at odds with technology, to a degree. It's an anachronism, and a vital one. It's a reminder that not everything needs to be taken for granted, and that sometimes the best ideas are the simplest ones: ride uphill until your eyeballs explode and the fastest time wins.

The National Championship Hill Climb is the apotheosis of amateur cycling. The season is compressed together into three, four or five minutes of mania, after which there is no more racing. There is no steady drift in form away from a 'target' event; it is the end. Only the darkness of winter follows. It is surely no surprise that the end of British Summer Time occurs on the same day. The hill climb sits in a space between amateur and professional sport, divested of outside worries, driven by a community of people giving freely of their time and removed from materialism.

There is strength in the maxim from *The Rider*. When I'm riding uphill I go through a range of experiences, as though I'm climbing up through the topography mentally, as well as physically. Hill climbs are a very heightened and brutal form of that experience. It is intense and fragmentary, existing in the momentary gaps between time itself. During the race time is everything, defined by the battle for vital seconds in a race against gravity and human frailty. And yet, wider notions of time, of lived time, people, relationships and work become silenced; vision becomes blurred and thoughts narrowed; there is only the climb. It is a distillation of all that is good about life itself. The attraction of wearing a cotton racing cap, tilted backwards, is clear.

In researching the book I was able to meet an amazing array of people. The contrast between the superhuman powers exhibited by the riders then, in their prime and ripping up Winnats Pass, and their fragility now, was a tough one. Some of them touched upon it, but to acknowledge frailty is to acknowledge mortality. Eric Wilson, four times National Champion, living in the lee of the Rake, spoke with melancholy:

> 'We're going back 60 years and it's a long time. And now I've got to come to terms with the gradual deterioration, as you get older. There's nothing you can do about it at all. I think people are very fortunate, people that I used to ride with, that are still active. I cannot go anywhere without having to fight. The lads kept having to wait for me at the top of the hills. It was not a question of not trying hard enough – that doesn't come into it – you're just not capable of it.'

You will get old, you will wear the bottom of your trousers rolled, you will ride slower uphill than you used to, these things are inevitable. But within that time frame and arc of existence, a hill climb is one of those rare things that allows you to state unambiguously: 'That was a real three minutes; I really lived in that three minutes. I was on the edge and experiencing something different.'

The paradox is that such a savage and unkempt experience can be so life-affirming.

Appendices - The Results

The National Hill Climb Championship

Year	Hill	Gold
1944	Brasted Hill Kent	F. H. Worthen, Manchester Clarion C & AC, 3'-12.8"
1945	Peaslows Hill Chapel-en-le-Frith	R. J. Maitland, Solihull CC, 3'-0.4"
1946	Holly Lane Derbyshire	V. Clark, Manchester Clarion C & AC, 3'-35.6"
1947	Winnats Pass Castleton	V. Clark, Coventry CC, 3'-23.8"
1948	Lansdowne Lane Weston, Bath	V. Clark, Coventry CC, 3'-42.6"
1949	Winnats Pass Castleton	R. J. Maitland, Concorde R CC, 3'-50.8"
1950	Barber's Hill Llangollen	R. Stringwell, Bramley Wheelers 4'-33.4"
1951	Saintbury Gloucestershire	R. Stringwell, Bramley Wheelers, 6'-26"
1952	Mow Cop Staffordshire	B. Robinson, Huddersfield RC 3'-41.8"
1953	Winnats Pass Castleton	R. Keighley, Shipley RC, 3'-43"
1954	Holme Moss West Yorkshire	W. L. Ingman, Norwood Paragon CC, 6'-46.2"
1955	Holly Lane Derbyshire	E. Wilson, Rossendale RC, 3'-12"
1956	Saintbury Hill Gloucestershire	W. L. Ingman, Norwood Paragon CC, 6'-13.8"
1957	Winnats Pass Castleton	E. Wilson, Rossendale RC, 3'-56.8"
1958	Monks Lane Bathford	P. J. Graham, West Pennine RC, 2'-46.2"
1959	Winnats Pass Castleton	G. Rhodes, Huddersfield RC, 3'-49.2"

Men's Results - 1944 – 2014

Silver	Bronze
V. Clark, Manchester Clarion C & AC	V. Taylor, Manchester Clarion C & AC
V. Taylor, Manchester Clarion C & AC, 3'-1.2"	J. D. Spink, West Bradford CC, 3'-3.4"
R. J. Maitland, Solihull CC 3'-38.4"	L. H. Dodd, Sheffield Phoenix CC, 3'-41.4"
R. J. Maitland, Solihull CC 3'-31"	F. H. Worthen, Manchester Clarion C & AC, 3'-35
R. Woore, Manchester Clarion C & AC, 3'-47.6"	B.J. King, Coventry CC 3'-48.4"
W. E. Penvose, Huddersfield ER 3'-53"	V. Clark, Coventry CC, 3'-53.8"
R. J. Maitland, Concorde RCC, 4'-35.2"	B. Robinson, Huddersfield RC, 4'-39"
B. Robinson, Huddersfield RC, 6'-30.2"	R. Procter, Army CU, 6'-43.4"
J. Pentecost, 3'-43.8"	R. Keighley, Shipley RC, 3'44.4"
R. Stringwell, Bramley Wheelers, 3'-48.8"	P. S. Boyd, Birkenhead CC,
E. Wilson, Rossendale RC, 6'-47.8"	B. Haskell, Huddersfield RC, 6'-52.8"
R. Keighley, Shipley RC, 3'-15"	A. Pursey, Medway RC 3'-17"
E. Wilson, Rossendale RC, 6'-17.4"	W. Bradley, Southport RCC, 6'-25.8"
A. Pursey, Medway RC, 3'-59"	W. Holmes, Hull Thursday RC, 4'-0.8"
E. Wilson, Rossendale RC, 2'-45.4"	W. Holmes, Hull Thursday RC, 2'-51.8"
R. Foster, Birdwell Wheelers, 3'-50.4"	P. J. Graham, West Pennine RC, 3'-55.6"

Year	Hill	Gold
1960	Saintbury Gloucestershire	E. Wilson, Rossendale RC 6'-21.2"
1961	Yorks Hill Kent	P. J. Graham, West Pennine RC 1'-56.2"
1962	Nick O' Pendle Sabden	P. J. Graham, West Pennine RC 4'-08"
1963	Winnats Pass Castleton	G. Sydney, Huddersfield Star Wheelers, 3'-18"
1964	Peaslows Hill Chapel-en-le-Frith	E. Wilson, Rossendale RC 4'-49.6"
1965	Dover's Hill Gloucestershire	G. Sydney, Huddersfield Star Wheelers, 4'-00"
1966	Winnats Pass Castleton	P. D. Greenhalgh, Nottingham Phoenix, 3'-11.2"
1967	Winnats Pass Castleton	P. Wildsmith, East Bradford CC, 3'-43.6"
1968	Dover's Hill Gloucestershire	P. Gannon, Leeds St. Christopher's CCC, 3'-59.6"
1969	Llywel Brecknockshire	G. Sydney, Huddersfield Star Wheelers, 3'-19.8"
1970	Nick O' Pendle Sabden	G. Sydney, Huddersfield Star Wheelers, 3'-59.6"
1971	Horseshoe Pass Llangollen	J. Clewarth, Kirkby CC 9'-17.8"
1972	Winnats Pass Castleton	G. Sydney, Huddersfield Star Wheelers. 3'-23.0"
1973	Dover's Hill Gloucestershire	G. Sydney, Huddersfield Star Wheelers, 3'-47.0"
1974	Holme Moss West Yorkshire	J. Waugh, Tyne RC 10'-41.2"
1975	Nick O' Pendle Sabden	G. Armitage, Oldham Century 3'-49.5"
1976	Horseshoe Pass Llangollen	J. Waugh, G.S. Strada-Lutz 9'-12.0"

Silver	Bronze
P. J. Graham, West Pennine RC 6'-23.6"	R. Foster, Birdwell Wheelers 6'-28.4"
R. Foster, Birdwell Wheelers 1'-56.4"	D. A. Patten, Tunbridhe Wheelers CC, 2'-3.4"
R. Foster, Birdwell Wheelers 4'-8.2"	D. Millar, Southport RCC 4'-8.4"
P. J. Graham, West Pennine RC 3'-22.2"	R. Foster, Birdwell Wheelers 3'-23.6"
E. Lightfoot, Merlin RC 4'-53.2"	G. Sydney, Huddersfield Star Wheelers, 4'-59.2"
P. J. Graham, Bury Clarion 4'-6.8" (tie)	R. Martin, Barrow Central Wheelers 4'-6.8"
P. Wildsmith, East Bradford CC 3'-22.0"	G. Sydney, Huddersfield Star Wheelers, 3'-22.6"
G. Clements, Wolverhampton RCC 3'-53"	Granville/Graham Sydney, Huddersfield Star Wh. 3'-54" (tie)
P. Wildsmith, East Bradford CC 4'-0.2"	G. Sydney, Huddersfield Star Wheelers, 4'-5.4"
C. Kearley, East Bradford CC 3'-22.2" (tie for 2nd)	R. Wilson, Birdwell Wheelers 3'-22.2" (tie for 2nd)
R. Wilson, Birdwell Wheelers 4'-5.4"	A. Gornall, Clayton Velo 4'-10.4"
D. Lloyd, Kirkby CC 9'-18.4"	W. Moore, Merseyside Wheelers 9'-35.8"
J. Clewarth, Kirkby CC 3'-27.8"	P. Wildsmith, East Bradford CC 3'-46.0"
J. Kershaw, Oldham Century 3'-49.6"	P. Wildsmith, East Bradford CC 3'-55.0"
C. Berry, Birdwell Wheelers 10'-45.8"	R. Martin, Kent Valley RC 10'-53.0"
P. Carbutt, Saracen RC 3'-50.4"	J. Waugh, Tyne RC 3'-51.8"
D. Pitman, Somerset RC 9'-14.6"	S. Johnson, Birkenhead NECC 9'-24.4"

Year	Hill	Gold
1977	Winnats Pass Castleton	J. Parker, Southport RC 3'-22.6"
1978	Dover's Hill Gloucestershire	G. Armitage, Oldham Century 3'-40.0"
1979	Haytor Vale Devon	J. Williams, G.S. Strada-Lutz 12'-44.6"
1980	Nick O'Pendle Sabden	M. Elliott, Rutland CC 3'-34.4"
1981	Horseshoe Pass Llangollen	J. Williams, Manchester Wheelers-Trumanns Steel, 9'-17.0"
1982	Dover's Hill Gloucestershire	J. Williams, Manchester Wheelers-Trumanns Steel, 3'-36.2"
1983	Weston Hill Bath	D. Webster, Manchester Wheelers-Trumanns Steel, 2'-50.4"
1984	Stanhope County Durham	D. Webster, Manchester Wheelers-Trumanns Steel, 9'-8.8"
1985	Challacombe Hill Devon	D. Webster, Manchester Wheelers-Trumanns Steel, 4'-22.4"
1986	Riber Hill Matlock	D. Webster, Manchester Wheelers-Trumanns Steel, 4'-48.8"
1987	Rosedale Chimney North Yorkshire Moors	P. Curran, Manchester Wheelers-Trumanns Steel, 5'-22.8"
1988	Nick O'Pendle Sabden	C. Boardman, Manchester Wheelers-Trumanns Steel, 3'-29.2"
1989	The Burway Church Stretton	C. Boardman, Manchester Wheelers-Trumanns Steel, 5'-01.8"
1990	Widecombe-in-the-Moor, Devon	C. Boardman, Manchester Wheelers-Trumanns Steel, 4'-10"
1991	Park Rash Kettlewell	C. Boardman, Manchester Wheelers-Trumanns Steel, 6'-47"
1992	St John's Chapel County Durham	S. Dangerfield, Leo RC-Shorter Rochford, 8'-44.9"
1993	Newlands Pass Cumbria	S. Dangerfield, Leo RC-Shorter Rochford, 6'-12.2"

Silver	Bronze
G. Armitage, Oldham Century 3'-23.0"	L. Moore, Port Sunlight Wheelers 3'-30.4"
C. Miller, Clayton Velo 3'-46.8"	J. Parker, G.S. Strada-Lutz 3'-48.9"
D. Pitman, Somerset RC 13'-4.0"	G. Armitage, Manchester Wheelers 13'-6.4"
J. Williams, Manchester Wheelers-Trumanns Steel, 3'-34.6"	G. Armitage, Manchester Wheelers-Trumanns Steel, 3'36.6"
M. Elliott, Rutland CC 9'-27.4"	C. Gough, Liverpool Century RC 9'-32.6"
K. Reynolds, G.S. Strada 3'-52.2"	D. Jarvis, Chesterfield Coureurs 3'-32.6"
M. Noble, Team Zoyland 2'-55.0"	P. Mason, San Fairy Ann CC 2'-57.2"
S. Marchant, South Eastern RC 9'-28.8"	K. Smith, Clayton Velo 9'-32.4"
S. Marchant, '34 Nomads 4'-27.8"	K. Smith, Clayton Velo 4'-28.6"
S. Marchant, '34 Nomads 4'-55.0"	C. Walker, Paragon RT 4'-56.4"
C.Boardman, Manchester Wheelers Trumanns Steel, 5'-23.0"	S. Marchant, '34 Nomads 5'-31.2"
P. Sheard, Bradford Wheelers 3'-43.0"	P. Curran, Manchester Wheelers - Trumanns Steel, 3'-43.6"
S. O'Brien, Manchester Wheelers -Trumanns Steel, 5'-13.1"	S. Marchant, CC Orpington 5'-19.0"
S. Marchant, South Eastern RC 4'-20"	S. Dangerfield, Wolverhampton Wheelers, 4'-28"
J. Wright, Tyne Velo 6'-59"	S. Dangerfield, Leo RC 7'-08"
J. Wright, Tyne Velo 9'-04.7"	P. Longbottom, G.S. Strada 9'-28.8"
J. Wright, North East RT 6'-16.0"	R. Reynolds-Jones, V.C. Bradford 6'-19.4"

Year	Hill	Gold
1994	Jackson Bridge West Yorkshire	J. Wright, North East RT- Hardisty Cycles, 3'-49.9"
1995	Ditchling Beacon East Sussex	S. Dangerfield, Leo RC - Shorter Rochford, 3'-45.2"
1996	Carlton Bank North Yorkshire Moors	S. Dangerfield, Parker International RT, 5'-39.6"
1997	Rowsley Bar Derbyshire	S. Dangerfield, Wheelbase CC 5'-12.4"
1998	Dover's Hill Gloucestershire	J. Henderson, Oxford University CC 3'-25.3"
1999	The Rake Ramsbottom	J. Henderson, Terry Wright Cycles - Raleigh R.T. 2'-22.1"
2000	Westclose Hill Rodney Stoke	J. Henderson, Terry Wright Cycles - Raleigh R.T. 5'-05"
2001	Y Bwlch Ruthin	J. Henderson, Southport C.C. 6'-45.2"
2002	Cat and Fiddle Cheshire	M. Lovatt, Compensation Group R.T. 19'-33.6"
2003	Halifax Lane Luddenden	J. Henderson, Southport C.C. 5'-19.2"
2004	Winter's Gibbet Northumberland	J. Dayus, Arctic-Shorter Rochford R.T., 6'-33.8"
2005	The Rake Ramsbottom	B. Greenwood, Recycling.co.uk, 2'-26.5"
2006	Peak Hill Sidmouth	J. Dobbin, Arctic-Shorter Rochford R.T., 4'-44.0"
2007	Cheddar Gorge Somerset	J. Dobbin, Arctic-Shorter Rochford R.T., 6'-51.5"
2008	Bank Road Matlock	M. Clinton, Mike Vaughan Cycles 2'-24.2"
2009	Pea Royd Lane Stocksbridge	D. Fleeman, Cervelo Test Team 3'-17.8"
2010	Dover's Hill Gloucestershire	D. Fleeman, Raleigh UCI 3'-41.1"

Silver	Bronze
S. Dangerfield, North Wirral Velo 3'-56.2"	R. Harris, Optimum Performance RT, 4'-03.4"
J. Wright, North East R.T. 3'-54.2"	C. Newton, North Wirral Velo-Kodak Prints, 4'-02.6"
S. Hulme, Team Freetown Pace 6'-01.4"	J. Henderson, Oxford University C.C., 6'-05.7"
J. Henderson, Oxford University C.C., 5'-19.2"	J. Wright, North East R.T. 5'-22.8"
J. Wright, Team Guru 3'-28.2"	G. Baker, Condor Cycles 3'-41.2"
J. Wright, Team Travelwise 2'-27.2"	R. Taylor, Chesterfield Coureurs 2'-33.9"
T. Anderson, Holme Valley Wheelers, 5'-11.9"	I. Stott, Blackburn & District CTC 5'-22.7"
T. Anderson, Holme Valley Wheelers, 6'-51.4"	C. Myhill, Chesterfield Coureurs 7'-14.7"
M. Hutchinson, Team MDT 20'-38.8"	I. Stott, Blackburn & District CTC 20'-58.5"
M. Lovatt, Life Repair CRT 5'-38.2"	D. Clarke, Team Endurasport 5'-38.9"
J. Dobbin, Arctic-Shorter Rochford R.T., 6'-35.8"	A. Coutts, Flanders-Afin.com 6'-41.1"
J. Henderson, Southport C.C. 2'-26.8"	D. Clarke, Rayon D'Argent 2'-31.9"
D. Clarke, Team Nippo KFS, 5'-07.3"	J. Dayus, Arctic-Shorter Rochford R.T., 5'-07.7"
D. Clarke, Blue Sky Cycles 6'-57.6"	M. Clinton, Mike Vaughan Cycles 7'-08.5"
W. Bell, Gemini BC 2'-25.2"	J. Henderson, Southport C.C. 2'-26.5"
M. Clinton, Mike Vaughan Cycles 3'-31.6"	J. Henderson, Southport C.C. 3'-39.4"
M. Clinton, Mike Vaughan Cycles 3'-47.7"	M. Smith, Team Corley 3'-55.3"

Year	Hill	Gold
2011	Long Hill Buxton	G. Gronlund, RST Racing Team, Trigon, 12'-49.0"
2012	The Rake Ramsbottom	J. Pullar, Wheelbase.co.uk MGD 2'-21.3"
2013	The Stang Langthwaite	T. Pettinger, Sri Chinmoy C.T. 7'-57.7"
2014	Pea Royd Lane Stocksbridge	D. Evans, Team Elite-Paul Bethell Electrical, 3'-24.2"

The National Hill Climb Championship

Year	Team
1944	Manchester Clarion C and AC (F. Worthen, V. Clark, V. Taylor)
1945	Solihull C.C. (R.J. Maitland, R.W. Bowes, T. Kempshall)
1946	Manchester Clarion C and AC (V. Clark, F. Worthen, D. Nield)
1947	Manchester Clarion C and AC (V. Clark, F. Worthen, D. Nield)
1948	Coventry CC (V. Clark, B.J. King, T. Lovell)
1949	Concorde RCC (R.J. Maitland, A.D. Newman, V.J. Martin)
1950	Concorde RCC (R.J. Maitland, A.D. Newman, A.S Jones)
1951	Huddersfield RC (B. Robinson, B. Haskell, T.M. Smith and G.L. Clark [tied for 15th])
1952	Huddersfield RC (B. Robinson, W.E. Penvose, B. Haskell)
1953	Bramley Wheelers (R. Franklin, E. Harrison, F. E. Buckley)
1954	Bramley Wheelers (R. Franklin, E. Harrison, F. E. Buckley
1955	Bramley Wheelers (V. F. Caswell, F.E. Buckley, R. Franklin)
1956	Bramley Wheelers (V. F. Caswell, F.E. Buckley, R. Franklin)
1957	Bramley Wheelers (N.A. Smith, F.E. Buckley, E.Harrison)
1958	Bramley Wheelers (N.A. Smith, F.E. Buckley, R. Franklin)
1959	Bramley Wheelers (N.A. Smith, V.F. Caswell, R. Franklin)
1960	Rossendale RC (E. Wilson, B. Clegg, R. Ashworth)

Silver	Bronze
R. Handley, Team Raleigh 12'-56.1"	M. Clinton, Mike Vaughan Cycles 12'-57.5"
G. Gronlund, RST Racing Team 2'-26"	M. Clinton, Mike Vaughan Cycles 2'-29"
J. Gullen, Team Hope Factory Racing, 7'-59.8"	M. Clinton, Mike Vaughan Cycles 8'-08.1"
M. Clinton, Mike Vaughan Cycles 3'-26.5"	A. Kenway, Team Zenith-www.buzzcycles.co.uk, 3-'26.5"

Team Results

Year	Team
1961	Featherstone RC (L.A. Grayson, K.B. Lycett, C.M. O'Rourke)
1962	West Pennine (P.J. Graham, G.C.Greenwood, D.O. Middleton)
1963	West Pennine RC (P.J. Graham, Doug & Derek Middleton)
1964	Huddersfield Star Wheelers (Granville and Graham Sydney (jun), A. Hinchcliffe)
1965	Huddersfield Star Wheelers (G. and G. Sydney, A. Hinchcliffe)
1966	East Bradford CC (P. Wildsmith, S. Holdsworth, I. Sutcliffe)
1967	Huddersfield Star Wheelers (G. and G. Sydney, S. Whiteley)
1968	Huddersfield Star Wheelers (G. and G. Sydney, S. Whiteley)
1969	Huddersfield Star Wheelers (G. and G. Sydney, D. Petroykus)
1970	Huddersfield Star Wheelers (G. and G. Sydney, S. Whiteley)
1971	Kirkby CC (J. Clewarth, D. Lloyd, D. Dailey)
1972	Huddersfield Star Wheelers (G. and G. Sydney, C. Porter)
1973	Huddersfield Star Wheelers (G. and G. Sydney, C. Porter)
1974	Birdwell Wheelers (C. Berry, R. Wilson, M. Clegg)
1975	East Bradford CC (P. Wildsmith, K. Sayles, S. Holdsworth)
1976	Kirkby CC (G. Harrison, A. Matthews, D. Cuming)
1977	Huddersfield Star Wheelers (P. Grimes, J. Lindley, C. Raw)

Year	Team
1978	Huddersfield Star Wheelers (P. Grimes, J. Lindley, J. Hutton)
1979	Manchester Wheelers - Trumanns Steel (G. Armitage, S.Wilkinson, B. Lowe)
1980	Manchester Wheelers - Trumanns Steel (J. Williams, G. Armitage, S. Joughin)
1981	Manchester Wheelers - Trumanns Steel (J. Williams, D. Webster, G. Armitage)
1982	Manchester Wheelers - Trumanns Steel (J. Williams, P. Longbottom, W. Mansfield)
1983	Manchester Wheelers - Trumanns Steel (D. Webster, P. Longbottom, R. Holden)
1984	Manchester Wheelers - Trumanns Steel (D. Webster, P. Curran, M. Webster)
1985	Manchester Wheelers - Trumanns Steel (D. Webster, P. Longbottom, M. Webster)
1986	Manchester Wheelers - Trumanns Steel (D. Webster, P. Curran, P. Longbottom)
1987	Manchester Wheelers - Trumanns Steel (C. Boardman, P. Curran, P. Longbottom)
1988	Manchester Wheelers - Trumanns Steel (C. Boardman, P. Curran, P. Longbottom)
1989	Manchester Wheelers - Trumanns Steel (C. Boardman, S. O'Brien, P. Longbottom)
1990	Manchester Wheelers - Trumanns Steel (C. Boardman, P. Longbottom, S. O'Brien)
1991	Manchester Wheelers - Trumanns Steel (C. Boardman, P. Longbottom, S. Hulme)
1992	Dinnington RC-Ideal Travel (W. Randle, N. Martin, J.Tanner)
1993	Leo RC-Shorter Rochford (S. Dangerfield, W. Moore, G. Taylor)

Year	Team
1994	North East RT-Hardisty Cycles (J. Wright, S. Tyson, G.Turnbull)
1995	North Wirral Velo-Kodak Prints (C. Newton, P. Manning, J. Ramsbottom)
1996	Middridge CRT-Middridge Engineering (D. Cook, S. Tyson, G. Stirzaker)
1997	Wheelbase CC (S. Dangerfield, M. Andrew, C. Golightly)
1998	Oldham Century (B. Green, S. Green, M. Flynn)
1999	Blackburn & District CTC (D. Ebrell, C. Helliwell, I. Stott)
2000	Blackburn & District CTC (D. Ebrell, C. Helliwell, I. Stott)
2001	Southport CC (J. Henderson, M. Sewell, R. English)
2002	Blackburn & District CTC (D. Collinge, C. Helliwell, I Stott)
2003	Arctic-Shorter Rochford RT (J. Dobbin, T. Bayley, A. Bird)
2004	Arctic-Shorter Rochford RT (J. Dobbin, D. Axford, T. Bayley)
2005	Arctic-Shorter Rochford RT (J. Dobbin, D. Axford, P. Bissell)
2006	Arctic-Shorter Rochford RT (J. Dobbin, J. Dayus, S. Nunn)
2007	Arctic-Shorter Rochford RT (J. Dobbin, D. Axford, P. Bissell)
2008	Blackburn & District CTC (A. Pinder, C. Edmondson, I. Stott)
2009	Blackburn & District CTC (A. Pinder, C. Edmondson, C. Helliwell)
2010	Raleigh UCI (D. Fleeman, M. Cuming, R. Handley)
2011	InGear Quickvit Trainsharp RT (M. Hutchinson, P. Tadros, C. Yates)
2012	Buxton CC-Sett Valley Cycles (L. Baldwin, S. Mansfield, C. Lea)
2013	Rapha Condor JTL (H. Carthy, R. Handley, M. Cuming)
2014	Team Zenith-www.buzzcycles.co.uk (A. Kenway, J. Clark, S. Marshall)

National Hill Climb Championship

Year	Hill	Gold
1998	Dover's Hill Gloucestershire	Nicole Cooke, Cardiff Ajax, 4'-37.5"
1999	The Rake Ramsbottom	Helen Dawson, Blackburn & District CTC, 4'-05.8"
2000	Westclose Hill Rodney Stoke	Tracey Maund, Cheltenham & County CC, 7'-09.0"
2001	Y Bwlch Ruthin	Susan Massey, Birkenhead North End CC, 11'-38.1"
2002	Cat and Fiddle Cheshire	Ann Wooldridge, Gloucester City CC, 27'-29.7"
2003	Halifax Lane Luddenden	Ruth Dorrington, Pete Read Racing, 8'-43.3"
2004	Winter's Gibbet Northumberland	Ann Bowditch, Guernsey VC, 8'-29.7"
2005	The Rake Ramsbottom	Ann Bowditch, Guernsey VC, 3'-34.6"
2006	Peak Hill Sidmouth	Ann Bowditch, ScienceinSport.com 6'-41.9"
2007	Cheddar Gorge Somerset	Caroline Kloiber, Chirio Foron D'Asolo, 8'-03.3"
2008	Bank Road Matlock	Lynn Hamel, The GreenRoomGroup.com 2'-59.6"
2009	Pea Royd Lane Stocksbridge	Anna Fischer, Maxgear RT, 4'-55.2"
2010	Dover's Hill Gloucestershire	Lynn Hamel, TeamNCA, 5'-04.0"
2011	Long Hill Buxton	Lynn Hamel, Herbalife/Wheelbase, 15'-38.6'
2012	The Rake Ramsbottom	Lynn Hamel, Herbalife-Leisure Lakes Bikes 3'-08.9"
2013	The Stang Langthwaite	Maryka Sennema, Kingston Wheelers CC 9'-49.2"
2014	Pea Royd Lane Stocksbridge	Maryka Sennema, Kingston Wheelers CC 4'-35.3"

Women's Championship 1998-2014

Silver	Bronze
Marianne Hesketh, Ribble Valley CRC, 8'-48.3"	
Catherine Hare, Luciano Fondriest, 8'-44.5"	Lynn Hamel, Kent Valley RC 8'-53.1"
Hannah Bussey, VC Meudon, 3'-51.9"	Jane Morris, Perth United CC 3'-58.5"
Lynn Hamel, Kent Valley RC 7'-02.1"	Jane Kilmartin, London Phoenix 7'-05.4"
Lynn Hamel, GreenRoomGroup. com, 8'-23.9"	Ann Bowditch, ScienceinSport.com 8'-38.5"
Claire Thomas, Edinburgh RC, 3'-25.1"	Marianne Britten, VC St. Raphael 3'-37.0"
Lynn Hamel, Team NCA, 4'-55.7"	Claire Cook, Paramount RT 5'-16.8"
Chrissy Radon, Team Zappi's 5'-14.7"	Michelle King, Cult Racing 5'-18.1"
Rebecca Slack, The Altitude Centre 15'-59.6"	Sarah Byrne, Abergavenny RC 16'-28.4"
Joanne Clay, Leek Cyclists' Club 3'-18.6"	Ann Bowditch, Guernsey VC 3'-23.4"
Lynn Hamel, Herbalife-Leisure Lakes Bikes, 10'-06.6"	Angela Hibbs, Tyneside Vagabonds CC, 10'-25.6"
Lou Collins, Beeston RC 4'-42.1"	Lynn Hamel, Trainsharp RT 4'-42.6"

Bibliography

Cooke, N., 2014, *The Breakaway*, London: Simon & Schuster

Deakin, R., 2009, *Wildwood*, New York: Free Press

Elliott, M. and Connor, J., 1990, *Sprinter*, London: Pelham

Fife, G., 2010, *Brian Robinson: Pioneer*, Norwich: Mousehold Press

Hawkes, J., 1952, *A Land*, New York: Random House.

Hewson, T., 2006, *In Pursuit of Stardom*, Norwich: Mousehold Press.

Joughin, S. and Allen, R., 2010, *Pocket Rocket: the Autobiography of Steve Joughin*, Colby: Nemesis Publishing.

Krabbé, T., 2002, *The Rider*, London: Bloomsbury.

Macfarlane, R., 2008, *The Wild Places*, London: Granta Books.

Macfarlane, R., 2012, *The Old Ways*, London: Penguin.

Messenger, C., 1998, *Ride and be Damned*, Harpenden: Pedal.

Simpson, T., 2009, *Cycling is my Life*, London: Yellow Jersey.

Syed, M., 2010, *Bounce*, London: Fourth Estate.

Thurston, J., 2013, *Lost Lanes*, Wild Things Publishing.

Warren, S., 2010, *100 Greatest Cycling Climbs*, London: Frances Lincoln.

Warren, S., 2012, *Another 100 Greatest Cycling Climbs*, London: Frances Lincoln.

Wray, F., 1927, *The Kuklos Papers*, London: J.M. Dent.

Wray. F., 1908, *The Vagabond's Notebook*, London: Daily Press.

Lionel Birnie and Ellis Bacon, 2014, *The Cycling Anthology 4*, London: Yellow Jersey